By the same author:
Modernization of Islam and the Creation of a Multipolar World
Order (Booksurge, 2008)
Karma, Mind, and Quest for Happiness (iUniverse, 2012)

CASINO CAPITALISM

•—◆—•

The Collapse of the US Economy
and the Transition to Secular Democracy
in the Middle East

DR. SUSMIT KUMAR

iUniverse, Inc.
Bloomington

Casino Capitalism
The Collapse of the US Economy and the Transition to Secular Democracy in the Middle East

For queries or comments regarding this book, readers may contact the author at susmitk1@gmail.com or www.susmitkumar.net

iUniverse books may be ordered through booksellers or by contacting:

iUniverse
1663 Liberty Drive
Bloomington, IN 47403
www.iuniverse.com
1-800-Authors (1-800-288-4677)

ISBN: 978-1-4697-3455-2 (sc)
ISBN: 978-1-4697-3457-6 (e)
ISBN: 978-1-4697-3456-9 (dj)

Library of Congress Control Number: 2012900554

Printed in the United States of America

iUniverse rev. date: 3/28/2012

Contents

Dedicated to Baba

PREFACE

• ◆ •

In a 1995 article published by the *Global Times*, Denmark, based on an analysis of the social, political, and religious environments in the Middle East, I predicted the global rise of Islamic militancy due to the 1980s US intervention in Afghanistan and a takeover of Middle Eastern and North African Islamic countries (including Saudi Arabia) by fundamentalist Muslims, which may result in a temporary revival of the caliphate system, and also its final outcome. I predicted that the global Islamic militancy would result in making the majority of Islamic nations secular and democratic, like Turkey: the world seat of the Islamic Caliphate since 1517, Turkey shed its fundamentalist rule in 1923 and has remained free ever since.[1] In a 1996 article in the same periodical, I wrote, "Afghanistan was a Waterloo for the USSR but it might become a Frankenstein for the US."[2] Both these articles are available at my blog (www.susmitkumar.net).

When Islamic fundamentalists intentionally crashed airliners into

---

(1)   Susmit Kumar, "Christian vs. Islamic Civilization—Another Cold War?" *Global Times*, Copenhagen, Denmark, December 15, 1995.
(2)   Susmit Kumar, "Forgotten Victims of U.S. Crusades to Save the World from Communism," *Global Times*, Copenhagen, Denmark, October, 1996.

the New York World Trade Center and the Pentagon, killing more than three thousand people on September 11, 2001, I sent proposals for a book, based on my 1995–96 articles, to several literary agents and publishing firms. None of them accepted my proposal, as I predicted the collapse of the American economy also, apart from the establishment of an Islamic empire, which would finally lead to modernization of Islam. None of the US publishing firms wanted to publish a book that predicted the collapse of the American economy. It is said that the 2011 bestseller *Aftershock: Protect Yourself and Profit in the Next Global Financial Meltdown* (by David Wiedemer, Robert A. Wiedemer, and Cindy S. Spitzer, Wiley, 2011) originally had a chapter that predicted the complete collapse of the American economy, which was taken out by the publisher.

Hence I decided to publish the book on my own, which came out in January 2008—*The Modernization of Islam and the Creation of a Multipolar World Order* (Booksurge). The book has 376 pages (500 words per page) and 640 endnotes. It took four years to write it. Chapter 6 ("The Collapse of the American Economy") was finished in early 2007. The present book is an extension of that chapter 6.

I take pleasure in acknowledging the generous help of Trond Overland in editing this book, as well as Garda Ghista, Firdaus Ghista, Professor Raj N. Singh and Professor Raj Bhatnagar of University of Cincinnati, Professor Dinesh Agrawal of Pennsylvania State University, and Dr. Ram S. Singh of Cincinnati for their helpful discussions in writing it. I am always thankful to my PhD advisor, Professor Stewart K. Kurtz of Pennsylvania State University, who taught me how to do research and also how to write a research paper/article. I would like to thank General Secretary of Ananda Marga Pracaraka Samgha for allowing me to quote extensively from various books of P. R. Sarkar. Above all, I am grateful to my mother, who inspired and guided me in more ways than I can ever say.

1

INTRODUCTION

Since 2010, the United States has proposed limits on "sustainable" trade surpluses and deficits. The proposal has been rebuffed by the BRIC (Brazil, Russia, India, China) countries and also Germany, which currently produces the second-largest trade surplus in the world. The US proposal is nearly the same as the one proposed by the British economist John M. Keynes and his team (the Keynesian stimulus plan is named after him) during the deliberations that led to the 1944 Bretton Woods Accord.

The Americans claim that China has been manipulating its currency yuan (renminbi) by keeping it undervalued. According to Paul Krugman, the Nobel Prize winner in economics and *New York Times* columnist, the United States needs to impose at least a 25 percent tax on Chinese items if China does not appreciate its currency significantly. Yes, it is true that China does manipulate its currency, but, on the other hand, the United States has been doing the same since the 1980s.

Let us first explore the following issues:

(1) During economic recessions the United States goes for budget deficit. Other countries in similar distress, however, are forced by the International Monetary Fund (IMF) to balance their budgets when they approach that institution for a loan. Generally a country applies for an IMF loan when it does not have enough FOREX (FOReign EXchange Reserve) to import goods or save its currencies against the onslaught of currency traders.

(2) During economic recessions the United States reduces it interest rate. At the moment it stands at near zero in order to spur growth and reduce unemployment. On the other hand, having to swallow the bitter pills of IMF, aid recipients are required to increase their interest rates by double digits, which leads to an increase in their unemployment rates and depresses their economies further. During the 1997 East Asian economic crisis, a popular phrase was used to characterize the IMF and its policies: For the average person the actual meaning of IMF was "I'M Finished." After watching IMF at work during the crisis, Joseph E. Stiglitz, the 2001 winner of the Nobel Prize in economics, wrote in April 2000:

> I was chief economist at the World Bank from 1996 until last November, during the gravest global economic crisis in a half-century. I saw how the IMF, in tandem with the US Treasury Department, responded. And I was appalled.[1]

> The IMF may not have become the bill collector of the G-7, but it clearly worked hard (though not always successfully) to make sure that the G-7 lenders got repaid.[2]

(3) In the IMF, major decisions, including the election of its managing director, require an 85 percent super-majority. The top three countries, having the highest votes, are the

United States (16.75 percent), Japan (6.24 percent), and Germany (5.81 percent).

(4) Why was the United States able to sell a trillion dollars worth of its Treasury Bonds in 2011, whereas Greece found it difficult to shore up a mere $30 billion in bonds?

(5) According to Economics 101, money should be invested where it gets the maximum return. However, the entire world, including China and Russia, deposits its money in the United States, where it gets nearly zero interest rate right now.

(6) The United States has record trade deficits, upward of $500 billion per annum during the 2000s, whereas countries like India, South Africa, and Vietnam cannot sustain even a modest trade deficit. According to Economics 101, the US dollar should have lost its value drastically, as the United States has had trade deficits since the 1980s, except for 1991 when it received a significant amount of money from allies in the 1991 Gulf War. Instead, since the 1980s the US dollar has risen sharply against all other currencies except for major economies such as Japan and Western European countries. When I arrived in the United States two decades ago, the exchange rate for the Indian rupee against the US dollar was 15. In December 2011, it was 51 rupees for one dollar—in the last twenty-two years the Indian currency has been devalued by 250 percent against the US dollar. In February 2011, Vietnam devalued its dong by 6.7 percent, the fourth time in the last fifteen months.

The root of all these complicated issues is found in the 1944 Bretton Woods Accord. At this planning meeting for the postwar era, the United States implemented its dollar as the world currency. We will see in the second section that the US economy in itself is not an exceptional economy. The exceptional thing about the American economy is that it has been able to print its currency whenever it so desires in order to fund budget and trade deficits, whereas others cannot do such a thing. However, the enormous piles of money that are accumulating are neither realistic nor sustainable.

THE 1944 BRETTON WOODS AGREEMENT AND THE UNITED STATES' $14 TRILLION CREDIT CARD

During the 1930s, countries used currency devaluations to increase their exports in order to reduce balance of payment deficits. But instead it resulted in a decline in world trade. At the time, Nazi Germany had bilateral trade agreements with several countries, while the members of the British Empire formed an exclusive trading bloc, known as the "Sterling Area." These agreements caused discriminations and obstructions in world trade.

Toward the end of World War II (WWII) there were two competing plans for the future of the global economic order—Britain's Keynes plan and United States' Harry Dexter White plan.

Keynes favored a world currency, to be called *bancor*, and managed by a global bank and an International Clearing Union. That "neutral" world currency would be exchangeable with national currencies at fixed rates of exchange. Under Keynes's plan, both debtors and creditors would be required to change their policies. A country with a large trade deficit would pay interest on its account and devalue its currency to prevent the export of capital. On the other hand, a country with a large trade surplus would increase the value of its currency to permit the export of capital. A country with a bancor credit balance more than half the size of its overdraft facility would be required to pay interest on it. Keynes went so far as to propose the severe penalty of confiscation of surplus if at the end of the year the country's credit balance exceeded the total value of its permitted overdraft.[3]

Under the White plan, the United States was given veto power in the workings of the IMF and the International Bank for Reconstruction and Development (IBRD, later incorporated into the present World Bank). The IMF was to be based in Washington, DC, and staffed by US economists and US Treasury officials mainly.

When the future of world trade was discussed, and the Bretton Woods conference was planned in the early 1940s, many Third World countries were still under colonial rule and had absolutely no say in those discussions. The main deliberations took place between the United States and Britain exclusively, and at Bretton Woods all other countries were invited simply for the formal signing-in ceremony. At the time of the conference the US gross domestic product (GDP) amounted to almost half of the world's GDP. The US gold reserves stood at $20 billion, almost two-thirds of the world's total of $33 billion.[4] Because of the two world wars the European countries were deeply in debt and had transferred huge amounts of gold to the United States. They also needed money from the United States for their postwar reconstruction. Therefore the United States was able to impose its will and its plan at Bretton Woods.

Under the Bretton Woods agreement, a system of fixed exchange rates was announced using the US dollar as a reserve currency. The United States committed to convert dollars into gold at $35 an ounce. At the conference itself the IMF and the IBRD were established. In 1971, the Nixon administration unilaterally cancelled the direct convertibility of the US dollar to gold and effectively ended the Bretton Woods system of international financial exchange.

Had Germany developed long-range missiles and destroyed US industries like it destroyed the British industries during World War II, the United States might not have emerged as the postwar economic superpower. However, the United States emerged as the right country at the right time. Had the same treaty been signed in the late 1950s or later, the United States would not have had the final say on the treaty, and a global currency and even an International Clearing House as proposed by Keynes may have come into existence.

John Maynard Keynes was a brilliant economist who foresaw a global crisis due to large trade imbalances that would lead to instability in the global economy. His proposals may have been construed as if he represented a country—the United Kingdom—in decline and in huge debt, a country that would be accumulating large trade deficits for the foreseeable future. It is worth mentioning that Keynes resigned from the British Treasury, as he was against the large reparation amount imposed on Germany in the 1919 Versailles Peace Treaty after World War I. The stupendous burden thus imposed on Germany is considered to be a main cause for the rise of Hitler.

Right now the Americans find themselves in the same situation as the Europeans were in then (i.e., in overpowering debt). The country needs funding for its economy to recover from the current economic crisis. Hence, if the United States and the Euro countries remain in economic crises, and there is another Bretton Woods conference, countries like China may impose their will, and the United States may be at the receiving end of the stick due to it being in massive debt.

The United States imports goods and services from other countries by simply giving them pieces of paper (i.e., newly issued dollars). In return, the manufacturing countries deposit the same pieces of paper in the United States. It is nothing but a Ponzi scheme run by the United States. According to economist Allan H. Meltzer at Carnegie Mellon University: [5]

We [United States] get cheap goods in exchange for pieces of paper, which we can print at a great rate.

However, the mountain of US bonds that foreigners are accumulating continue to lead the country into deeper debt in order for it to fund its import binge. According to William R. Cline, a scholar at the Institute for International Economics: [6]

Sooner or later, the rest of the world will decide that the US is no longer a safe bet for lending more money.

According to Lou Crandall, chief economist at Wrightson ICAP, which analyzes Treasury financing trends: [7]

While the current market for [US] Treasuries is booming, it's unclear whether demand for debt can be sustained. There's a time bomb somewhere, but we don't know exactly where on the calendar it's planted.

Due to the exponential rise in money supply, the US Federal Reserve Bank decided in March 2006 to cease publication of the amount of its entire supply of money (M3). For their analysis, economists define three different forms of money supply in an economy—M1, M2, and M3.

(1) M1: All physical money, such as coins and currency, demand deposits, which are checking accounts, and Negotiable Order of Withdrawal (NOW) Accounts. It is a very liquid measure of the money supply (i.e., money that can quickly be converted to currency).

(2) M2: It is M1 plus all time-related deposits, savings deposits, and noninstitutional money-market funds. It is a measure of amount of money in circulation. It is used by economists in their forecast of inflation.

(3) M3: It is M2 plus all large time deposits, institutional money-market funds, short-term repurchase agreements, and other larger liquid assets. It is a measure of the entire supply of money within an economy.

Figure 1.1 shows the US M3 from 1960 to 2006 (January data for each other). Since the Reagan years, it has been increasing exponentially. During 1980–96, the annual increase in M3 varied between $200 billion and $300 billion a year, and then in the early years of the Bush administration in the 2000s, it increased to $500 billion to $850 billion a year.

In early 2011, the daily amount of global currency trading was about $4 trillion—85 percent of it was in US dollars, down from the high of 90 percent in 2001. At the same time, the daily trading of US Treasury Bonds was about $580 billion; whereas British gilts and German bonds were only $34 billion and $28 billion, respectively. Had there been a global currency, all these transactions would have happened in the "bancor," and all the countries would have kept their FOREX in that global currency as well, and not in US dollars. Also, the United States would have been in the same boat as countries such as Thailand, Indonesia, Mexico, India, and Vietnam (i.e., the United States would not have been able to fund its twin deficits by just printing its own currency).

Let us have a look at the importance of the US dollar in global trade. Most of the global trade is conducted in US dollars. During recent years India has been purchasing crude oil worth $12 billion a year from Iran. Prior to the US economic sanctions against Iran, India paid Iran in dollars for its crude oil imports via a US bank. When the sanctions were enforced, banks trading in dollars started refusing to be the medium of transfer of money from India to Iran to avoid punishment for acting against the sanctions. Finally, in early 2012, after several months of backlog in payment, Iran had to accept a major portion of the payment in India's rupee for its petrol export and invest the amount in India, as no other country will accept Indian rupee because of its frequent devaluations.

Figure 1.1 **US M3 Money Supply (1960-2006; January data)**

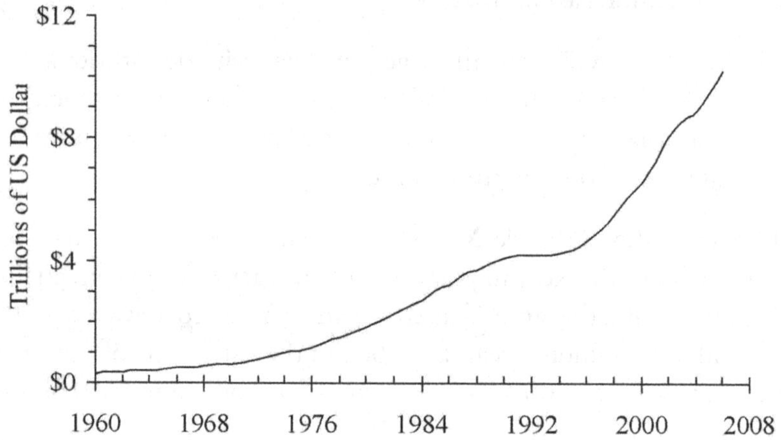

Source: www.federalreserve.gov

If a country such as India does not have enough US dollars to pay for its imports, then it has to devalue its currency to increase its exports. For instance, the manufacturing cost of a Ralph Loren brand of shirt may be 100 Indian rupees (i.e., $2 at the present exchange rate of $1 to 50 rupees) in India, whereas in Bangladesh the manufacturing cost of the same item could be $1.50 measured in Bangladesh's currency. If India devalues its currency by 100 percent (i.e., the exchange rate now becomes $1 to 100 rupees), then the manufacturing cost of the same cloth would be reduced to $1 in India. India's share of exports would increase at the expense of Bangladesh (it may even result in the shutdown of Bangladesh's cloth industry), and India would earn more dollars. On the downside, India's imports would become costlier. Say, before such a devaluation, petrol costs 200 rupees ($4) a gallon at the local pump.

After the devaluation it would cost 400 rupees a gallon (i.e., the same $4 a gallon). India imports 70 percent of its petrol; therefore, the petrol price is determined by the import price. Such doubling of the price of petrol would increase the cost of transportation, leading to an increase in consumer goods prices. Devaluation of every one rupee (against the dollar) impacts the cost of diesel, gas, and petrol by 80 billion rupees ($1.7 billion) per year.[8] In January 2012, state-owned oil companies in India were losing 435 crore rupees ($100 million) each day, as they are forced to sell diesel, domestic LPG, and kerosene much below the cost to keep inflation in check.[9] Apart from this, the real estate and other businesses would also be devalued by half in dollar terms, turning them into takeover targets of foreign investors. A sharp devaluation or frequent devaluations result in flight of capital. During the 1997 East Asian crisis and the 1998 Russian currency crisis, the wealthy people of those countries converted their local money into dollars and exported it, causing the crisis to deepen further. The United States, however, just prints its currency and gives it to all its trading partners as payment for its imports.

Had there been a global currency, the US economy would have collapsed in the 1980s; Reaganomics would have died in its infancy. Reaganomics was paid for by Japan (the main takers of US dollars at the time) during the 1980s and into the early 1990s, and since then by China primarily.

Therefore, we may conclude that capitalism was never successful in the United States. For the last thirty years the US economy has been thriving due to its manipulation of its currency and the global trade.

At present the situation is changing fast. In 2011 the BRIC countries signed an agreement to grant loans to each other in their own national currencies and not in US dollars. The BRIC deal has far-reaching geopolitical importance, as it will undermine the status of the dollar as a reserve currency. Russia and China presently trade oil in rubles. China has replaced the United States as the main trading partner of several countries in Africa, Asia, and Latin America, and China is now requesting them to trade in their own currencies or in yuan rather than in the US dollar. Firms in Russia, Vietnam, and Thailand have already started trading in Chinese currency instead of in the American currency.

Tables 1.1 and 1.2 below show the budget surplus/deficit and balance on current account of two groups of EU countries and the United States. The balance on current account is the sum of the balance of trade (exports minus imports of goods and services), net factor income (interest and dividends) and net transfer payments (such as foreign aid). Euro-GroupA countries (Germany, Holland, Belgium, Austria, and Finland) are not affected much by the current economic downturn. On the other hand, Euro-GroupB countries have suffered badly. The latter group of countries is now known as PIIGS (Portugal, Ireland, Italy, Greece, and Spain) and economists are predicting that in the very near future, France will also join this group, needing to be bailed out.

Table 1.1a **Government Fiscal Balances in Euro GroupA Countries (2001–10)**
(in percent of GDP)

	2001	2002	2003	2004	2005	2006	2007	2008	2009	2010
Germany	-2.8	-3.6	-4.0	-3.8	-3.3	-1.6	0.3	0.1	-3.0	-3.3
Holland	-0.3	-2.1	-3.2	-1.8	-0.3	0.5	0.2	0.5	-5.5	-5.3
Belgium	0.4	-0.2	-0.2	-0.4	-2.8	0.1	-0.4	-1.3	-6.0	-4.2
Austria	-0.2	-0.9	-1.7	-4.6	-1.8	-1.7	-1.0	-1.0	-4.2	-4.6
Finland	5.0	4.0	2.3	2.1	2.5	3.9	5.2	4.2	-2.9	-2.8

Source: *Organization for Economic Co-operation and Development* (OECD)

Table 1.1b **Government Fiscal Balances in Euro GroupB Countries and the US**
(2001–10) *(in percent of GDP)*

	2001	2002	2003	2004	2005	2006	2007	2008	2009	2010
France	-1.6	-3.2	-4.1	-3.6	-3.0	-2.3	-2.7	-3.3	-7.5	-7.0
Italy	-3.1	-3.0	-3.5	-3.6	-4.4	-3.3	-1.5	-2.7	-5.3	-4.5
Spain	-0.7	-0.5	-0.2	-0.4	1.0	2.0	1.9	-4.2	-11.1	-9.2
Greece	-4.4	-4.8	-5.7	-7.4	-5.3	-6.0	-6.7	-9.8	-15.6	-10.4
Portugal	-4.3	-2.9	-3.1	-3.4	-5.9	-4.1	-3.2	-3.6	-10.1	-9.2
Ireland	1.0	-0.3	0.4	1.4	1.6	2.9	0.1	-7.3	-14.3	-32.4
US	**-0.6**	**-4.0**	**-5.0**	**-4.4**	**-3.3**	**-2.2**	**-2.9**	**-6.3**	**-11.3**	**-10.6**

Source: *Organization for Economic Co-operation and Development* (OECD)

Table 1.2a **Balance on Current Account in Euro GroupA Countries (2001–10)**
(in percent of GDP)

	2001	2002	2003	2004	2005	2006	2007	2008	2009	2010
Germany	0.0	2.1	1.9	4.7	5.1	6.5	7.9	6.7	5.7	5.6
Holland	2.4	2.5	5.5	7.5	7.3	9.3	8.7	4.8	4.9	7.2
Belgium	3.4	4.6	4.1	3.5	2.6	2.0	2.2	-2.5	0.3	1.0
Austria	-0.8	2.7	1.7	2.2	2.2	2.8	3.6	3.2	3.1	2.6
Finland	8.6	8.8	5.2	6.6	3.6	4.5	4.2	3.0	2.3	3.1

Source: *Organization for Economic Co-operation and Development* (OECD)

Table 1.2b **Balance on Current Account in Euro Group B Countries and the US (2001–10)** *(in percent of GDP)*

	2001	2002	2003	2004	2005	2006	2007	2008	2009	2010
France	1.9	1.4	0.8	0.6	-0.4	-0.5	-1.0	-2.3	-1.5	-1.8
Italy	-0.1	-0.8	-1.3	-0.9	-1.7	-2.6	-2.4	-3.4	-2.1	-3.2
Spain	-3.9	-3.3	-3.5	-5.3	-7.4	-9.0	-10.0	-9.6	-5.1	-4.6
Greece	-7.3	-6.8	-6.6	-5.9	-7.4	-11.3	-14.5	-14.5	-11.0	-10.4
Portugal	-9.9	-8.1	-6.1	-7.6	-9.5	-10.0	-9.4	-12.1	-10.9	-9.9
Ireland	-0.7	-0.9	0.0	-0.6	-3.5	-3.5	-5.3	-5.3	-3.0	0.5
US	**-3.9**	**-4.3**	**-4.7**	**-5.3**	**-6.0**	**-6.0**	**-5.2**	**-4.9**	**-2.7**	**-3.2**

Source: *Organization for Economic Co-operation and Development* (OECD)

Until the start of the present economic downturn in 2008, the government fiscal balances, which denote the budget surplus/deficit, of both groups, except Greece, were nearly the same. But there is a stark difference between these two groups in their balance on current account. Euro-GroupB countries have recurring negative balances on current account during the 2000s, whereas Euro-GroupA countries have positive balances on current account during the same period. Within the Euro zone, France's share of exports fell to 13.4 percent in 2009, from 17 percent in 2000; Italy's share fell to 10.1 percent from 11.9 percent. The German share increased during the period.[10] Since the current economic downturn started, the budget deficits of Euro-GroupB countries have worsened.

Major European economies, such as Germany and France, are trying to save the Euro-GroupB countries by giving them billions of Euros for support. Apart from redeeming the Euro, they would like to save their own banks as well, as these banks would lose a lot of money should the countries in trouble default on their loans. These are the same banks that funded the spending binge in the troubled countries.

One remarkable point we get from the tables below is that the US economy resembles the economies of Euro-GroupB but is still surviving, as it can print its currency to fund its deficits, whereas the Euro-GroupB countries cannot do such a thing, as the Euro is managed by the European Central Bank (ECB).

With a debt-to-revenue ratio of 312 percent, Greece is in dire straits at present. However, the debt-to-revenue ratio of the United States is 358 percent, according to Morgan Stanley. The Congressional Budget Office estimates that interest payments on the federal debt will rise from 9 percent of federal tax revenues to 20 percent in 2020, 36 percent in 2030, and 58 percent in 2040. Only America's "exorbitant privilege" of being able to print the world's premier reserve currency gives it breathing space. But this very privilege is under mounting attack from the Chinese government.[11]

In several of the crises-stricken European countries, a collapsing housing industry, as in the United States, is the main reason for their economic downturn. Five years ago, Spain and Ireland, which are receiving a bailout from IMF and EU, were running budget surpluses with low national debts. But the private sectors in these countries were increasingly borrowing from overseas, and most of these investments were in the housing industry instead of creating productive industries generating profits. When their housing industries collapsed, their private sector debts were converted into national debts. In a monetary deal there is always a probability that it may result in loss. But in these kinds of investments, if the government does not make sure that all the foreign investors are paid in full, the rating agencies would downgrade the rating of the country. One of the IMF bailout conditions is that outside debts need to be repaid in full. Therefore the financial sector is in a position to take excessive risk while feeling protected against any downside risk. They invest in countries where they can get maximum return, and if the recipient of their investments defaults, rating agencies and the IMF make sure that the investors get all of their money back. If a country restricts investments to go to productive industries only, which will generate incomes to help pay for the loans, the investors argue that the country has strict regulations.

Right now several European countries are facing an economic crisis similar to the 1997 East Asian crisis (i.e., they are not generating enough dollars to pay for the investments by private bankers). Government in Greece, Ireland, Portugal, and Italy did not take these loans. Instead, private firms or individuals took the loans, and when private firms/ individuals go bankrupt, the governments had to own these private loans. In the similar situation in the United States in 2008–9, the (Bush and later Obama) administration owned the loans of Wall Street bankers. This has nothing to do with "socialism," as claimed by conservatives. Common people, who had nothing to do with these loans, have to suffer due to benefit reduction by the government and job losses.

Argentina went through an economic crisis in 2001. Instead of bowing to IMF dictates, it defaulted on $100 billion, mostly of foreign debts, and the investors had to take haircuts on their investments. At the height of the crisis in 2001, four Argentinian presidents took oaths and resigned in just ten days. At that time, Argentina's fiscal deficit and debt were only 3.2 percent and 54 percent, respectively, of its GDP. Argentina, whose main exports are agriculture products, now runs a trade surplus due to the global steep rise in prices of such products.

When someone defaults on a loan, his or her credit rating goes down drastically, and he or she may not even get a loan for the next several years. If one applies the same logic to the Wall Street bankers and investors, the government and the Fed should charge them a very high tax rate as well as interest rate, because there is always a risk that they may create another 2008 type banking crisis in the future.

The Collapse of the Present Model of Global Trade

Table 1.3 below shows the balance on current account of the BRIC countries, as well as South Africa and Vietnam. Except for China and Russia, they all have sizeable negative balances on current accounts. The positive balance on Russia's current account is due to an increase in oil prices and other minerals, which are its main exports. During the late 1980s and 1990s, Wal-Mart got rid of family-owned stores in American cities. Similarly, since the 2000s China has been forcing the manufacturing plants for mass consumption items in other countries to close. It has resulted in trade imbalances in several countries.

Table 1.3 **Balance on Current Account in Selected Countries (2003–10)**
(in percent of GDP)

	2003	2004	2005	2006	2007	2008	2009	2010
China	2.8	3.6	7.1	9.3	10.6	9.6	6.0	5.2
Russia	8.2	10.1	11.1	9.5	5.9	6.2	4.1	4.9
Brazil	0.8	1.8	1.6	1.2	0.1	-1.7	-1.5	-2.3
India	1.5	0.1	-1.3	-1.0	-0.7	-2.0	-2.8	-3.2
South Africa	-1.0	-3.0	-3.5	-5.3	-7.0	-7.1	-4.1	-2.8
Vietnam	-4.9	-3.5	-1.1	-0.3	-9.8	-11.9	-6.6	-3.8

Source: *World Economic Outlook*, IMF

In 2008, Vietnam's export to China was $4.5 billion, whereas imports from China were $15.7 billion. In February 2011, Vietnam devalued its currency by 6.7 percent, the fourth devaluation of the dong in fifteen months. In 2010, India imported $40.8 billion worth of items, mainly finished products, from China, whereas its export to China was only $20.9 billion worth of items, mainly minerals. Countries like India are surviving due to remittances from people living overseas and from foreign investments.

As shown in Table 1.4, the trade deficit of India is increasing every year. In just five years, the trade deficit of India quadrupled from $28 billion in the 2004–5 (April through March) financial year to $118.4 billion in the 2008–9 (April through March) financial year. Although in the next two financial years the trade deficit dropped slightly due to the 2008 Great Recession, it had increased to $118.7 billion in just the first eight months (April through November) of 2011, and it may surpass $150 billion during the 2011–12 (April through March) financial year.[12] On the other hand, the trade surplus of China increased from $177 billion in 2006 to $298 billion in 2008, as shown in Table 1.5. Due to the 2008 Great Recession and subsequent economic crises in the United States and European countries, the trade surplus of China has dropped since reaching a record high in 2008. Due to large overseas remittances and foreign investments, India is able to fund its trade deficit. The drop in overseas remittances and foreign investments put pressure on India's currency. Overseas remittances to India were $45 billion and $58 billion in 2008 and 2010, respectively, whereas for China, these numbers were $35 billion and $57 billion, respectively.[13] In India the majority of Hindu gods and (India's) national flags are "Made in China." During the Diwali festival of lights, cheap Chinese multicolored lights are replacing the traditional earthen *diyas*. As shown in Table 1.6, India's trade deficit with China has been increasing year after year. With an increase in number of consumers, the trade deficit of India has the potential to surpass the US trade deficit level (i.e., $600 billion to $700 billion a year), which is unsustainable for India as, unlike the United States, it cannot print its currency to fund it.

Table 1.4 **Exports, Imports, and Balance of Trade of India (in billions)**

Financial Year (April-March)	Exports	Imports	Trade Balance
2004–05	$83.5	$111.5	-$28.0
2005–06	$103.1	$149.2	-$46.1
2006–07	$126.4	$185.7	-$59.3
2007–08	$163.1	$251.6	-$88.5
2008–09	$185.3	$303.7	-$118.4
2009–10	$178.8	$288.4	-$109.6
2010–11	$251.1	$369.8	-$118.7
2011 (Apr-Nov)a	$192.7	$309.5	-$116.8

Source: Department of Commerce (www.commerce.nic.in), Government of India; (a) "Trade deficit spans to $117 b in April-Nov period," *Deccan Herald*, January 2, 2012.

Table 1.5 **China's Trade Surplus (in billions)**

	Trade Surplus
2006	$177.5
2007	$261.8
2008	$298.1
2009	$195.7
2010	$181.5
2011	$160.0

Source: "China trade surplus," *AFP*, January 5, 2012.

Table 1.6 **India's Trade with China (in billions)**

Financial Year (April-March)	Exports	Imports	Trade Balance
2006–07	$8.3	$17.5	-$9.2
2007–08	$10.9	$27.1	-$16.2
2008–09	$9.4	$32.5	-$23.1
2009–10	$11.7	$30.8	-$19.1
2010–11	$19.6	$43.4	-$23.8
2011 (Jan-Dec) a	$23.4	$50.0	-$27.1

Source: Department of Commerce (www.commerce.nic.in), Government of India; (a) "India-China trade hits all time high of USD 73.9 bln in 2011," *Deccan Herald* (PTI), January 29, 2012.

Indians, who purchase cheap imported items, do not realize that they are in fact paying much more than the sticker price. In India, people use the Indian rupee when they pay storeowners, who in turn purchase imported items in the world market. The importers pay in US dollar when they buy these items in world markets, and these dollars are provided by banks in India that are authorized to do transactions in foreign currencies. Hence, in the end, India has to get these dollars from somewhere, say from the dollars earned by exporters or foreign investors. If India does not have enough dollars to pay for imports, it has to devalue its currency so that exporters can export more. Whenever there is a price rise in commodities such as petrol, opposition parties and common people blame the government for the price rise, whereas they should blame their own countrymen, who are purchasing imported items.

In the late 1980s, the conversion rate of Indian currency was 1:15, whereas in November 2011 it was 1:51 (i.e., about 250 percent in the last twenty-two to twenty-three years). Just in the last six months of 2011, the rupee had a record fall of 17 percent, from 1:44 to 1:51. The main reason behind this devaluation was the sharp drop in foreign investment, which tumbled from $6.5 billion in June to $616 million in September.[14] Indian companies borrow money in foreign currencies from outside the country because of lower interest rates. Indian companies borrowed close to $29 billion in foreign currencies, through ECBs

(External Commercial Borrowing) and FCCBs (Foreign Currency Convertible Bonds) in the first eleven months of 2011, as against such loans worth $18 billion during the entire 2010. Hence, the sharp fall of about 17 percent in the value of the rupee made the cost of repaying these foreign loans costlier by a similar margin. For example, an Indian company would have to pay an amount of about Rs 51 billion (based on conversion rate of 1:51) toward the principal amount to a bondholder of $1 billion, while a similar loan amount would have been worth about Rs 44 billion at the beginning of 2011. According to Jagannadham Thunuguntla, SMC Global Securities' strategist and head of research, the additional burden due to the rupee depreciation could be of Rs 252 billion ($5 billion) for the Indian companies on their ECBs worth about $30 billion raised in 2011. The possibility of such a scenario increases the risk of loan default by their issuer companies.[15]

In 1991, India had to go to the IMF to get a loan because its FOREX was worth only three weeks of essential imports, and India was on the verge of default. One of the main reasons for this economic crisis was imports of luxury items during the late 1980s under the Rajiv Gandhi administration. India had to airlift sixty-seven tons of its gold reserves to London as collateral in order to get $2.2 billion from the IMF. In addition, India had to liberalize its economy and sell several of its profit-making public firms at throwaway prices to US firms such as Enron.

Brazil follows in India's footsteps. The country's previous positive balance on current account is going into deep red due to its increasing trade deficit. Brazil's exports, mainly minerals, are not increasing at the rate of its imports due to the increase in the number of consumers in the country.

By mid-2011, China's FOREX was $3.2 trillion. In recent years it has been increasing at the rate of $400 billion to $500 billion a year. Five and ten years from now China's FOREX will be $5.5 trillion and $7 trillion, respectively. With this much money China will control the United States in every sphere. If China starts to dump its trillions of FOREX dollars in the international market, the US interest rate (mortgage rates, bank loans, credit card rates, student loans, etc.) will skyrocket, with huge consequences for the United States and the global economy.

According to the president of the Council on Foreign Relations, Richard Haass, China may bring down the United States in the same way the Eisenhower administration brought down its close ally Britain during the 1956 Suez crisis. Haass said, "Essentially the US took advantage of Britain's Sterling problem to exercise economic leverage over the British government, and that led to a hasty retreat (despite defeating the primitive Egyptian army on all the fronts, the invading forces had to withdraw). So one can imagine a situation nowadays, where, say, there is a crisis over Taiwan between the US and China—which holds a significant number of dollars—and one can imagine the Chinese might be prepared to threaten the dollar, make some comments to weaken it unless the US backs off some of its support of Taiwan."[16]

Even without the 2008 economic crisis, China would have emerged as the dominant economic force by being the largest lender in the world, and almost all major consumer countries would have to declare bankruptcy to China after a couple of decades or so. Therefore, the current global economy model is not sustainable.

Suppose China emerges as the sole economic power after the present global economic crisis that now batters the United States and the Euro countries. Its currency, the yuan, could then become the global currency. Then China will be replacing the United States as the world economic superpower, whereas nearly all other countries will be facing the same old economic crises every now and then. Therefore it is in the best interest of every country to implement the 1944 Keynesian main principles in full (i.e., to create a global currency and limit trade imbalances).

KRUGMAN'S LONG DEPRESSION OR
THE GREAT DEPRESSION II

The severity of the 2008 economic global downturn shocked almost all. It started with the crisis in the subprime loans in 2007, which led to huge losses in securities sold against these subprime loans. With mounting losses, interbank lending froze. The housing bubble, which had been rising in the preceding six to seven years, crashed too, and housing prices collapsed all over the country. Within a few months, share prices dropped by more than half from a record high. The crisis quickly spread to most of the industrialized world. Several US and European banks suffered huge losses, and some were forced to file for bankruptcy.

In mid-2010, economist Paul Krugman claimed that the US economy was in the early stages of a third depression, and it would probably look more like the Long Depression of the nineteen century, which followed the Panic of 1873, than the much more severe 1930s Great Depression. According to him, the cost—to the world economy and, above all, to the millions of lives blighted by the absence of jobs—will nonetheless be immense. [17]

There is a major difference between the 1930s Great Depression and the coming Great Depression. During the 1930s Great Depression, the Keynesian stimulus (i.e., generating employment by government spending) worked. Unlike right now, during the 1930s Great Depression, both consumer debt and government debts were not high. At present the Keynesian stimulus alone is not going to solve the problem because the United States is completely dependent on the import of consumer items.

By the end of 2011, the economy seemed to have stabilized due to the $1.5 trillion stimulus money provided by the Bush and Obama administrations. During the 1930s Great Depression, too, the economy had temporarily improved because of two stimulus packages provided by the Roosevelt administration. US unemployment was 25 percent in 1933 and 15 percent in 1940 measured by the fact that in those days only one person in the family used to work. The real numbers were actually much higher reckoned by present standards. Mass unemployment in the United States ended only after the outbreak of World War II, when the US economy started to churn out arms and armaments initially for the European allies and later for its own country as well.

One need not be a rocket scientist to analyze the present US economy. From the 1980s, US firms started to send manufacturing jobs to East Asian countries in order to reduce costs and increase profits. Until the mid-1990s, information technology sector jobs were created in the United States, but henceforth those jobs were also outsourced to English-speaking countries such as India and the Philippines in order to fulfill Wall Street's expectations. Although Americans were losing jobs, the American economy boomed because of the tech stock bubble during the 1990s. The budget surplus during the Clinton administration's last years was mainly due to jobs created in the tech sector, which resulted in a rise of revenues.

After the collapse of the tech stocks in the early 2000s, the US economy kept booming because of the housing sector bubble. Prior to the subprime crisis, people were making money by selling homes to each other. From 1950 to 2000, existing homes grew in value by less than 0.5 percent per year, after adjusting for inflation. From 2000 to 2006, home prices rose at an average annualized rate of 8.2 percent above inflation and peaked with a 12.3 percent jump in 2005.[18] Suppose you buy a house worth $200,000 with a down payment of $10,000, and the price of the house increases by 10 percent in a year. By selling the house, you can make say about $10,000 after deducting transaction costs (i.e., you can get 100 percent return in a year; or after a year you can get a $20,000 home equity loan to spend). According to the National Association of Realtors, the average down payment for the first-time home buyers was 10 percent in 1989, whereas in 2007, it was only 2 percent.[19] Hence for a 2 percent down payment (i.e., $4,000 down payment for a $200,000 home), you could have had 500 percent return in a year. In case of sale, the $10,000 transaction cost is paid to the real estate agents and the banks involved in the transaction. Although this $20,000 would be immediately spent in the economy, raising the spending level by $20,000, on the negative side this also increased the overall debt by $20,000, which would be paid by the next owner. Apart from home loans, banks were showering Americans with several other kinds of loans also, such as for appliances, furniture, and cars. Hence these two bubbles kept the US economy booming although the people had lost quality jobs. People were using their homes as ATM cards.

During the housing sector bubble, individuals were making money in tens of thousands of dollars due to the rise in home prices. At the same time, hedge funds were making hundreds of millions of dollars in the commercial real estate sector bubble, which started to crash in 2009. Job losses resulted in closures of stores, malls, and offices, which caused a significant drop in commercial real estates prices. The commercial real estate market always lags behind the general economy. Between 2005 and 2007, $1.5 trillion in commercial property traded hands.

The volume of sales soared from $78 billion in 2001 to $498 billion in 2007. Between 2005 and 2008, nearly three quarters of San Francisco's top downtown office buildings were bought and sold. Scott Lawlor, a hedge fund manager doing business in commercial real estate, was producing more than 40 percent a year for investors from 2000 to 2007. For example, he bought a building in hedge-fund haven Greenwich, Connecticut, in 2003, brought in tenants at higher rents and sold it for twice the purchase price in 2006. But Lawlor had to bite the dust once the economy crashed in 2008. He was forced to foreclose on the Hancock Tower, a sixty-two-story building in Boston's Black Bay, which was under its fourth owner in six years in 2009 after his foreclosure. Due to the crash of the commercial real estate market, its value dropped by more than half in just two years—from $1.7 billion in 2007 to $700 million in 2009.[20] The commercial real estate crash dealt another blow to the already struggling financial industry. In 2009, banks had about $1 trillion of commercial real estate loans and an additional $530 billion in construction loans.[21]

Hence, the late 1990s and 2000s economy presented a bubble economy funded by borrowed money. In 1990, the average American household's debt was 83 percent of its income and in 2000 it was 92 percent of its income. In 2007 it had gone up to 130 percent of income.[22] Therefore, although Americans were able to immediately spend money worth 38 percent of their household's income during 2000 and 2007, they had increased their debt by the same amount. The prosperity during the 2000s was based on borrowed money. In early 2010, the average British household's debt was 170 percent of its income.

From the peak value of $9 trillion in 2006, the loss of home values was $1 trillion in 2009 and $1.7 trillion in 2010, an increase of 63 percent over the last year. The increase in loss was less due to the home buyer tax credit plan until the first half of 2010—first half loss $700 billion and second half loss $1 trillion. And, 23.2 percent of single family homes were underwater in the third quarter of 2010 as compared to 21.8 percent in 2009.[23] "Underwater" is a technical term for the phenomenon when a borrower owes more than his house is worth.

Due to the Bush administration's tax policy, the wealth distribution is now skewed in favor of the ultrarich. The top 1 percent of US households owns nearly twice as much of America's corporate wealth as they did just fifteen years ago. More than 40 percent of employed Americans work in very-low-paying service jobs.[24]

After the collapse of the housing sector bubble, as Americans have lost their purchasing power, US firms are losing sales, and, hence, they have to lay off employees. Fifty-five percent of Americans have lost a job, taken a pay cut, or faced cutbacks in paid hours on the job since the start of the 2008 Great Recession.[25] This has led to a severe economic downturn. Due to the crash of home values as well as job losses, the credit scores of people have gone downhill—and have damaged their credit ratings. Even if interest rates are kept near the record low, people will not be eligible for loans.

During previous recessions, although there were job losses and share prices had dropped, home values did not collapse all over the country on the scale witnessed in the economic downturn of 2008–9. Back then people were able to use home equity to get cash to spend.

At present the financial systems are also badly damaged. They are not in a position to lend to consumers and businesses to the level they used to lend before the 2008 economic crisis. Job losses and the housing crisis have affected commercial real estate too, due to foreclosure of malls and offices. This has given another blow to the already struggling financial system. Due to these reasons the economy will be marked by high unemployment and weak growth for years.

The housing market crash has affected local governments due to a decrease in property tax collections. This has led to the firing of police officers, teachers, and firefighters all over the United States. Cities such as Detroit, once the proud auto capital of the world, have become like Third World countries' slums. States have been affected, too, due to the decrease in revenue collections. Although California boasts to have the tenth largest economy in the world, it is on the verge of bankruptcy.

State and local administrations have received substantial amounts from the federal stimulus plan under the Bush and Obama administrations. But now, by the end of 2011, the stimulus money will be ending, which will lead to exasperation of the economic situation at both state and local levels.

Even by cutting the welfare schemes substantially, the federal budget deficit will increase over the years. Under the Paul Ryan plan, which aims to cut welfare schemes substantially, the federal deficit will increase by $5 trillion over the next ten years. Hence the United States will remain under scrutiny for further rating downgrades.

According to Harvard economist Kenneth Rogoff, the August 5, 2011, downgrade of the United States to AA-plus by S&P was generous, and other rating agencies have been cowering not to follow suit.[26]

After the rating downgrade in mid-2010, the Greeks were paying 13 percent and 12 percent interest rates on ten-year and two-year bonds, respectively. Americans, on the other hand, were paying 3 percent and 0.4 percent on ten-year and two-year bonds, respectively. In 2011, the United States paid $250 billion to its bond holders. For each point rise in interest rate, the annual interest payment rises by $140 billion on a $14 trillion debt. For a 3 percent rise in the interest rate, the interest payment will rise by $400 billion a year, nearly the same as the defense budget. If the United States had to pay the same interest rate as crisis-struck European countries are paying (i.e., more than 10 percent), it would have run out of money after only having paid interests on its loans, with nothing left in its budget to spend at all.

Interest on the federal Treasury bond is a benchmark for most of the debts in the country. As of 2009, total debts owed by US households, businesses, and governments in the country amounted to $50.7 trillion, more than 3.5 times the gross domestic product. Every 1 percent increase in the rate results in an increase of $500 billion on all debts in the country.

At the end of World War II, the US federal debt was 122 percent of GDP, but state and local debts were minimal. Due to near double-digit growth rates, along with a high savings rate and inflation due to demand for consumer goods in the following six years, the federal debt went down to three-fourths of GDP.

In March 2009, the Pentagon for the first time held a series of economic war games exercises. The soldiers were Wall Street traders and executives, economists, and academics. The weapons were stocks, bonds, and currencies. The participants were divided into teams: the United States, China, Russia, Japan, the European Union, and so on. Then the teams were presented with different scenarios—North Korea is imploding, a major global economy is melting down—and told to do what was in their best interests. The intelligence experts watched as the economic conflicts played out.[27]

What the exercises showed was that the United States consistently lost to China in economic warfare. Part of the reason was that the United States could be easily distracted by expensive side conflicts that sapped its economic strength. But the more important reason was that China could inflict real pain on the United States without feeling it at home. For instance, by simply moving the maturities of some of its $850 billion in Treasury holdings from ninety days to sixty days, it could cause chaos in the US stock markets. Or China could sell just a trickle of its US financial assets and signal that it didn't have confidence in the US economy, setting off a panic. [28]

In capitalism, emphasis is on maximizing profit and not welfare of human beings. Hence manufacturing units will move to the place where profit will be at a maximum. Therefore, it is natural that jobs, especially manufacturing jobs, are going to countries like China. Reagan dubbed communism as evil. However, communism failed due to its inefficiency, whereas what we are witnessing right now is that capitalism is much more evil. Not only does it destroy its own people, it also creates its own Frankenstein, China.

After India got independence from Britain in 1947, Prime Minister Jawahar Lal Nehru was riding high, like a leader of a superpower, in international politics. But when he ordered Indian troops, against warnings by his top-level generals that Indian troops were not prepared for a full-scale war with China, to destroy newly erected Chinese military small posts along the disputed Indo-China border, then Chairman Mao Zedong decided to teach him a lesson and invaded India all along the border in 1962. Everywhere the Chinese troops decimated the Indian troops, who did not have even proper clothes and equipments to fight at high altitude in cold climate. According to newly declassified papers, Nehru was willing to ditch his Non-Alignment Movement, of which he was one of the three founders, when he sent two letters in succession, pleading with US President Kennedy for military aid, which included providing radar installations and bombers, to be manned by Americans for air cover for his troops. Nehru was so shocked by the humiliating defeat that he had a paralytic attack; he died within two years due to heart failure.

According to reliable sources and also confirmed by Shashi Tharoor, a former UN undersecretary and now a political leader of the ruling

Indian Congress Party to which Nehru also belonged, the United States had offered India in 1953 to take a permanent seat, having veto power, in the United Nation Security Council (UNSC) held by the Republic of China (Taiwan) at that time. It is worth noting that the People's Republic of China (i.e., Communist China) was seated at the United Nations only in November 1971. But Nehru urged that it should be offered to Beijing instead. During the 1950s, the Nehru administration gave the slogan—"Hindi-Chini Bhai Bhai"—the Indians and the Chinese are brothers! India was one of three countries, apart from the USSR and Yugoslavia, to vote at the Security Council in favor of the Soviet motion in 1950 to give the seat of China, along with the veto power, to the communist People's Republic of China (PRC) and to expel Taiwan from the United Nations. The defeat of this motion led to the USSR boycott of UNSC. But the Soviet action backfired when the United States was able to get a UNSC nod to fight invading North Korean troops in South Korea. Had the Soviets not been boycotting the UNSC, it would have vetoed the resolution for a UN action against North Korea. For this very reason Nehru considered the invasion of China a backstabbing; it was a great and fatal shock to him.

Once Mao said he did not fear nuclear war because even if half of the Chinese population would be killed, the other half would rule the world. The lobbing of missiles over the Taiwan Strait during the 1996 Taiwanese presidential elections showed that the present Chinese administration is no better than Chairman Mao. Hence, China can take a risk by getting rid of the superpower status of the United States, even when it would affect their economy badly.

The Euro crisis has the potential to start a chain reaction that can lead the global economy into a tailspin. The PIIGS countries, along with the United Kingdom, are selling their public sector firms, such as airports, national post offices, manufacturing plants, roads, banks, utility (gas and electricity) firms, lands and beaches in something that looks like fire sales. By September 2010, the unemployment rate in EU27 was close to 10 percent, up by more than one-third over 2007 unemployment rates: United Kingdom (8 percent), Spain (20 percent), Greece (11.6 percent), Portugal (10.8 percent), Lithuania (17.3 percent), and Latvia (20.1 percent). The EU27 had twenty-three million unemployed between them at this point. Like the United States, Europeans are also cutting back on spending, a policy that will increase unemployment and set in motion a vicious circle of further problems.

We will see in this book that there is no option for the United States and other Western countries but to restart domestic manufacturing and service sector units, which they have outsourced, although inflation will go through the roof, and their living standards will go down drastically.

CASINO CAPITALISM

At the onset of the 2008 recession, the economies of the East European countries were on the verge of collapse. In an October 2008 speech, Romanian President Traian Basescu pinned the blame on "corrupt" outsiders. He said, "There were smart guys coming to Romania, who had studied at Harvard and Oxford, and they invented how to increase the value of one's shares without actually having money."[29] His statement describes in brief the working of Wall Street bankers and hedge fund managers. Until the start of the 2008 economic downturn, hedge funds were creating havoc in Third World countries, for instance the 1994 Mexican peso crisis and the 1997 East Asian crisis. Now they are doing the same in the United States and the European Union.

With the advent of Internet technology and the subsequent integration of national and global economies in the last couple of decades, brilliant brains have devised algorithms to generate money for millionaires and billionaires. These sophisticated mathematical and statistical methods work by moving money from one place to any another place in the world by the click of a mouse button. This creates financial instruments (derivatives, credit default swaps, etc.), that resembles casino games, which create trillions of dollars of investments on paper. The hedge funds play these casino games, and the ultimate losers are the common people.

The moneymaking instruments at Wall Street are not the birthrights of the bankers and investors. They simply use these instruments as long as the government permits their use. The government enacted laws to restrict short selling after short sellers were blamed for the 1929 Wall

Street crash. Some of these restrictions were in effect until 2007, when the Securities and Exchange Commission (SEC) removed them.

Also, the government is not printing any special money for the Wall Street bankers and investors. Rather, the outrageous amount of money that these people are making comes from the pockets of common people. John Paulson, a New York hedge fund manager, made $3.7 billion in 2007 by betting against questionable subprime mortgage securities during the collapse of the mortgage market. George Soros and James Simons made $2.9 billion and $2.8 billion, respectively, the same year in similar ways. Almost all of their monies were taxpayers' money because they received this money from the AIG (American International Group), which had insured those mortgage securities (also termed as derivatives), and AIG needed to be bailed out by the government due to mounting losses. The AIG bailout was a backdoor bailout of financial institutions including Goldman Sachs, JPMorgan Chase, and Morgan Stanley. Instead of getting "haircuts," they were paid in full. This betting method employed by these hedge fund managers was illegal until 2000, when a Republican-controlled Congress made it illegal to regulate or hinder it by passing the Commodity Futures Modernization Act. In 2008, Alan Greenspan, the Fed chairman when the 2000 act was passed and actually a force behind its enactment, admitted his mistake in opposing the regulation of these kinds of derivates. Had the government not passed the Commodity Futures Modernization Act of 2000, these hedge fund managers would not have made these outrageous amounts of money.

Even if AIG would not have required taxpayers' money to be bailed out and the company would have paid these tens of billions of dollars to hedge fund managers from its own account, AIG would have to get this money from somewhere, as government does not money especially for AIG. If you had followed the trail of the money within AIG, the trail would have ended in the pockets of ordinary people—the source of all this money. Moreover, these companies' income has little social value, as they do not create jobs, except for a few secretaries and a few analysts. Later in this section and also in chapter 5, we will see how Wall Street bankers and investors are making money from everyone, even from a homeless person when he buys some consumer item such as bread, corn, gas, etc.

Suppose a person owns a large piece of land, and a river runs through it. If he decides to use all the water of the river, the people downstream will not get any water. Unless the government outlaws this kind of behavior by people living upstream and "regulates" the use of river water to ensure its proper use, there will be no end to the suffering of the people living downstream. Similarly, the government needs to regulate the financial industry to properly distribute the money.

Wall Street and other financial institutions have become the modern-day Las Vegas and Atlantic City—casinos where only the ultrawealthy and people working there can win. In traditional casinos most of the games are biased in favor of the owners, and amateur players rarely end up winning. Similarly, at Wall Street and other financial institutions, top executives and hedge funds earn multimillion dollars, whereas common people mostly only think that they are winning, and, suddenly, due to a financial setback they realize that everything is gone. As the majority of firms have opted out of pension plans, and working people are dependent on their 401(k)s for their retirement, heavily invested in stocks, the whole scenario gives a very bleak picture of the future of retirees in this country.

When you squeeze the juice out of a fruit, then what remains in the fruit? That's what the hedge funds have done with the United States and the global economy. This also shows the self-destructive nature of capitalism.

The dice are loaded in favor of the bankers and the ultrarich. Lower- and middle-class people work hard every day to earn their salary and pay government taxes in thousands of dollars annually, whereas some people, working and investing in financial sectors, earn millions and billions of dollars by the click of a mouse button using sophisticated mathematical and statistical methods to move money from one place to any another. Another irony is that people who earn money in financial sectors pay only 15 percent federal taxes, claiming their incomes as capital gains rather than regular income, where tax rates are at least twice as high. Warren Buffett famously said that he pays only 15 percent tax, whereas the people working for him pay almost twice this amount. During the economic boom period, people making money in the financial sector claim that they are behind the economic boom. In reality, they are squeezing the juice out of the fruit, and when that juice is gone there is not much left of the general economy. During economic recessions and depressions the government has to clean the garbage left by the financial sectors, the moneymaking tools used by millionaires and billionaires, by spending trillions of dollars of taxpayers' money, which could have been used for development programs.

Due to the rise in investments in commodity markets, the global prices of commodities such as gas, corn, wheat, rice, and potatoes are going through the roof. These prices are not determined by demand and supply but by investors, who in almost all cases do not take physical possession of these commodities, except maybe precious metals, at all. In mid-2011, the gold price was up by 40 percent from a year earlier. This tremendous rise in gold price is not because of a sudden increase in the number of users of gold or a sudden drop in supply. The rise of price is due to investors. The same is true for the steep rises in consumer items such as gas, wheat, onions, corn, and potatoes.

Let us take the example of gold. Suppose the gold price is $1,200 an ounce, and a group of investors invest $5 billion in gold at this price. In a year, the gold price jumps to $2,400 an ounce and, at this price, investors decide to sell their holdings. Due to the sell on such a massive scale, it is natural that gold price will crash, as there will not be enough buyers to buy $5 billion worth of gold on such short notice. Say the gold price crashes to $2,000 to $2,100 an ounce. After selling their gold holdings, the investors will make anywhere from $3 billion to $5 billion on their $5 billion investment. Now, after the crash of gold prices, the losers will be the end users (i.e., those who buy gold for their own use) and people who bought the gold at its peak price (i.e., at $2,400 an ounce) thinking that the price would keep rising. This will give you an idea about how Wall Street bankers and investors are making money. The government is not printing any special money for them. They are getting money from the pockets of ordinary people by playing casino games. You may think that it is okay, since people generally buy gold as an investment and, hence, if these ultrarich people are making money from investment-minded people, then we should not worry about it. No, you are wrong. These Wall Street bankers and hedge fund managers are playing the same casino game with almost all commodities that we use every day (e.g., rice, wheat, onions, sugar, potatoes, gas—anything you can think of). Even a homeless person pays this "Wall Street tax" when he buys a food item in the local store with his meager money.

In November 2010, silver and copper were 44 percent and 25 percent, respectively, above May 2010 prices. In late 2010, JPMorgan Chase bought $1.5 billion worth of copper contracts, more than half of 350,000 tones of reserves, on the London Metal Exchange, pushing the price of immediate delivery of copper to a record level. In 2008, twenty-seven barrels of crude were being traded every day on the New York Mercantile Exchange for every one barrel of oil that was actually being consumed in the United States.[30]

Food prices have skyrocketed. The World Bank's food price index rose by 15 percent between October 2010 and January 2011, and was 29 percent above its level a year earlier. In early 2011, wheat and corn rose 85 percent and 87 percent, respectively, in just one year at the Chicago Board of Trade.[31] The money invested in commodity index funds and commodity derivatives went up from $13 billion in 2003 to $250 billion in early 2008. It is alleged that Goldman made a $1 billion profit in trading in the food market in 2009. In 2010, Armajaro, a hedge fund, was said to have bought 240,000 tons of cocoa beans, driving the price of cocoa still higher.

In India, food prices have tripled in the last four years. In 2009, the total turnover of the potato at commodity exchanges in India was four million tons, but the actual delivery was only seven thousand tons. That means 99.82 percent of the trade was mere speculation on paper.[32] Out of the 8,038.42 billion rupees turnover of 2009 at India's National Commodity Exchange (NCDEX), delivery was 0.28 percent (2.2 billion rupees).[33]

It is worth noting that the required down payment for purchase of a commodity on a future date is only 10 percent. Hence one can buy $1 billion worth of a commodity (petrol, wheat, corn, rice, copper, silver, etc.) with only $100 million at one's disposal. If the price goes up by 10 percent in a week, the commodity speculator can make $100 million by selling the contract (i.e., 100 percent return in just one week).

Due to wrong bets in energy trading, Amarnath Advisors LLC, a $9 billion hedge fund founded in 2000, lost $5 billion within a week in September 2006, which led to its collapse. In 2010, the Federal Energy

Regulatory Commission found Brian Hunter, the head of its energy division, guilty of market manipulation in energy futures.

In national newspapers, you can find numerous articles by economists on how you can make money in commodity trading. If an investor is making money in the commodity market, he never takes physical possession of the commodity but is taking money from the pockets of common people who are the end users. Conservatives rail against the government and do not want to pay taxes. The question then arises why should common people pay the "Wall Street tax" at the time of purchasing consumer items in the market?

The trillions of dollars of the Federal Reserve's QE (Quantitative Easing) programs are causing havoc in emerging countries such as India, Brazil, and Vietnam, and even in China, as investors can borrow dollars in the United States at a negligible interest rate and invest in foreign countries, a practice called "carry trade." Rise in inflation forces governments in emerging countries to raise interest rates in order to reduce money supply, but the rise in interest rates affects the economic growth in these countries. Hence it is a Catch-22 situation for them: If they do not increase their interest rates, inflation will increase.

The banking crisis that began in 2008 related to credit-default swaps, raises a question of whether this is just a precursor to what can happen in the future if hedge funds and investment banks keep creating trillions of dollars of investments on paper. If that situation continues, the same scenario will happen again and again. The government will have to come up with trillions of dollars of bailout funds every time for the mischief of these casino hedge fund gamblers. We do not know what kind of zombies (i.e., special moneymaking mathematical and statistical software) are being created inside the Wall Street and other financial systems. Such "time bombs" may lie dormant for years, only to explode under certain conditions. For instance, Long-Term Capital Management (LTCM), a US hedge fund, lost a whopping $4.4 billion following the 1998 Russian financial crisis, leading to a massive bailout by other major banks and investment houses supervised by the Federal Reserve. LTCM was liquidated in early 2000.

The Federal Reserve had to rescue LTCM, otherwise it would have led to a wider collapse of the financial markets. After its founding in 1994, LTCM had annualized returns of over 40 percent (after fees) in its first years. Its board of directors' members included Myron Scholes and Robert C. Merton, who shared the 1997 Nobel Prize in Economic Sciences. Before the crisis, LTCM had a leverage ratio of 25 to 1 ($120 billion in positions with $4.8 billion in capital). Due to its astounding annual returns, banks were providing a nearly unlimited amount of credit to LTMC at very low interest rates. The LTCM software, using mathematical and statistical techniques developed in-house, was based on the assumption of small fluctuations in interest rates. On August 17, 1998, the Russian government devalued the ruble, defaulted on domestic debt, and declared a moratorium on payment to foreign creditors. The LTCM software could not handle this much large fluctuations in Russian currency. By the end of September 1998, LTCM had just $400 million in capital. With liabilities still over $100 billion, this translated to an effective leverage ratio of more than 250 to 1.[34]

Rise of China due to Reaganomics—A Treason

Reaganomics is the biggest fraud created in the history of the United States. Not only did it create large debts, it also transferred money from the middle class to the richest 2 percent. Without the 1944 Bretton Woods Agreement, which made the US dollar the global currency, Reaganomics would have died in its infancy. Reaganomics was paid for initially by Japan during the 1980s to the early 1990s, and thereafter mainly by China, which is a potential enemy of the United States. In a similar situation, when the Soviets needed money for their "glasnost" (freedom of speech, transparency in government) and "perestroika" (reconstruction of the economy, economic reforms) campaigns during the late 1980s, German banks stopped giving loans and instead started demanding repayments, causing the Soviet economy to collapse.

Reagan was a great "socialist," who transferred money to the rich from the middle-class people. Reagan raided the Social Security trust fund to give tax breaks to the rich. Democrats are accused of being a tax-and-spend party (i.e., they are for tax increases so that the government can spend that money on social welfare programs). On the other hand, the Republican Party is pro tax-cut and spend (i.e., they will cut the taxes, but they will increase the spending, mainly by increasing defense spending—remember Bush Jr.'s two unfunded wars and unfunded Medicare B plan). Unlike the Democrats' tax-and-spend policy, which causes little or no budget deficits while all the money transactions remain inside the country, the Republican cut taxes and spend policy has created large budget deficits, which have now put the country at the mercy of foreign investors such as China, another Soviet-like adversary in the making. The Republicans' tax-cut and spending policies, therefore, amount to high treason.

President Bush's tax cuts for the rich transformed the January 2001 projected ten-year $5.6 trillion budget surplus into trillions of dollars of deficit in the early 2000s. When the economy booms, and there is a budget surplus, their administrations give tax cuts to corporations and wealthy people, claiming that the extra money belongs to all Americans. But when the economy is in recession, they again give tax cuts to corporations and wealthy people, claiming that they are needed to jump-start the economy. In chapter 4 we will see how similar tax cuts during the 1920s have been cited as some of the main reasons for the 1930s Great Depression.

After the midterm elections in 2002, when Dick Cheney started proposing another round of tax cuts, Treasury Secretary Paul O'Neill told him, "the government is moving towards a fiscal crisis" and explained what rising deficits meant for economic and fiscal soundness. Cheney replied, "Reagan proved deficits don't matter." A few weeks later, President Bush asked O'Neill to submit his resignation[35] and found a Treasury secretary who would rubber-stamp his tax cuts. In addition to O'Neill, Bush also got rid of Colin Powell, as both of them were against the invasion of Iraq. It is worth noting that O'Neill, a lifelong Republican, successfully ran Alcoa, the world's largest aluminum producer, for twelve years as its CEO and chairman.

As we will see in chapter 4, it was Reaganomics that created the recession in the late 1980s. Had there been no advent of information technology, Reaganomics as well as the US economy would have collapsed in the early 1990s.

Banks give credit card loans to an extent that a person can pay only the interest on the loans from his or her monthly paycheck. They are not interested in getting the principal back; rather, they go for the maximum interest payment. Therefore, if the person suffers an economic setback, he or she will have no option but to declare bankruptcy. Reaganomics is based on the same principle. During good times the country accumulated debts to such an extent that now it may have a problem paying even the interests on the accumulating debt without risking a severe economic crisis in the country. An individual can declare bankruptcy and get rid of all loans, but it will be a disaster for the global economy if a country like the United States declares bankruptcy.

Reaganomics has created a deadly cancer in the American economy that has no cure. Within a few years, China will have such a large amount of dollars that it will be in a position to dictate US policy in every sphere, and it seems certain that China is going to take the United States down.

If you tell a lie a hundred times, it becomes a truth. Commercial media, especially conservative media like Fox News, work on the same principle. They brainwash Americans. Even after several months of the release of his long-form birth certificate, confirming his birth in Hawaii, more than half of Americans still had doubts about President Barack Obama's birthplace being in the United States.[36] Still, more than half of Americans believe that Saddam Hussein was behind the 9/11 attacks in 2001 and also that he had weapons of mass destruction (WMD) despite numerous reports to the contrary by congressional investigations. Prior to the 2003 Iraq invasion, everyone in the media underscored the tunes of the Bush administration about Saddam Hussein having the weapons of mass destruction. Anyone in the media who was against this misinformation was simply being fired. Phil Donahue, who was trying to have a balanced conversation (both pro and con) in his talk show before the 2003 Iraq war, was fired by MSNBC. Using similar propaganda, conservatives have made the F-grade Ronald Reagan an A-grade president and are claiming Reaganomics, a treacherous and failed theory, to be a success and the force behind the economic boom during the Clinton administration in 1990s. Jimmy Carter was a victim of conservative propaganda too.

By similar massive propaganda, conservatives have brainwashed Americans by claiming that by reducing the size of government, the economy booms when more money goes to people who can spend it more wisely. As we will see in chapter 3, had the Bush administration not gone for two wars (Iraq and Afghanistan) and increased the size of government, the American economy would have been in recession throughout the eight years of his administration.

RISE OF THE EAST

Until the advent of the Industrial Revolution, the economies of China and India were far ahead of others, including European countries. Put together, China and India's economy was more than half of the global GDP, more than a quarter each. Civil wars, and the Japanese attacks in the late 1800s and early 1900s on China and the subjugation of India by the British, led to their downturn. Now, after nearly three hundred years, they are again in a position to dominate the global economy. China has already emerged as a leader in the global economy, and it is just a question of time before India may overtake China, due to the latter's graying population and decrease in working population resulting from its one-child policy.

Reaganomics is one of the main reasons behind the rise of China. Also mainly due to the 2008 Great Recession, which was the result of the deregulation of the financial industry created by Republicans, China has arrived at the global stage much sooner than predicted. In 2011, Gerard Lyons, chief economist and group head of global research at Standard Chartered, said:

The last decade could be characterized by the three words 'Made in China.' In this next decade, it will be "Owned by China."[37]

According to a 2011 IMF estimate, China's GDP will surpass the United States' GDP in purchasing power parity (PPP) terms in 2016. Although the per capita income of China is one-twelfth that of the United States in nominal terms, this ratio is just one-fourth in PPP terms. Due to its double-digit growth rate, China's per capita income is going to be only half that of the United States in the next two decades because of the latter's meager one or two percent growth rate. With the decline in the value of the US dollar, it may happen much earlier.

In 2011, the per capita GDP of China was 19 percent of that of the

United States, compared with 4 percent when Chinese economic reform began just over thirty years ago. According to the IMF, China's share of global GDP (measured in current prices) will pass the 10 percent mark in 2013. Goldman Sachs continues to forecast that China will overtake the United States in terms of GDP in 2027. China recently overtook the United States as the world's biggest market for cars (14 million sales a year, compared to 11 million one year ago), and its demand is projected to rise tenfold in the years ahead. Once China was mainly an exporter of low-price manufactures. Now that it accounts for fully a fifth of global growth, it has become the most dynamic new market for other people's stuff.[38]

In 2011, China overtook the United States and Japan in terms of filing new patent applications. This is part of a wider story of Eastern ascendancy.[39] In 2008, for the first time, the number of patent applications from China, India, Japan, and South Korea exceeded those from the West. The United States is losing high-tech manufacturing jobs, mainly to Asian countries. According to a National Science Board report published in January 2012, the number of high-tech manufacturing jobs in the United States declined by 687,000, or 28 percent, between 2000 and 2010.[40]

The last time a change in the leadership of the global economy took place was after World War II, and it was a smooth transition from the United Kingdom to the United States. Prior to that, the economic superpower leadership struggle between Germany and the United Kingdom had led to the two world wars, which had sapped the economies of both the countries, and this led the United States to claim the position. This time around the change may or may not happen smoothly and without any war.

It is perhaps in the interest of China that it should lay low and let the US and Western economies collapse and then claim the leadership. On the other hand, if it takes any adventurous step like attacking Taiwan, India (to grab sparsely populated regions on their disputed borders), and/or its neighbors for grabbing the controversial islands in the South China Sea, taking advantage of a weak United States and Europe, China will be destroyed on par with the destruction of Germany in the previous two world wars. However, if China takes military action against its neighbor(s) it may not result in another world war. Instead,

China could be devastated due to the economic sanctions imposed on it by nearly all major countries. Economic sanctions against China will have an effect on other countries, too, but will lead to the complete collapse of the Chinese economy.

MIDDLE EAST AND NORTH AFRICAN COUNTRIES—EARLY 1900S EUROPE

The rise of Islamic fundamentalism worldwide took most by surprise when on September 11, 2001, Islamic fundamentalists intentionally crashed airliners into the World Trade Center in New York and into the Pentagon, killing more than three thousand people. On that day, US National Security Adviser Condoleeza Rice was scheduled to outline a Bush administration policy that would address "the threats and problems of today and the day after, not the world of yesterday." The focus was largely on missile defense, not terrorism from Islamic radicals. The address was designed to promote a missile system as the cornerstone of a new national security strategy. It contained no mention of al-Qaeda, Osama bin Laden, or Islamic extremist groups, according to former US officials who saw the text. The speech was postponed in the chaos of the day. It mentioned terrorism, but did so as one of the dangers from rogue nations, such as Iraq, that might use weapons of terror, rather than from the extremist cells now considered to be America's main security threat.[41]

In 1995, I published an article based on the analysis of the social, political, and religion environments in the Middle East in *Global Times* (Denmark). I wrote:

The United States has sowed the seeds of the next Cold War by employing the low-cost war strategy in Afghanistan. Although a rise in Islamic fundamentalist movements world-wide was inevitable, US involvement in Afghanistan only hastened the process ...

The rise in Islamic fundamentalist movements world-wide is inevitable. Iraq just delayed this rise by waging the eight-yearlong war with fundamentalist Iran. Large-scale unemployment and acute poverty in the general population and corruption in high places is giving rise to militancy. Earlier, these reasons were responsible for the rise in communist movements in countries like India, Vietnam, Yemen, Chile, and Nicaragua. Nowadays, the unemployed and poor masses are swayed to militancy in the name of religion, giving rise to religious militancy. The rise of some Hindu militant groups in India, the Islamic Salvation Front in Algeria, Hamas in Palestine, the Islamic Group in Egypt, and An-Nahda (*Renaissance*) in Tunisia are some examples of this rise in religious militancy world-wide. This trend is especially dangerous in the case of Islamic states because Islam and its holy book, the Quran, do not differentiate between state and mosque or between politics and theology. It is a general feature even in a country like India, where Muslims are about 12 percent of the population, that clergy give a political lecture after the Friday prayer in the mosque …

After the fall of oil-rich countries like Saudi Arabia to Islamic militants, Islamic clerics will try to establish an Islamic empire like the old Ottoman Empire founded during the 14th and 15th Centuries.

Although fundamentalist Islamic states and powerful Islamic clerics will be the losers of a Cold or Third World War, Islam as a religion will emerge victorious and shed its 7th century image, becoming a new 21st century religion more tolerant to women and non-Muslims.

[W]hen ordinary people fail to find relief from radical Islamic regimes, they will force a change in leadership and we will see the emergence of a number of Mustafa Kemals. These Kemals will bring drastic social and religious changes, and the West will help them financially. [42]

Based on this article, I published a book *The Modernization of Islam and the Creation of a Multipolar World Order* (Booksurge, January 2008). In this book, one chapter was on the global economy (chapter 6—"The Collapse of The American Economy"). I analyzed the global economy data of the last couple of hundred years and concluded that the US economy would collapse, leading to the next Great Depression. I predicted that due to money woes, the United States (and its Western allies) would not be able to influence the coming transition in Islamic countries except applying economic sanctions.

Sharia is Islamic law. It is based mainly on the *hadith*, or sayings of Muhammad. In non-Muslim countries, especially in the United States and Western Europe, sharia is considered to be an evil because it does not provide any rights to non-Muslims and restricts rights of Women. But almost all religions had similar legal codes in the past.

After the killing of Osama bin Laden, newspapers published the photo of President Obama and his national security team huddled around a conference table in the White House Situation Room watching the real-time Navy Seal team attack on the bin Laden compound. Two women, including Secretary of State Hillary Clinton, were in the photo. While publishing this photo, an ultraorthodox Hasidic (a branch of Orthodox Judaism) New York newspaper, *Der Tzitung,* edited both women out of the picture, claiming that the photos did not display women, in accordance with their own anachronistic policy. In some Jerusalem bus routes, women are required to ride in the back of the bus only. In a December 2011 closed-door meeting of the Saban Forum at the Brookings Institution's Saban Center, US Secretary of State Hillary Clinton said that the attitudes of a growing and increasingly powerful ultra-Orthodox community in Israel, particularly its attitudes toward women, are reminiscent of Iran. She gave the segregated busing on some routes as an example.[43]

In the United States, fundamentalist Christians claim that the country should be run on rules based on the Christian faith, and it should not grant any religious rights to non-Christians. They openly claim that everyone except good Christians is certain to go to the hell.

Hindus also used to have their own legal code, *Manu Smirti,* similar to *sharia.* When Manu Smirti was written, the caste of a person was based on occupation and was not hereditary. For example, Krishna was born in a Vaishya family, whereas one of his uncles, Maharishi Garga, who gave him the name Krishna, was a Brahmin, as he was a priest, and his maternal uncle, the tyrannical king Kansa, whom he killed, was a Kshatriya. There are four traditional Hindu castes— Brahmins (scholars, teachers, fire priests), Kshatriyas (kings, warriors, law enforcers, administrators), Vaishyas (agriculturists, cattle raisers, traders, bankers), and Shudras (artisans, craftsmen, service providers). Certain people, like foreigners, nomads, forest tribes, and the chandalas (who dealt with disposal of the dead), were excluded altogether and treated as untouchables. According to Manu Smirti, a person could marry only within his own caste, as well as a person below him in the caste system (e.g., Brahmins could marry with any from the other three castes, but not vice versa). Also, the punishment given by a legal court depended on the caste of the convict. For instance, if a Brahmin was found guilty of killing a shudra, he had to just donate a few animals as punishment, whereas a shudra was to be given the death penalty. All non-Hindus were considered as below shudras. Brahmin means one who knows Brahma (i.e., God), and hence he was considered to be more valuable to society than others. According to Manu Smirti, doctors/ physicians had to live outside the villages, as they were considered filthy because during those days surgery was considered to be a very dirty job. At present the majority of Hindus in India and elsewhere do not even know about Manu Smirti, although its unhealthy influence on their society is tremendous.

The majority of religions came into existence only in the last couple of thousand years, and nearly every one claims that only its followers will go to the Heaven or have a successful afterlife, and the rest are certain to go to the Hell. In a word, they are mutually exclusive. But the exponential rise in scientific knowledge in the last two hundred to three hundred years undermines their essential scriptural claims. Now we know that human beings roamed the planet even two hundred thousand years ago, and there might be billions of planets like Earth where human-like creatures might be.

A scientific theory is considered valid only if it is reproducible—that is, if it has the following three characteristics:

(1) Universal—the theory is applicable to all.

(2) Time independent—the theory should be valid today, millions of years ago, and millions of years after.

(3) Space independent—the theory should be valid at all the places.

For instance, Einstein's famous mass-energy equation $E=mc^2$ is a scientific law because you will get the same results as me if we are doing experiments at two different places to verify this law, and this law is not time dependent (e.g., it is valid, say, even after ten thousand years).

Suppose I have come up with a scientific theory claiming some kind of output on the basis of some assumptions. Then everyone should get the same output at any place and any time if they follow the same assumptions. If you or anybody else gets a different result under the conditions assumed, then my theory is invalid.

One point worth noting is that when a scientist comes up with a new scientific law, he is just discovering it and not creating or inventing it, as the newly discovered law is already there in the universe since time immemorial. From the point of view of religion and spirituality, therefore, we need a theory that is progressive and consistent with the age of the universe and is not limited by historical or geographical circumstances. It stands to reason that if there is a God, he would love each and every one the same—not just those born recently—and he would give everyone—people living here two hundred thousand years ago or human-being-like creatures on millions and billions of planets—equal opportunity to go to heaven or hell or move in any other way. Like any good theory, spiritual theory needs to be free from the distorting influences of time and place, too. In my book, *Karma, Mind, and the Quest for Happiness* (iUniverse, 2012), I have explained one spiritual theory, the theory of Karma, which conforms to all of the three requirements of a scientific theory.

Islam is the only religion that is being enforced by several countries today having Muslim majority population. Quran and sharia discriminate against non-Muslims and give limited rights to women. Quran and sharia impose *jizya*, a tax, on non-Muslims, and Muslims are not required to pay this tax. The Ottoman Empire (1299–1923) and Muslim rulers in India since the eleventh century imposed *jizya* on non-Muslims. In Persia, jizya was paid by the Zoroastrian minority until 1884. In North Africa also, jizya was collected by Islamic rulers until the late nineteenth century. Conversion by Muslims to other faiths is forbidden under sharia, and converts are considered apostates. Non-Muslims, however, are allowed to convert to Islam. In several Islamic countries there are numerous cases in which sharia courts have forced Muslims who converted to other religions to remain Muslims, and they are given prison terms. In several Islamic countries, a non-Muslim gets only a fraction (ranging from one half to one-tenth) of what a Muslim gets in a similar legal settlement in courts. In sharia courts, non-Muslims cannot even represent themselves. Saudi Arabia implements the Quran and hadith in toto. No other religion is allowed in Saudi Arabia. Although American soldiers are in the country to protect the kingdom from outside threat, soldiers who wear a cross or a Star of David must keep the symbols hidden, and they must worship in private. Fifteen out of nineteen hijackers who conducted the attacks on September 11, 2001, in the United States were from Saudi Arabia.

Until the Middle Ages (1300 AD), nearly all Christian rulers in Europe and the Middle East were enforcing Christianity and imposing restrictions on non-Christians (please see chapter 8 for more details). The Hindu rulers of India, too, ruled by discriminating religious terms. Gradually, by sociopolitical enlightenment, it was realized that it is wrong to limit religious freedoms, and secularism became the norm. This evolution can be termed as the modernization of those religions. Non-Christians are able to practice their religions freely in the Christian majority United States not because their forefathers fought for their religious freedoms but because of the secularization of the majority of Christians. Such a secular majority is missing in nearly all Islamic countries. Even in non-Muslim majority countries such as India, Muslims have separate civil codes, based on their sharia. Once, a Muslim of India criticized an article on my blog that proposed provisions for a uniform civil code in a country's constitution. I asked him, "Why do you want only the civil code of sharia (for example, a man to have up to four wives, denying alimony to divorced women, and divorcing the wife by just uttering the word 'divorce' three times) and not the criminal code of sharia? Why does the government not implement the criminal code of sharia on Muslims, i.e., if the court convicts a non-Muslim, then he shall have to go to jail, whereas if the convicted person is a Muslim, his limbs (hand/leg) will be cut off, an eye may be taken out, or death by stoning may be administered according to sharia?"

Prophet Muhammad was a great person. He united the entire Arab population, which had been divided into several clans, under one umbrella. It is wrong to criticize him for his deeds, as whatever he did was relevant at the time (please read chapter 8 for more details). For instance, he provided an eye for an eye judgment in the Quran as there was no prison system wherein a convict could serve a term at the time. We should blame the present-day people who are following these seventh-century practices. Except for the divinity aspects of Muhammad's revelations, the Quran consists of the social practices of seventh-century Arabia.

Two factors, the coming global economic depression and global Islamic fundamentalism, are going to redefine human civilization in the same way as the 1930s Great Depression and the two World Wars redefined human civilization. The 1930s Great Depression resulted in the rise of Hitler, who tried to establish the "Third Reich," an awesome colonial power like Britain's, which would rule over the world for a thousand years. In the first half of the last century, the independence movements in the European colonies were on the rise, which would eventually have ended colonialism. Hitler was simply trying to turn back the clock. Instead of achieving his goal, he helped pave the way for thriving democracies in most of Europe and the decolonization in Asia and Europe.

The collapse of the US economy will lead to radical political changes in the world, not the least in the Islamic world, which would open up for the modernization of Islam. During the period of modernization of Islam, the world may be experiencing turmoil while it moves toward stability. Europe, India, the United States, Israel, and perhaps even China will constitute war fronts, particularly for homegrown terrorists. If Pakistan's nuclear arsenal falls into the hands of Islamic militants, we may witness large-scale nuclear attacks on these countries. But in the end the modernization of Islam will be a major step toward the integration of human civilization.

Until 1900, no one could predict that democracy would replace kingdoms in most European countries, or that Asian and African countries would gain independence within five to six decades. Because of the two world wars, most European kingdoms were replaced by vibrant democracies, and colonial rulers had to leave most of Asia and Africa due to the destruction wrought on their economies.

In order to give birth to a beautiful child, a woman has to go through pangs of labor. Europe went through a crisis in the first half of the last century. World Wars I and II were necessary in order to change the global socioeconomic and political environments of those times, in Europe in particular. Had those world wars not occurred, much of Europe might still be ruled as kingdoms, and most Asian and African countries might still be awaiting independence from their colonial masters.

Today, Islamic civilization is going through what Europe went through during 1914–45. The creation, first, of Israel in 1948, and the invasion of Iraq, in 2003, have catalyzed deep changes that will result in its modernization. Outside forces cannot impose anything for long in any country. The solution has to come from within. At the end of this crisis, Islam will soon cease to be the guiding force wherever it now leads, and the majority of Islamic nations will become secular and democratic, like Turkey. Until World War I, Turkey, whose population is 99 percent Muslim, had been the seat of the Ottoman Empire (1299–1922), an Islamic empire, and the Islamic caliphate. It is now a secular, democratic nation since 1923.

Until 2010, nobody would have thought of the drastic changes happening in Middle Eastern and North African Islamic countries, dubbed the Arab Spring. After the fall of dictators such as Hosni Mubarak of Egypt, Ben Ali of Tunisia, Ali Abdullah Saleh of Yemen, and Muammar Gaddafi of Libya, every ruler in this region now looks vulnerable.

After the defeat of the Ottoman Empire in World War I, Britain and France divided the Ottoman Empire into several countries, forty in number right now, and installed their lackeys as rulers in these countries. Later on, military generals (such as Nasser in Egypt, Gaddafi in Libya, Qasim and then Saddam in Iraq, and Assad in Syria), overthrew several of those rulers and established their dictatorial rules. At the time, these generals were hailed as heroes in their countries. Over the years these military dictators behaved in the same way as the leaders they had overthrown, and this has led to the disenchantment of their masses. In almost all countries in this region, the median age of the population is below thirty years. Due to the advent of the World Wide Web and its accessibility in almost every corner of the globe, these young people lead the Arab Spring throughout the region after having watched how their own country lagged far behind others in terms of economic and living standards. After watching the World War I defeat and disintegration of his Ottoman Empire by the Western powers, Mustafa Kemal, an Ottoman army officer, faced a similar situation. Until the advent of the industrial revolution in Europe in the eighteenth century, the Ottoman Empire, founded in 1299, was far ahead of European countries, especially during its prime years. After the disintegration of the Ottoman Empire, Kemal saw no option but to modernize his country, which led him to the establishment of a secular and democratic Turkey in 1923. The establishment of modern Turkey was a result of World War I, the first war that had left scars on most of the global population and in which millions had lost their lives. The then-European colonies, such as India, also lost hundreds of thousands of their population as Europeans used them to fight their enemies. Hence the coming drastic change in the Islamic countries, especially in the Middle East and North Africa, will not be a calm affair. This transformational change will take place only after a violent shake-up in these countries and will leave scars in several non-Muslim countries as well, especially in those having a sizeable Muslim population.

The present global Islamic militancy may lead to a temporary establishment of an Islamic empire in the Middle East and North Africa, with fundamentalist Islamic parties taking power in democratic elections. These ruling parties will try to turn back the clock by imposing sharia rules, which is nothing but seventh-century Arabian culture. But like Hitler's Third Reich, it will lead to the formation of secular and democratic nations, such as Turkey, in the region. Hence the current rise in Islamic militancy worldwide does not reflect Samuel Huntington's "clash of civilizations,"[44] but is instead a violent prelude to the modernization of Islam, and a major step toward the integration of human civilization.

DEMOCRACY NEEDS A TUNE-UP

Like communism, common political democracy is a relatively new phenomenon. In several Western nations, women were denied voting rights until the last century. In Switzerland, women obtained voting rights toward the end of the twentieth century. In one region of that country it happened as late as in 1990, by central government decree. Although democracy is the best of all "-cracies," it has deficiencies, due to which incompetent persons like US presidents Reagan and Bush Jr. could get elected. Democracy is far from successful in the United States, the world's most developed democracy, or in India, the world's largest democracy. For instance, more than half of the elected officials in India at both state and central levels are noted criminals. Almost 99 percent of Indian cabinet ministers would go to prison if corruption and criminal charges were impartially and vigorously investigated. Democracy needs major reforms.

Also, the lagging economic growth of India (vis-à-vis China) and the drubbing of US and other Western economies are putting a question mark on the liberal democratic system. Russia toyed with liberal democracy during the 1990s, and it resulted in its GDP reduced by half. During his second presidential bid in 1996, Russia's then-President Boris Yeltsin, the architect of the dissolution of the USSR and hailed as a hero in the West, had his popularity in single digits for several months. Then he sold the crown jewels of the country, mining industries, to a small group of people known as oligarchs, making them overnight billionaires, just for a couple of hundreds of millions for his election, which he finally won by spending this money. Had Yeltsin done the same in a Western country, not only he but all of these oligarchs would have been behind bars for the remainder of their lives. Yeltsin was afraid that once he left office he might have to face corruption charges. Hence he chose Vladimir Putin, an unknown person on the national stage, as his successor because he would to save himself and his inner circles. In his previous post, Putin helped his boss, St. Petersburg Mayor Anatoly Sobchak, to flee overseas when Sobchak was about to be arrested on corruption charges.[45] Russia under authoritarian Putin has progressed economically at a rate nobody could have imagined.

The sudden rise of authoritarian China has taken everyone by surprise too. In October 2009, Putin sent some members of his ruling United Russia party for a special meeting with representatives of China's Communist Party to get a crash course so that he could emulate the workings of China in Russia.

According to a US diplomatic cable released by WikiLeaks, all important decisions in China are taken by the Politburo of the ruling Communist Party, consisting of twenty-four men and one woman. According to the cable, "true democracy" prevails in the Politburo, as all the decisions are taken by consensus system, in which members can exercise veto power. They discuss as long as it takes for all to agree on an issue.

The Chinese economy is divided into two categories. At the lower level, the private sector dominates industries such as factory-assembled exports, clothing, and food. At the higher level, major industries such as finance, communications, transportation, mining, and metals are still run by the central government. In China, the major portion of the $585 billion stimulus package after the 2008 recession, spent on infrastructure, went to government-owned firms. In the mid-2000s, the central government opened the passenger airline industry to private investors. By 2006, there were eight private and three state-controlled airlines. Then the state-controlled airlines started a price war. The state-controlled fuel firms refused to provide private-owned airlines jet fuel on the same generous terms that were given to the three state-controlled airlines. The private-owned airlines were not allowed to book flights using the only computerized reservation system, partly owned by state-controlled airlines. After the 2008 recession, when the private-owned airlines faced financial difficulties, the Chinese government bought all private-owned airlines, except one, and turned them into state-controlled firms.[46] On the other hand, after the airline industry was opened to private investors in India, the services of the state-controlled airline, Air India, were withdrawn from lucrative routes, which were given to private-controlled airlines, and that is the main reason why the state-controlled airline now runs in deep red.

In 2011, a mass movement against corruption raised its voice in India. Perhaps due to this movement, corruption on the individual level will go away in India, and the country will become like the United States, where the entire Congress is owned by the ultrarich. Although individual corruption throughout society is low in the United States, as the probability a person committing an illegal act will be caught is high, a corrupt political-business nexus does exist, but of a different type than in India and other Asian countries. As politicians need a lot of money to run for office, s/he has to accept donations from multinationals and the ultrawealthy. Once elected, s/he works more for these multinationals and the ultrawealthy, and less for the average citizen. Though politicians receive only peanuts—a few thousands of dollars—in donations, their benefactors in return get millions, if not billions, of dollars in the form of budgets and other government provisions like tax breaks and no-bid contracts.

Ronald Reagan and George Bush Jr. transferred massive amounts of money from the government exchequer to the ultrarich, effectively bankrupting the nation. Had they done the same in a corporation they would have been given life sentences. Only for the 2003 invasion of Iraq on bogus evidences, Bush Jr. would have been court-marshaled and given life imprisonment in an African or any other country. According to people close to him, George Bush Jr.'s knowledge was limited to baseball mostly. For his deposition before the 9/11 commission, Bush went with Cheney, as he could not have given any answer himself regarding his administration.

When asked about the working condition in the Bush administration, Paul O'Neill, George W. Bush's first Treasury secretary, said that he had worked in the US administration for fifteen years and also at major companies in the world, but he had never seen anything like this (i.e., the way the Bush administration was functioning).[47] According to him, Presidents George H. W. Bush (Bush Sr.) and Gerald Ford used to hear both pros and cons from cabinet members, and then they used to make their decisions.[48] In his book *The Price of Loyalty*, O'Neill discussed the president's complete lack of inquisitiveness and pertinent experience and how the president took no interest in discussions during cabinet meetings. George Bush Jr. was not reading reports or even short memos sent by his cabinet secretaries; he asked no questions. According to O'Neill, "[The] President was like a blind man in a roomful of deaf people." O'Neill had previously worked in both the Nixon and Ford administrations. He found Bush utterly different from his predecessors and unresponsive in large and small meetings.[49]

Like Bush Jr., Reagan did not have any knowledge of what was being done in his name by his administration, as he had no knowledge in any field except entertainment. Although conservative Republican Ronald Reagan is generally held in the "near-to-great" category of US presidents, according to Henry Kissinger, the former secretary of state and national security advisor:

> Reagan knew next to no history. He treated biblical references to Armageddon as operational predictions. Many of the historical anecdotes he was so fond of recounting had no basis in fact, as facts are generally understood. In a private conversation, he once equated Gorbachev with Bismarck, arguing that both had overcome identical domestic obstacles by moving away from a centrally planned economy toward the free market. I advised a mutual friend that Reagan should be warned never to repeat this preposterous proposition to a German interlocutor.

> The details of foreign policy bored Reagan. When you talk to Reagan, you sometimes wonder why it occurred to anyone that he should be president, or even governor. But what … historians have to explain is how so unintellectual a man could have dominated California for eight years, and Washington already for nearly seven.[50]

Donald Regan, Reagan's secretary of the Treasury and later chief of staff, criticized Reagan for his lack of attention to economics:

> In the four years that I served as Secretary of the Treasury, I never saw President Reagan alone and never discussed economic philosophy or fiscal and monetary policy with him one-on-one … The President never told me what he believed or what he wanted to accomplish in the field of economics.[51]

Communism restricts fundamental rights, whereas in capitalism, people have fundamental rights, but their voices are not heard. Although politicians win due to the participation of common people in elections, they work for the ultrarich and multinationals, as they need money to win despite knowing full well that their policies are harmful for the country. They have no other option but to sell themselves to the highest bidder.

In any of the Third World countries, including India, the present form of democracy is a complete failure. The main reason is that after getting independence, there was only the transfer of political power from the colonial powers (i.e., a small group of people replaced the colonial rulers, whereas everything remained the same).

A "true" democracy consists of both a "political democracy" and an "economic democracy." The democratic system, defined by Western standards, defines the first only (i.e., political democracy). Right now both faculties of democracy are controlled by vested interests, mainly by the ultrarich and large firms. In the next section and also in chapter 12, we will discuss a socioeconomic theory, PROUT (PROgressive Utilization Theory), formulated by Indian thinker P. R. Sarkar. PROUT defines these two types of democracy in detail. The present liberal democratic system can be improved by incorporating some features of PROUT.

PROUT

Over the past decade and a half, American corporations have been saving more and investing less in their own businesses. A 2005 report from JPMorgan Research noted with concern that, since 2002, American corporations on average ran a net financial surplus of 1.7 percent of the gross domestic product—a drastic change from the previous forty years, when they had maintained an average deficit of 1.2 percent of GDP. More recent studies have indicated that companies in Europe, Japan, and China are also running unprecedented surpluses. The reason for all this saving in the United States is that public companies have become obsessed with quarterly earnings. To show short-term profits, they avoid investing in future growth. To develop new products, buy new equipment, or expand geographically, an enterprise has to spend money—on marketing research, product design, prototype development, legal expenses associated with patents, lining up contractors, and so on. Rather than incurring such expenses, companies increasingly prefer to pay their executives exorbitant bonuses or issue special dividends to shareholders, or simply engage in pure financial speculation. But this means they also short-circuit a major driver of their continued growth.[52]

Germany has only 7.5 percent unemployment, unlike the nearly double-digit unemployment in United States and other EU countries, and the lowest any time after the unification. During the 2008 recession, the German government offered money to firms to retain workers and cut working hours instead of producing layoffs. Hence, Germany came out of recession early. Its manufacturing sector still contributes about 25 percent of its GDP as compared to only 11 percent in the case of the United States. German corporate boards have generally equal numbers of management persons and workers, and hence the future of a firm is decided by stakeholders instead of shareholders. For this very reason Germany is still the world's second-largest exporter and has not faced the same severe crisis that countries such as the United States and other Western nations have been facing due to emergence of the global Chinese workshop.

Capitalism is now on the verge of collapse. In capitalism, emphasis is on maximizing profits and not on increasing the welfare of human beings. Hence, manufacturing units are constantly shifted to places where profits will be maximized. This has also led to shifting of massive amounts of money to the developing countries, which amounts to something like the "Marshall Plan II" (after World War II, the United States offered economic aid under the Marshall Plan to Western European countries for the reconstruction of their war-devastated economies). However while shifting jobs overseas, the United States and other Western countries forgot the "purchasing power" factor of economics. Along with the jobs, the people's purchasing power went overseas too.

Due to its soaring profits year after year, the Amazon Internet bookstore is one of the darlings of Wall Street. But one of the main reasons behind its profits is the low-paid workers in its warehouses. In 2011, twenty current and former employees at an Amazon warehouse in Allen Town, Pennsylvania, said that they were forced to work in brutal heat at breakneck pace while hired paramedics waited outside in case anyone became dangerously dehydrated. A local doctor treated employees at the facility for heat-related health problems and wound up filing a complaint with federal regulators regarding work conditions there. More than a dozen workers collapsed inside the local warehouse there because of the summer heat. Many of the warehouse's employees were temporary and were hired through a staffing company. If they did not meet packing quotas they faced daily threats of contract termination. A corps of other temporary workers was poised to replace any freshly fired Amazon employee.[53],[54] Despite having $546 billion in combined profits between 2005 and 2010, the four biggest oil companies—Exxon Mobil, Chevron, Shell, and BP—reduced their US workforce by 11,200 employees during the same period. [55]

Had Amazon been a privately held firm, it would not have been subjected to Wall Street pressure of generating profits every quarter. The company would then have employed staff permanently instead of exploiting low-paid temporary workers. This story of low-paid temporary workers is true with a majority of firms in the country. Permanent employed staff would have been earning much more than the low-paid temporary workers and at year-end they would have received bonuses. Such employees would have spent their money in the market, say by either renting or buying homes and buying cars. The local, state, and federal coffers would have also generated more taxes from the permanent employees. Purchases of high-priced items such as cars would have generated jobs in places like Detroit. In this way permanent employment would have created a series of economic activities all over the country. According to Tony Krasienko, mayor of Lorain (Ohio), which had 10.6 percent unemployment in late 2011, "For every manufacturing job there are between five and seven ancillary jobs created within the community that support those manufacturing jobs."[56] Similarly, a job loss or reduction in an employee's salary results in job losses within the community.

Apple's stock has risen astronomically in the last six years, from $45 in 2005 to $427 in 2011. After surpassing Exxon in August 2011, Apple has become the most valuable company in the market in terms of market capitalization. According to a *New York Times* article, Apple's revenue in 2011 topped $108 billion, a sum larger than the combined state budgets of Michigan, New Jersey, and Massachusetts. But almost all of the seventy million iPhones, thirty million iPads, and fifty-nine million other products Apple sold in 2011 were manufactured overseas. In 2011, it earned over $400,000 in profit per employee, more than Goldman Sachs, Exxon Mobil, or Google. Apple employs forty-three thousand people in the United States and twenty thousand overseas, a small fraction of the over four hundred thousand American workers at General Motors in the 1950s, or the hundreds of thousands at General Electric in the 1980s. Many more people work for Apple's contractors: an additional seven hundred thousand people engineer, build, and assemble iPads, iPhones, and Apple's other products. But almost none of them work in the United States. Instead, they work for foreign companies in Asia, Europe, and elsewhere, at factories that almost all electronics designers rely upon to build their wares. According to Jared Bernstein, an economic adviser to the White House until 2011—"Apple's an example of why it's so hard to create middle-class jobs in the U.S. now. If it's the pinnacle of capitalism, we should be worried."[57]

Due to the Wall Street pressure, every firm tries to squeeze money out of each and every place within the organization to generate profit, which they can give to Wall Street, where this money goes to the coffers of the rich. Hence Wall Street has now become a machine that transfers the money of middle-class people to the ultrarich. If your 401(k) money invested in shares on Wall Street is increasing, then part of this money is coming from the pockets of low-paid workers in firms like Amazon.

"Free trade," championed by the United States and embraced by most of the countries in the last thirty to forty years, is a ploy by Wall Street and the ultrarich to make money for themselves. Yes, Americans are getting "cheap goods" imported from overseas, but this import also replaces their well-paying jobs by "cheap jobs." A household needs to balance its budget and cannot afford to continue to pile on debts. If debts grow too large and the household is unable to pay even interests on the debt, then it has to sell its assets, such as the house, cars, furniture, etc. The same statement is true for a country as well.

Keynes's proposal, to keep trade deficit and trade surplus in check, aligns with Prout's principle of barter trade. According to Prout, barter trade is most suitable for developing countries that have a surplus of goods—raw materials or manufactured goods. It would be a way for them to generate economic and industrial growth gradually. Barter trade would also work as a hedge against inflation and help to relieve economic depression should there be one. Constant deficit in money-based foreign trade tends toward generating inflation. If real growth takes place outside the country, the home market will be punished by rising prices over time imposed by foreign agencies. Countries that import much of their basic foodstuffs and simply export their raw materials unrefined are most inflation-prone. Conversely, when raw material is processed at home into various products both for domestic markets as well as export, it increases local employment, develops own knowhow, etc. Also, barter trade, as opposed to money-based trade, would help to regenerate economic dynamics where economic depressions threaten to build or have already taken hold. It would cut through the economic morass and deliver the basics to the people so that life can go on and fresh growth may germinate.

According to Brad Setser, an economist with Roubini Global Economics in New York: [58]

> In order to pay for its imports the US needs to attract foreign capital at the rate of about $20 billion a week [i.e., to finance $1 trillion dollar twin deficit a year, consisting of a $600 billion trade deficit and a $400 billion budget deficit]. This is equal to selling three companies the size of the maritime firm that was supposed to be purchased by Dubai Ports World.

According to Peter Morici, a professor at the University of Maryland's business school in College Park: [59]

> We are basically selling off the furniture to pay for Thanksgiving dinner. Foreigners could own within the next decade more than a fifth of the nation's total $35 trillion or so in assets of every kind—corporations, businesses and real estate.

Therefore it is wrong to claim that capitalism has been successful in the United States. If a person needs $3 billion every day to run the family, then he or she cannot claim to be a successful businessperson.

In the Proutistic economy emphasis is on the welfare of human beings and not on profits. Prout focuses on the increase of people's "purchasing capacity," not on the GDP, which is not the correct measure for the economic growth of a country. According to Prout, a country should never be dependent on imports for any of its essential items, and it should find alternatives for each essential. In the case of the United States a major thrust of its defense policy is geared toward defending global petroleum supplies, especially in the Middle East. In recent decades the United States has spent tens of trillions of dollars for this purpose, which can be considered as a subsidy for its domestic petroleum market. Apart from the money spent, hundreds of thousands of brave US young men and women have lost their lives or have been crippled for life in the Middle East just for the sake of petroleum. Instead of spending this much money, it would have been better for the United States to go for another Manhattan Project to search for a substitute for the gasoline. (To force Japan to surrender, the United States formed a group of the best scientists to create the nuclear bomb in the early 1940s. This project was called the Manhattan Project.) The emphasis should have been to explore nonconventional sources of energy such as ethanol- and hydrogen-powered autos, solar energy, wind energy, geothermal energy, biogas energy, wave power, tidal power, and ocean thermal energy conversion. As the United States has some of the best brains in the world, this research would certainly have yielded results. Brazil is a perfect example in this case; there are no longer any light vehicles in Brazil running on pure gasoline.

According to Prout, a country or community should not import a mass consumer product if it can be produced locally. Also, no jobs should be outsourced.

2

•◆•

A Short History of the Global Economy

According to Angus Maddison, an economic historian, India was the world's leading economic power from the year 0 to 1000. Two thousand years ago India was the world's largest economy with a 32.9 percent share of the worldwide GDP and 28.9 percent in the eleventh century, closely followed by China. From 1500 to 1600, India was second only to China in terms of world GDP share and remained among the top-producing countries until as late as the seventeenth century. In 1700, when most parts of India were ruled by Mughals, India had a 24.4 percent world GDP share, higher than Europe's 23.3 percent. In 1700, China was ruled by the Qing dynasty and had about one-fourth of the world GDP. But their respective shares dropped to less than 5 percent by 1950.[60]

The world center of economic capital has changed over the last four thousand years from one city to another. According to Nicholas Kristof of the *New York Times*:

The most important city in the world in the period leading up to 2000 B.C. would be Ur, Iraq; in 1500 B.C., perhaps Thebes, Egypt. There was no dominant player in 1000 B.C., though one could make a case for Sidon, Lebanon. In 500 B.C., it would be Persepolis, Persia; in the year 1, Rome; around A.D. 500, maybe Changan, China; in 1000, Kaifeng, China; in 1500, probably Florence, Italy; in 2000, New York City; and in 2500, probably none of the above. Today Kaifeng is grimy and poor, not even the provincial capital and so minor it lacks even an airport. Its sad state only underscores how fortunes change. In the 11th century, when it was the capital of Song Dynasty China, its population was more than one million. In contrast, London's population then was about 15,000.[61]

Until seven hundred to eight hundred years ago, the various continents exhibited little difference in wealth and poverty. The industrial revolution in Europe, however, created vast differences in wealth between rich and poor countries as their colonies were deprived of the use of the "new technologies." For thousands of years, until about 1800, there had been virtually no sustained economic growth anywhere in the world and only gradual increases in human population. The world population rose from about 230 million in AD 1 to 270 million in AD 1000, and to 900 million in AD 1800. The first millennium saw no significant increase in living standards on a global scale, and perhaps a 50 percent increase in per capita income in the eight-hundred-year period from AD 1000 to AD 1800. In the two centuries following, however, the population rose by six times, to 6.1 billion, and world per capita income rose by nine times.[62]

Between 1800 and 2000, US per capita income increased by twenty-five times while that of Western Europe increased by fifteen times. Differences between rich and poor countries increased at a rate not seen in the past. For example, as of 1820 the ratio of the per capita income of the United Kingdom, the world's wealthiest nation at the time, to that of the world's poorest region, Africa, was about four to one, whereas by 1998, the same ratio was twenty (for the United States) to one (for Africa). The key for US growth has been *consistency*. The US economy grew about 1.7 percent per year from 1820 to 1998, increasing its per capita income from $1,200 in 1820 to $30,000 in 2008 (in 1990 dollars), or twenty-five times, whereas in Africa growth in the same period has been only 0.7 percent per year, increasing its per capita income from $400 in 1820 to only $1,200 in 2008, or three times.[63]

Part of the reason for this is the slave trade, because of which Africa lost a large number of its working population, adversely affecting the African economy. Table 2.1 shows how severely the size of the population leveled off during the slave-trade years:

Table 2.1 **Distribution of World Population in Various Continents from 1650 to 1900** *(in millions)*

	1650	1750	1850	1900
Africa	100	100	100	120
Europe	103	144	274	423
Asia	257	437	656	857

Source: Rodney, Walter, *How Europe Underdeveloped Africa*, Howard University Press, Washington, DC, 1982, p. 97.

In the pre-Industrial Revolution era, India was a rich country. Hence in 1492, Queen Isabella of Spain gave money to Christopher Columbus to find an alternative route via sea to India from Europe so that the European traders could bypass the risky land route via the present-day Middle East, called "The Silk Road." At that time the tribesmen in the Middle East, Iran, and Afghanistan used to loot and kill European traders on their business trips to India. But instead of finding a sea route to India, Columbus stumbled upon the "New World," the Americas. As he was attempting to visit India, the Europeans named the native population in the Americas "Red Indians."

During the fourteenth and fifteenth centuries, the Ottoman Empire was technologically and culturally ahead of Christian Europe, which was undergoing famines and plagues that killed almost half of the population at that time. The Ottoman Empire boasted large cities with well-lit roads and drainage. It had universities with libraries. It was ahead of Europe in mathematics, medicine, and cartography. It was using gun casting, lighthouses, and mills. In the mid-1800s, the empire went downhill, however, and had to take loans from Europe before it was dissolved in the aftermath of World War I.

Portugal and Spain initiated Europe's expansion overseas in the sixteenth century. Portugal succeeded in getting control of shipping lanes in the Indian Ocean by taking over trading ports and sea forts, but being a small country it was not interested in colonization. Portugal controlled Malacca, on the narrow strait between the Malay Peninsula and Sumatra, Ceylon (the present-day Sri Lanka), and Goa and Diu in India, as well as Macao on the south coast of China. After Columbus accidentally discovered the Western Hemisphere in 1492, Spain went on to colonize most of the Western Hemisphere. European countries, mainly Britain and France, colonized most of Africa and Asia.

As shown in Tables 2.2 to 2.5, the economies of Third World countries like India and China were comparable to those of present developed countries until 1750, but due to exploitation of their resources and trade restrictions, their economies declined. Internal civil wars and Japan's attacks, in the late 1800s and early 1900s, on China, and the subjugation of India by the British, led to their ruin. Today, after nearly three hundred years, the two giants of Asia are about to dominate the global economy once again.

For more than two centuries, until the first half of the twentieth century, European countries controlled almost all of Asia and Africa, and they were also in direct control of the trade of Latin America. They thrived on exploiting the manpower and natural resources of their colonies. The restrictions they imposed on their colonies allowed them to safeguard their own industries. During the eighteenth century, for example, the British imposed trade restrictions on Indian textile exports, which were better than British machine-manufactured textiles, to safeguard their own textile industry.

For more than one and a half centuries after its independence in 1776, the US economy developed behind the high tariffs imposed on imports by the Tariff Act of 1789 to protect it from the more technologically advanced European countries.

As shown in Table 2.2, the total industrial potentials of China and India in 1750 were 41.7 and 31.2 (on a scale of 100 for the United Kingdom's industrial potential), respectively, whereas that of all of Europe was only 29.6. At that time, the United States was just starting its industries from scratch. But these numbers declined sharply for Third World countries (China 33.3 and India 13.1) as they had to face the onslaught of colonial powers, whereas the industrial potentials of Europe combined and the United States in 1913 went up to 527.8 and 298.1, respectively. The per capita levels of industrialization in 1750 tell the same story: it had been nearly equal (7 to 9) throughout the world, but it declined sharply (between 2 to 3) for the Third World countries, whereas it went up drastically for European countries (between 60 to 90) and the United States (126).

Table 2.2 **Total Industrial Potential (UK in 1900 = 100)**
(Triennial Annual Averages, except for 1913)

	1750	1800	1830	1860	1880	1900	1913
DEVELOPED COUNTRIES	34.4	47.4	72.9	143.3	253.1	481.2	863.0
Europe	**29.6**	**41.2**	**63.0**	**120.3**	**196.2**	**335.4**	**527.8**
Belgium	0.4	0.7	1.3	3.1	5.7	9.2	16.3
France	5.0	6.2	9.5	17.9	25.1	36.8	57.3
Germany	3.7	5.2	6.5	11.1	27.4	71.2	137.7
Italy	3.1	3.7	4.2	5.7	8.1	13.6	22.5
Russia	6.4	8.3	10.3	15.8	24.5	47.5	76.6
Spain	1.6	2.1	2.7	4.0	5.8	8.5	11.0
Sweden	0.3	0.5	0.6	1.4	2.6	5.0	9.0
Switzerland	0.2	0.4	0.8	1.6	2.6	5.4	8.0
Great Britain	2.4	6.2	17.5	45.0	73.3	100.0	127.2
Outside Europe	4.9	6.2	9.9	22.9	56.9	145.9	335.2
Canada	-	-	0.1	0.6	1.4	3.2	8.7
US	**0.1**	**1.1**	**4.6**	**16.2**	**46.9**	**127.8**	**298.1**
Japan	4.8	5.1	5.2	5.8	7.6	13.0	25.1
THIRD WORLD	92.9	99.4	111.5	82.7	67.0	59.6	69.5
China	**41.7**	**48.8**	**54.9**	**44.1**	**39.9**	**33.5**	**33.3**
India	**31.2**	**29.0**	**32.5**	**19.4**	**8.8**	**9.3**	**13.1**
Brazil	-	-	-	0.9	0.9	2.1	4.3
Mexico	-	-	-	0.9	0.8	1.7	2.7
WORLD	127.3	146.9	184.4	225.9	320.1	540.8	932.5

Source: Bairoch, P., "International Industrialization levels from 1750 to 1980," *Journal of European Economic History* 11 (fall 1982), p. 292.

Table 2.3 **Per Capita Levels of Industrialization (UK in 1900 = 100)**
(Triennial Annual Averages, except for 1913)

	1750	1800	1830	1860	1880	1900	1913
DEVELOPED COUNTRIES	8	8	11	16	24	35	55
Europe	**8**	**8**	**11**	**17**	**23**	**33**	**45**
Belgium	9	10	14	28	43	56	88
France	9	9	12	20	28	39	59
Germany	8	8	9	15	25	52	85
Italy	8	8	8	10	12	17	26
Russia	6	6	7	8	10	15	20
Spain	7	7	8	11	14	19	22
Sweden	7	8	9	15	24	41	67
Switzerland	7	10	16	26	39	67	87
Great Britain	10	16	25	64	87	100	115
Outside Europe							
Canada	-	5	6	7	10	24	46
US	**4**	**9**	**14**	**21**	**38**	**69**	**126**
Japan	7	7	7	7	9	12	20
THIRD WORLD	7	6	6	4	3	2	2
China	**8**	**6**	**6**	**4**	**4**	**3**	**3**
India	**7**	**6**	**6**	**3**	**2**	**1**	**2**
Brazil	-	-	-	4	4	5	7
Mexico	-	-	-	5	4	5	7
WORLD	7	6	7	7	9	14	21

Source: Bairoch, P., "International Industrialization levels from 1750 to 1980," *Journal of European Economic History* 11 (fall 1982), p. 294.

Table 2.4 **Shares of "New Technology" Industries in the Total Manufacturing Output by Regions** *(in percent)*

	Developed Countries (excluding Japan)			Third World (excluding Japan)	World (including Japan)
	UK	Other Countries	Total		
1750	0–1	0	(a)	0	(a)
1800	**6–10**	**1–3**	**2–4**	**(a)**	**1–2**
1830	32–40	6–10	12–17	0–1	4–6
1860	60–70	18–24	29–36	0–1	17–23
1880	62–74	30–38	40–48	1–3	30–28
1900	**68–78**	**49–57**	**52–61**	**4–9**	**49–56**
1913	72–80	55–65	60–65	10–19	54–62

(a) Less than 0.5 percent.

Source: Bairoch, P., "International Industrialization levels from 1750 to 1980," *Journal of European Economic History* 11 (fall 1982), p. 288.

Table 2.5 **Relative Shares of Different Countries And Regions in Total World
Manufacturing Output (in percentages)**
(Triennial Annual Averages, except for 1913)

	1750	1800	1830	1860	1880	1900	1913
DEVELOPED COUNTRIES	27.0	32.3	39.5	63.4	79.1	89.0	92.5
Europe	**23.2**	**28.1**	**34.2**	**53.2**	**61.3**	**62.0**	**56.6**
Belgium	0.3	0.5	0.7	1.4	1.8	1.7	1.8
France	4.0	4.2	5.2	7.9	7.8	6.8	6.1
Germany	2.9	3.5	3.5	4.9	8.5	13.2	14.8
Italy	2.4	2.5	2.3	2.5	2.5	2.5	2.4
Russia	5.0	5.6	5.6	7.0	7.6	8.8	8.2
Spain	1.2	1.5	1.5	1.8	1.8	1.6	1.2
Sweden	0.3	0.3	0.4	0.6	0.8	0.9	1.0
Switzerland	0.1	0.3	0.4	0.7	0.8	1.0	0.9
Great Britain	1.9	4.3	9.5	19.9	22.9	18.5	13.6
Outside Europe	3.9	4.2	5.3	10.2	17.8	26.9	35.9
Canada	-	-	0.1	0.3	0.4	0.6	0.9
US	**0.1**	**0.8**	**2.4**	**7.2**	**14.7**	**23.6**	**32.0**
Japan	3.8	3.5	2.8	2.6	2.4	2.4	2.7
THIRD WORLD	73.0	67.7	60.5	36.6	20.9	11.0	7.5
China	**32.8**	**33.3**	**29.8**	**19.7**	**12.5**	**6.2**	**3.6**
India	**24.5**	**19.7**	**17.6**	**8.6**	**2.8**	**1.7**	**1.4**
Brazil	-	-	-	0.4	0.3	0.4	0.5
Mexico	-	-	-	0.4	0.3	0.3	0.3
WORLD	100.0	100.0	100.0	100.0	100.0	100.0	100.0
WORLD: absolute volume (a)	127.3	146.9	184.4	225.9	320.1	540.8	932.5

(a) On the basis of the UK In 1900 = 100.

Source: Bairoch, P., "International Industrialization levels from 1750 to 1980," *Journal of European Economic History* 11 (fall 1982), p. 296.

The main reason for the decline was that the Third World countries were deprived of the use of the new technologies that came out from the Industrial Revolution, (Table 2.4) which were fueling economic growth in the Western Hemisphere. India, for example, experienced no per capita growth from 1600 to 1870, the period of growing British influence. Per capita economic growth from 1870 to independence in 1947 was a meager 0.2 percent per year, compared with 1 percent in the United Kingdom.[64] The share of the new technology industries in the total manufacturing output in Third World countries was only 1 to 2. In the Western countries it was 50 to 80. This discrepancy led to a sharp decline in the share of Third World countries in the global economy. In 1750, the total share of Third World countries in the global economy was 73 percent (led by China and India—32.8 percent and 24.5 percent, respectively), whereas it was just 7.5 percent in 1913. On the other hand, these numbers for the Western countries (Europe and the United States combined) were 23.3 percent and 86.6 percent in 1750 and 1913, respectively.

During the colonial period, India's education system, designed by the British, was there to churn out third- and fourth-grade employees instead of scientists and technocrats to serve the British. There were very few schools and colleges throughout India during British rule. Until the 1920s, Bihar, the second most populous state in India, having nearly three times the population of Britain, had just one university with five or six colleges throughout the state and one primitive engineering college. This same university managed all the high schools also, thirty to thirty-five in number.

The British devised an Indian administration that would rule the Indians, effectively creating a system where a small group of corrupt Indian middlemen, of the police force and land owners (zamindars), could assist them in their colonial rule. The British ruled India by creating fear among Indians. The same mentality has persisted until now. When India received its independence in 1947, there was simply a transfer of power from the British to a small group of Indians. Everything else remained the same. Instead of being ruled by the British, now the Indian masses were ruled by an Indian elite, which used the same corrupt administrative system. The British ruled India by fear psychosis, and after independence Indian bureaucrats continued the same pattern. In buildings in the United States we see Thanks for Not Smoking, whereas in India it becomes, Smokers Will Be Fined 500 Rupees.

Although the British constructed the railway system throughout India in the late 1800s and early 1900s to facilitate them in moving freights from one part of India to another, passenger trains were very few. During the 1930s, Hitler's Germany constructed autobahns (the national motorway system), having speed limit of nearly 80 miles an hour, throughout the country. In the 1950s and 1960s, the United States duplicated the autobahns by establishing the Interstate Highway System. In India, on the other hand, until the 1960s there were no paved roads outside cities. Our ancestral home in Bihar was in a village that is about twenty kilometers from the district city and the nearest railway station. Until the 1960s, we had to use a bullock cart to go home from the railway station. The story is the same in all countries that obtained independence after long periods of colonial rule.

The United States supplied billions of dollars worth of munitions and foodstuffs to the Allies during World War I, and the Allies had to borrow money on the New York and Chicago money markets to pay it back. European economies were destroyed by the war, which did, however, benefit countries like the United States, Canada, and Australia, which were spared fighting the war on their own soil.

World War II gave the United States the opportunity to become a superpower by default both in terms of wealth and military power. During the war, American industry became military-based. Automobile production lines in Detroit were reconfigured to churn out military tanks, navy battleships, and fighter planes. For the first time, women joined the workforce in droves, as the men had gone to Europe and East Asia to fight the Axis powers. By the late 1940s, the US GDP was almost half of the world's GDP, and American companies were working at full capacity. This contrasts dramatically with postwar Europe, where most factories had been completely destroyed. In addition, technological advances in both ocean and air transport during the war made the transportation of goods cheap. This relatively newfound technology drastically reduced transportation time also between the various continents, from months to a few hours, which helped in integrating the American economy with the world economy.

World War II also saw the emergence of the Union of Soviet Socialist Republics (USSR), which initially demonstrated tremendous economic growth. Soviet rulers claimed that they would surpass the economic might of the West, but after a few decades the Soviet economic miracle fizzled out once the drawbacks of communism, including inefficiency and relatively poor productivity, crept into the Soviet economy. This finally led to the collapse of the Soviet empire in 1991.

3

• ◆ •

THE POST–WORLD WAR GLOBAL ECONOMY

At the end of World War II, the United States completely destroyed Japanese industry and infrastructure by massive bombing. After the Korean War in the early 1950s had ended in a stalemate, the United States had to supply its massive army stationed in South Korea with consumer goods and military items. To accomplish this, it sent state-of-the art machinery to Japan and later to South Korea to take advantage of its cheap labor and proximity to the war theater. This helped Japan get started on the road to becoming the economic superpower it is now, rivaling even the United States. The Korean War was in effect a Marshall Plan for Japan and South Korea. Toyota, for example, was rescued from ruins because of the orders for trucks from the US Department of Defense.

A huge increase in petroleum prices after the 1973 Arab-Israeli War shocked US industry. During the 1970s (especially during the Carter period), unemployment and interest rates were both very high, with the latter running into double digits. This caused American industry to start shifting production of consumer items to Third World countries in order to take advantage of their cheap labor. The four Asian Tigers—Taiwan, Hong Kong, South Korea, and Singapore—were the first beneficiaries of this transfer of production.

The shifting of production units occurred slowly in the early 1980s but picked up speed in the late 1980s because American industry could not compete with Asia's cheap labor. The four original Asian Tigers were too small to satisfy all demands of the huge American consumer market, however. Chinese were a majority of the population in the Asian Tigers except for South Korea. Hence, as the demand for consumer items increased, Chinese businessmen started building production units in other Asian countries where they controlled the business. The next batch of Asian Tigers consisted of Malaysia, Indonesia, and Thailand. About one-third of the Malaysian population is Chinese. Although only about 4 percent of the Indonesian population is Chinese, they controlled more than 60 percent of the business there. The Chinese also controlled a majority of the business in Thailand. These countries subsequently experienced double-digit growth for about a decade. In the 1960s, East Asia had only 4 percent of world GNP, compared to North America's 37 percent. By the early 1990s, they were equal, at about 24 percent of world GNP.

It is a misconception that Western businessmen, including those from the United States, kick-started the Chinese economic miracle in 1979 by investing Western money. According to a 1997 article in *China Daily*, out of a total foreign investment of $36 billion in the previous five years, Chinese investors from Taiwan, Southeast Asia, Hong Kong, Europe, America, and Canada poured in almost 75 percent of this amount, and the rest came from non-Chinese sources. The same proportion is said to apply to the foreign investment of $96 billion made during the twelve years leading up to the period of economic reforms.[65]

Everything was fine with the Asian Tiger economies until the entry of China in the global consumer market. With the influx of money earned from exports to the United States, labor costs increased, and so did labor union power. Investors then fled to low-labor-cost countries like China. Chinese labor costs were about one-fourth those in other Asian countries.

Another factor in China's success stemmed from the Nixon years.

In order to defeat the USSR the United States had followed up on Kissinger's strategy of creating friendship with China and gave it most favored nation (MFN) status for trade. After China's entry into the picture, other Asian countries started losing market share. Three original Tigers, namely Taiwan, Hong Kong, and Singapore, were small nations and were able to switch their focus from low-tech exports (toys, shoes, etc.) to services and high-tech exports. Their economies were not much affected by the entry of Malaysia, Thailand, Indonesia, and, finally, China, Burma, Vietnam, and India. All these countries were competing with each other, however, in a global market where consumer demand volume was increasing more slowly than the production of these items.

The 1985 Plaza Accord

After the 1973 Arab-Israeli War, Arab countries imposed an oil embargo on the United States, raised the price of crude oil, and cut back oil production. Although they eventually ended the embargo, oil prices quadrupled within a few months to $12 a barrel. This led to oil rationing in the United States and inflation. During the Carter administration, inflation ran high. After the 1979 Iranian Revolution, oil peaked at more than $39 a barrel. The high oil prices and inflation led to Reagan's victory in the 1980 presidential election. The Reagan administration instituted a policy of massive tax cuts to help counter the inflation but also increased defense expenditures, causing annual growth in the budget deficit. At the same time, American manufacturing jobs started shifting to East Asia, leading to an increase in the US trade deficit. In order to reduce or finance the trade deficit, the United States had to either attract foreign investment by increasing interest rates or increase exports by depreciating the dollar. Increases in interest rates would adversely affect the domestic economy; hence, in order to depreciate the dollar, five nations—France, West Germany, Japan, the United States, and the United Kingdom—signed the Plaza Accord in 1985.

As per the accord, the Japanese yen appreciated rapidly, and the dollar depreciated at a rate that led to the shifting of Japanese manufacturing plants to low-labor-cost countries such as Taiwan, Singapore, and then, later on, countries such as Indonesia and Thailand. In the late 1980s, in order to stop a further rise in the yen, the Bank of Japan decided on a low interest rate and spent yen to buy dollars in the currency markets. This resulted in increased Japanese investment in the United States, fueling the "bubble economy" and a collapse of the Japanese economy in the early 1990s. Nevertheless, Japanese money had propped up the Reagan administration, allowing it to operate in spite of budget deficits, as well as the US economy in general. Had Japan not financed the budget and trade deficits at that time, Reaganomics would have collapsed. A similar situation is occurring right now, with China financing US deficits.

Japanese real estate prices skyrocketed in the late 1980s. The Nikkei (the Japanese stock exchange) average tripled during this period. Total Japanese land values ballooned to a point where they were theoretically four times greater than those of the entire United States, even though the United States is twenty-five times larger and full of the natural resources that Japan lacks.[66]

Due to the Plaza Accord, however, the dollar was continuing to slide in 1987 while the yen and German mark were continuing to appreciate, creating problems in international financial markets. In order to stop its slide, all G-7 members except Italy signed the 1987 Louvre Accord. Private investors exited the US market as a result. In fact, during most of 1987, private capital ceased to flow to the United States on a net basis, and foreign central banks were obliged to finance roughly two-thirds of the $163.5 billion current account deficit. The Federal Reserve raised interest rates in autumn that year in a further effort to stem the dollar's fall and calm financial markets. The Germans and Japanese offset the Fed's action, however, by following suit, and the resulting flight of capital from US financial markets triggered the October stock market crash.[67]

JOB LOSSES DUE TO OFFSHORING

The offshoring of American manufacturing jobs during the 1980s and 1990s can be termed the "Wal-Mart Phenomenon," as large department stores such as Wal-Mart, Kmart, and most other firms selling manufactured consumer items tried to reduce prices by shifting manufacturing to the Third World, where they could take advantage of low wages. As discussed earlier, these jobs first went to the four Asian Tigers and then to countries such as Thailand, Indonesia, and Malaysia, and, finally, to China. This global shift has resulted in a massive loss of manufacturing jobs in the United States. Although there was a small net gain in manufacturing jobs during the last five years of the Clinton administration, the first five years of the Bush Jr. administration saw these jobs decline by about 3 million (Table 3.1).

Table 3.1 **US Job Gained (Lost) 1990 to 2005** *(in thousands)*

Sector	1990–95	1995–2000	2000–05
Government	1,211	1,162	1,129
Education & Health Services	2,321	1,836	2,214
Financial Activities	230	853	472
Information	110	766	(434)
Leisure & Hospitality	985	1,305	971
Other Services	301	619	305
Professional and Business Services	1,778	3,723	222
Transport and Warehousing	348	569	(50)
Utilities	(61)	(68)	(31)
Wholesale Trade	87	581	(279)
Retail Trade	520	1,347	(134)
Construction	(186)	1,534	329
Natural Resources and Mining	(110)	(59)	13
Manufacturing	**(516)**	**47**	**(2,999)**
Total	7,018	14,215	1,728

Source: Ward, William A., *Manufacturing Productivity and the Shifting U.S., China, and Global Job Scenes—1990 to 2005*, Clemson University Center for International Trade Working Paper 052507, August 4, 2005.

Not only has China become a major manufacturing center, it is a major assembly center as well. Parts manufactured in other countries go to China as intermediate products to be assembled, and the final products are shipped out from there. This allows China to run a huge trade surplus with the United States, though it has trade deficits with other East Asian countries.

A decade ago, Taiwan controlled the computer components market and relied on domestic manufacturing. Today, Taiwanese companies produce 80 percent of computer motherboards, 72 percent of notebook computers, and 68 percent of LCD monitors, with most of the assembly taking place in China. "Everyone has moved to China," says Tony Yang, an executive at Aopen of Taiwan, a maker of computers and parts. "Our suppliers, our buyers, their main production facilities have all been relocated. Wages in Taiwan are just too high."[68]

Several Third World countries are also losing manufacturing jobs to Asian countries, mainly China. For example, South Africa lost 70,000 jobs in the apparel sector in four years (2002–6) because of imports from low-cost Asian producers. Thousands of jobs have also been lost in South Africa's electronics sector because of cheap imports. China has eclipsed the United States to become its largest trading partner. Trade between South Africa and China increased from $8 billion in 2006 to $20 billion in 2011. According to Ebrahim Patel, general-secretary of the Southern African Clothing and Textile Workers Union, every breadwinner supports an average of six persons, and that means the 70,000 textile jobs lost in South Africa are affecting almost half a million people in a country already suffering from high unemployment.[69] In India, until recently, weaving was the second-most-common occupation, behind farming. Many of these weavers, whose families have practiced weaving for generations, now face ruin because of newer factories in China. In the eastern villages and cities of the state of Uttar Pradesh, 175 weavers committed suicide in 2005, despondent over their recent change in fortunes.[70]

American productivity increased during the mid-1990s due to the advent of information technology. Information technology, along with the invention of the Internet, created many jobs as well. This had a downside, however, since anyone anywhere in the world with a computer can do the job that an American does in the office on a computer. Because labor costs in the Third World are just a fraction of those in America, the United States started losing service sector jobs too. In the era of the Internet, when more than half of US households had their money on Wall Street and everyone was becoming conscious of various firms' performance, every CEO came under pressure to show quarterly earnings meeting the predictions of Wall Street pundits. Falling short of expectations would mean losing their jobs. We may call it the "Wall Street Phenomenon." The main characteristics of this phenomenon include CEO's sending jobs outside the United States in order to save their own jobs, millions of dollars in CEO bonuses to reward quarterly profits, and the loss of millions of quality American jobs. It also includes record CEO turnover levels—15.3 percent out of the world's 2,500 largest public companies in 2005, a 4.1 percent increase from 2004 and 70 percent above the 9 percent turnover rate in 1995.[71]

BUSH ADMINISTRATION (2000–08)— AN ECONOMIC DISASTER

Figures 3.1 to 3.4 show a snapshot of the US economy over the last forty to fifty years. From the 1940s to the 1960s, the job growth rate was very high, from a high of 38 percent during the 1940s to a low of 24 percent during the 1950s. The high job growth rate in the four decades, starting from the onset of World War II, was due to massive government spending during World War II, which resulted in double-digit growth rates for next couple of decades. After World War II, the United States was the leading economic power and largest exporter in the world.

The USSR also witnessed similar double-digit growth rates for about a decade and a half after World War II. From the early 1950s to the mid-1960s, the Soviet Bloc's economic growth was astounding. Its GDP increased at a tremendous rate following the planned economy program of transferring a large amount of manpower from the agricultural sector into industry. In many respects, the region was transformed more than Western Europe during those first postwar decades, although that may have been chiefly due to the fact that it was so much poorer and underdeveloped to begin with. Russia's steel output, a mere 12.3 million tons in 1945, soared to 65.2 million tons in 1960 and to 148 million tons in 1980, making the USSR the world's largest producer of steel. Electricity output rose from 43.2 million kilowatt-hours to 292 million, and then to 1.294 billion kilowatt-hours during the same period. Automobile production jumped from 74,000, to 524,000, and then to 2.2 million units. The list of production increases could be added almost indefinitely. The Soviet Bloc achieved an average of more than 10 percent annual growth in industrial output during the period. Its space program, which included the successfully launching of the world's first space vehicle, "Sputnik," even surpassed the American space program. The United States had to work hard to close the "space gap."[72]

In the 1970s, however, growth behind the Iron Curtain reduced to a rate of 3 to 4 percent. The previous high rate of growth had been due primarily to the use of vast, reallocated pools of labor and capital, and these had become utilized to their full extent, unable to provide further dramatic increases in productivity. Japan, by using modern technology such as computers, telecommunications, and robotics instead of relying so much on labor, was able to surpass the USSR in terms of GNP, as was the West. In comparison, Soviet equipment was outdated.

Premier Mikhail Gorbachev attempted to reform the Soviet economy in the 1980s with glasnost and perestroika, for which he needed money. Western banks, especially German, initially gave the Soviet Union loans but subsequently stopped, leading to economic crisis in the USSR. The Soviet intervention in Afghanistan in the 1980s also contributed to the financial black hole.

Lower crude oil prices during the late 1980s further exacerbated the situation, oil being the primary Soviet export. The USSR's government now borrowed heavily to modernize its economy. These two factors led to a rise in Soviet external debt: in 1985, oil earnings and net debt were $22 billion and $18 billion, respectively; by 1989, these numbers had become $13 billion and $44 billion, respectively. By 1991, when external debt was $57 billion, creditors (many of them major German banks) stopped making loans and started demanding repayments, contributing to the collapse of the Soviet economy.[73]

Had oil prices increased, like they have during the Putin administration in the last ten years, or had German banks financed Gorbachev's perestroika like Japan financed Reagan's deficits, the USSR and communism would not have collapsed in 1991. It is just Republican propaganda that this collapse was due to Reagan's military buildup. Had Japan not financed American deficits in the 1980s, the US economy and capitalism would have collapsed before communism did.

After the oil shock and the inherent deficiencies in capitalism, the

US economy went through a turbulent period during the 1970s. Then the Reagan administration increased defense funding and reduced taxes for the rich, resulting in budget deficits. Republicans started to demonize the government. Reagan was himself a millionaire, paying high taxes. As he did not have any idea about the economy or the functioning of the government, he became a puppet in the hands of the ultrarich, who used him to do whatever they wanted (e.g., lower taxes). Reagan, a Hollywood actor, knew how to deliver speeches written by others. Hence he was able to convince Americans that government is an evil organization. But his policy resulted in the economic recession at the end of his presidency. It is worth noting that when his deputy, George H. W. Bush (Sr.), became the president, he raised taxes on the ultrarich despite pledging "Read my lips: no new taxes" at the Republican convention to nominate the presidential candidate. Any rational president would try to control the soaring national budget deficit in the long-term interests of the country. A rise in the tax rate on the ultrarich and the advent of information technology helped the Clinton administration to balance the budget and even generate a budget surplus in the last two years of the administration.

Apart from this, as capitalism's emphasis is on profit, industry started to generate megamergers and also started the shifting of jobs to overseas countries, leading to trade deficits year after year. During the 1980s Japan funded the twin deficits of the United States—budget and trade. We will discuss this further in the next chapter.

When George Bush Jr. took over, he did what the ultrarich—who had funded his election—wanted. Like Reagan, Bush Jr. had little general knowledge in any field. His expertise was said to be baseball only. He went on to reduce the tax rate and expand the size of government, cementing the current economic problems of the United States.

As shown in Figure 3.1 the job growth was about 20 percent during the 1980s and 1990s, but in the 2000s, it was zero. As shown in Figures 3.2 to 3.4 the government size and government expenditure increased during Republican administrations (i.e., 1980–92 and 2000–2008) [One point worth noting is that in Figure 3.4 the number of employees on the vertical axis starts from 600,000 and not 0.]. They increased the size of government. At the end of the Johnson administration (i.e., 1968), the total number of executive branch civilian employees (EBC) was 2,289 K—1,317 K department of defense (DOD) and 972 K civilian agencies (CA) (where K stands for thousands). After the end of the Vietnam War, although the DOD reduced to 1,010 K at the end of the Nixon-Ford administrations (1976), the CA increased to 1,147 K, an 18 percent increase in eight years. These numbers at the end of the Carter administration (1980) were 960 K DOD and 1,201 K CA, and the EBC (2,161 K) was nearly the same as at the end of the Nixon-Ford administrations (2,157 K EBC). But the Reagan administration increased DOD employees to 1,050 K, a nearly 10 percent increase, bringing the EBC to 2,222 K. Due to the end of the Cold War, the DOD went down to 952 K at the end of the Bush Sr. administration (1992), but the CA number increased by 10 percent to 1,274 K, making the total (2,225 K) nearly the same as that at the end of the Reagan administration. But due to the onslaught of the Republican-controlled Congress to reduce the size of government, the Clinton administration ended with a nearly 20 percent drop in EBC to 1,778 K (651 K DOD and 1,127 K CA). But, again, the next Republican administration (i.e., the Bush Jr. administration) increased the EBC (1,960 K) by 10 percent —670 K DOD and 1,289 K CA.

Had the Bush Jr. administration not gone for two wars and implemented Medicare Part B, the economy would have been in recession throughout his eight-year administration. In the first two years of his administration there were job losses. Then followed five years where a few jobs were created. Only 464,000 jobs were created from 2000 to 2009 as compared to the 21.7 million jobs that were created from 1989 to 1999.[74] In George W. Bush's last year as president there were huge losses in jobs.

On the other hand, when there is a Democrat in the White House (1992–2000 and at present), Republicans pressure him to reduce the size of government and the budget deficit so that the economic downturn would bring a bad name to Democrats. Any reduction in the size of the government and the budget deficit result in job losses. But the advent of information technology helped President Clinton in getting the economy out of the recession created due to the tax cuts during the Reagan administration.

During the 1950s, '60s and '70s, the number of private-sector jobs increased about 3.5 percent a year. During the 1980s and '90s, the number grew 2.4 percent a year, whereas during the 2000s private-sector jobs grew by just 0.9 percent.[75] These data prove that Reaganomics destroyed the economy.

In the first decade of the twenty-first century, Texas, North Carolina, Virginia, and Georgia, having economies based on raw materials, government, and senior citizens, had the fastest growth in the country. The losers were states such as California and Michigan, which produced manufactured goods. Although California still enjoys having the largest state economy, with a $1.9 trillion GDP, Texas had the biggest increase in its GDP, which is now second in the country with more than $1 trillion. This is a proof of the erosion of the country's manufacturing base.

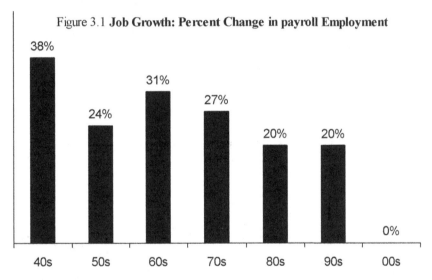

Figure 3.1 **Job Growth: Percent Change in payroll Employment**

Source: Irwin, Neil, "Aughts were a lost decade for U.S. economy, workers," *The New York Times*, January 2, 2010.

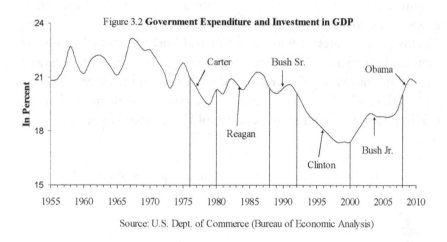

Figure 3.2 **Government Expenditure and Investment in GDP**

Source: U.S. Dept. of Commerce (Bureau of Economic Analysis)

Figure 3.3 **Private Sector Gross Job Gains and Losses At The End of Each Quarter**

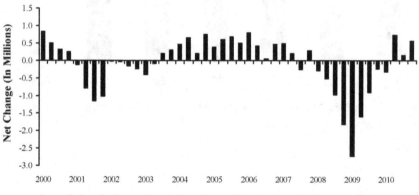

Source: Business Employment Dynamics Data, Bureau of Labor Statistics, U.S. Department of Labor

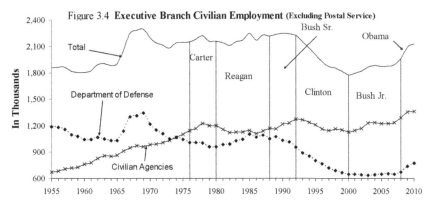

Figure 3.4 **Executive Branch Civilian Employment** (Excluding Postal Service)

Source: U.S. Office of Personnel Management

4

• ◆ •

State of the US Economy, 2011

The debt crisis started by the Reagan administration has become unsustainable. Although the Clinton administration was able to balance the budget, it was unable to rein in the BOP deficit, which increased from $140 billion in 1997 to $673 billion in 2008.[76] In economics, the BOP measures the payments that flow between any individual country and all other countries. By 2011 the United States needed more than $2 billion of foreign investment per day, on average, to finance its trade deficit. Generally, money should flow from rich countries to poor countries because the returns in poor countries are higher than in rich countries. For the last couple of decades, however, the reverse has been true. Developing countries like China, Russia, and Brazil are financing the United States.

Figure 4.1 shows the US debt from 1960 to 2010. The chart clearly shows that the debt rose at a faster rate during Republican administrations. The curve was concave during the Clinton administration, when the increase in debt was at its slowest. The Bush administration, to compound the difficulty, increased US fiscal debt from $5.6 trillion to $10 trillion due to tax breaks and increasing defense expenditures. A person saves during sunny days so that savings will help him during rainy days. He will try not to accumulate debts during sunny days. But during a period of economic growth, the Bush administration increased the national debt to such an extent that now, after the 2008 economic downturn, the government does not have the option to go for a substantial stimulus in order to jump-start the economy. Apart from this, the economic downturn drastically reduced the revenue collection at all levels—federal, state, and local—adding to the increase in budget deficit. States have, therefore, received substantial federal stimulus to mask the crisis. For instance, from the 2009 $154 billion jobs bill, $46 billion went to the states as aid. In 2011, forty-one states had a shortfall of about $180 billion.[77] On average the state revenue dropped by 30.8 percent between fiscal years 2008 and 2009. States and local governments have been cutting school funding, laying off police officers, firefighters, etc. Cuts in education are providing temporary relief from governments' monetary crisis, but the cuts generate a long-term disaster, as students are the future of the country.

The debt of Japan is also very high, twice its $5 trillion GDP. After the collapse of its real estate bubble in 1990, Japan spent more than $6 trillion on infrastructure during the following decade without having a convincing recovery. This caused Japan to accumulate debt to the tune of 190 percent of its GDP, the highest among the developed countries. Japan owes most of this debt to its own citizens. Only 10 percent is owed to foreigners, whereas 46 percent of US government debt is owed to foreigners. Japan has a high saving rate, whereas the United States has negligible savings. In early 2011, Japanese household assets was $17 trillion, more than three times its GDP, and hence it has a significant amount of domestic savings to fund its government bonds. Unlike the United States and some of the hardest-hit European countries, Japan has a steady flow of foreign earnings from a current account surplus. Japan is also the world's largest creditor country, with net external assets of $2.73 trillion.[78]

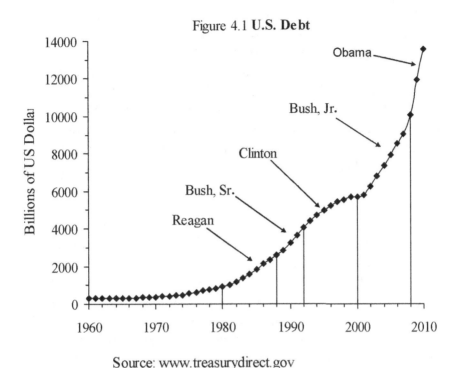

Figure 4.1 **U.S. Debt**

Source: www.treasurydirect.gov

According to the Economic Policy Institute, a US think tank, the average family's net worth dropped by 41 percent from 2007 to 2009. Net worth is a measure of a family's total assets, including real estate, bank balances, stock holdings, and retirement funds, minus all of their liabilities, such as mortgages and other consumer debt.[79] After getting a big hit on their net worth in the 2008 Great Recession, consumer spending has dropped drastically. Consumer spending accounts for two-thirds of the US GDP.

According to the Center for Economic and Policy Research, American households have lost an estimated $5 trillion of wealth from the housing market collapse, which will cut annual consumption by more than $400 billion.[80] US consumers have started saving more and paying debts. The savings rate was 1.2 percent of disposable income in early 2008, whereas by the end of the second half of 2009, it rose to 5.2 percent. Every dollar that Americans save is one dollar less for consumption, which results in decreasing economic output. According to the McKinsey Global Institute, when savings goes up by a percentage point, spending decreases by more than $100 billion.[81]

The 2008 Great Recession has caused an exponential rise in the federal budget deficit. While wages and other job-related income fell by a record $206 billion in 2009 to $7.84 trillion, transfer payments from the government such as unemployment checks and Social Security burgeoned by $231 billion to $2.1 trillion. Meanwhile, the amount of taxes that individual Americans paid plummeted by $325 billion to $2.1 trillion as a result of middle-class tax cuts and because nearly six million people were thrown out of work and are no longer paying payroll taxes. Economists in the US Department of Commerce said that the unprecedented drop of $256 billion in private wages—the mainstay of consumers in ordinary times—in 2009 was particularly dramatic. It was more than forty times larger than the drop in wages during the 2002–3 recession in the United States. With more than eight million workers laid off during the recession, unemployment benefits have quadrupled from $34 billion in January 2008 to $124 billion at the end of last year. As a result of record US government borrowing, total debt in the United States has soared to an all-time high of 370 percent of yearly economic output, far exceeding its peak of 300 percent during the Great Depression. While the government was lavishing aid, banks were cutting credit to consumers by a record $250 billion, nearly as much as the amount consumers gained from government transfer payments. In particular, many workers who were nearing retirement age and got laid off started to draw Social Security benefits. The number of retirees taking Social Security at the age of sixty-two grew by a record 19 percent in 2010, helping to push up Social Security outlays by $100 billion. Analysts expect those spending levels to stay high and even continue to increase as more baby boomers retire.[82]

Figure 4.2 shows the US BOP as a percent of GDP from 1930 to 2010, and Figure 4.3 shows the BOP in billions of dollars from 1990 to 2010. The BOP has deteriorated very fast since 2000, with the beginning of the Bush administration, and is now in uncharted territory. In terms of percent of GDP, this is the first time in American history the BOP has been allowed to drop to this level. Due to the 2008 recession, the US BOP situation improved slightly, but again it has started to drop further in 2010 as economic activity in the country picked up.

During the mid-1980s, when the US BOP started going into what was then also uncharted territory, the United States had to sign the 1985

Plaza Accord (shown as the vertical line in Figure 4.2) which resulted in a controlled depreciation of the dollar in order to increase its exports. At that time, all the main players in the global economy—Japan, West Germany, France, and the United Kingdom—were dependent on the United States for their security and therefore helped it in this endeavor. At present however, China and Russia are the world's largest and third largest FOREX holders, respectively, and most of their FOREX is in dollars. They may not always do what the United States wants; they have also seen the fate of the "bubble economy" of the late 1980s and 1990s in Japan due to the Plaza Accord and will likely hesitate to sign a similar accord. They may even prefer to see the US economy collapse rather than having a desire to save it.

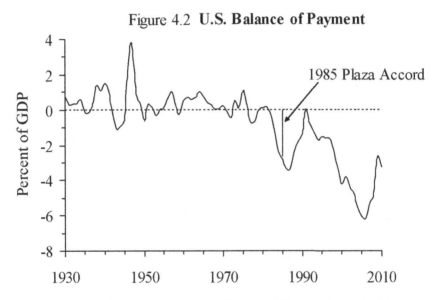

Figure 4.2 **U.S. Balance of Payment**

Source: U.S. Dept. of Commerce (Bureau of Economic Analysis)

Figure 4.3 **U.S. Balance of Payment**

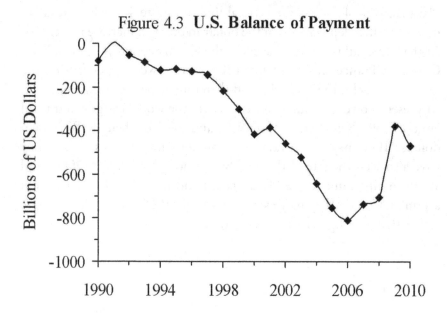

Source: U.S. Dept. of Commerce (Bureau of Economic Analysis)

In the last two decades, world trade has increased tremendously, especially since 2000, as shown in Figure 4.4. There was a dip in world trade in 2008–09 due to the 2008 global recession, but again it has started to increase. Let us see who is benefiting from this growth in world trade and who is losing as a result of the US free trade policy.

Figures 4.5 and 4.6 show the trade deficits of selected countries. Clearly it is China who is benefiting, while the losers are the Americans, who are increasing their debt each year by $500+ billion. All countries, except the United States, the United Kingdom, and India (from 2004 onwards), have a trade surplus. The UK trade deficit is due to the fact that its governments have been following the principles of Reaganomics initiated by the Thatcher administration. The main reason behind the trade deficit of India is the import of gasoline and consumer items due to the sharp increase in the number of consumers. India needs to follow in the footsteps of Brazil and find a substitute for petrol as soon as possible. Otherwise it may face an economic crisis. In Brazil, no small vehicles run on pure gasoline but use ethanol-mixed gasoline made available all over the country. Apart from this, India is becoming a consumer country like the United States rather than an export giant like China.

In 2010, the US trade deficit with China was $273.1 billion (imports $364.9 billion, exports $91.9 billion). In the same year, the total US trade deficit was $497.8 billion. Even at the height of the Great Recession in 2009, US imports from China stood at $296 billion, whereas its exports to China amounted to only $70 billion. An appreciation of the Chinese currency is not going to help the United States. China let its currency rise by 20 percent from 2005 to 2008 and then halted its rise in 2008. Despite the 20 percent appreciation of the Chinese currency, the US trade deficit continued to increase from 2005 to 2008. Also, even if China appreciates its currency to a significant degree, other countries, such as Vietnam and Bangladesh, will start to export to the United States the items that would become costlier to manufacture in China.

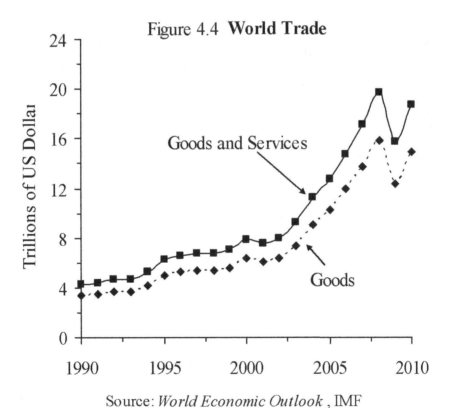

Figure 4.4 **World Trade**

Source: *World Economic Outlook*, IMF

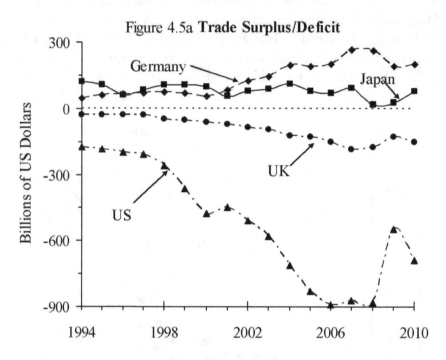

Figure 4.5a **Trade Surplus/Deficit**

Source: *World Trade Organization (WTO)*.

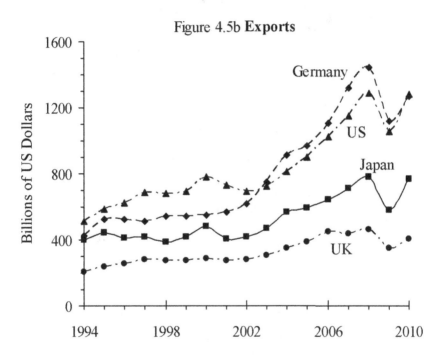

Figure 4.5b **Exports**

Source: *World Trade Organization (WTO)* .

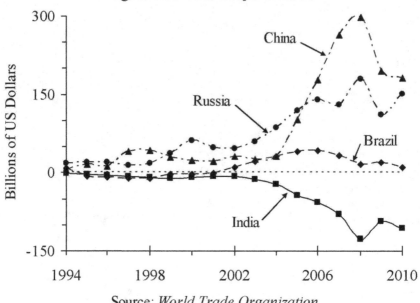

Figure 4.6a **Trade Surplus/Deficit**

Source: *World Trade Organization*.

Figure 4.6b **Exports**

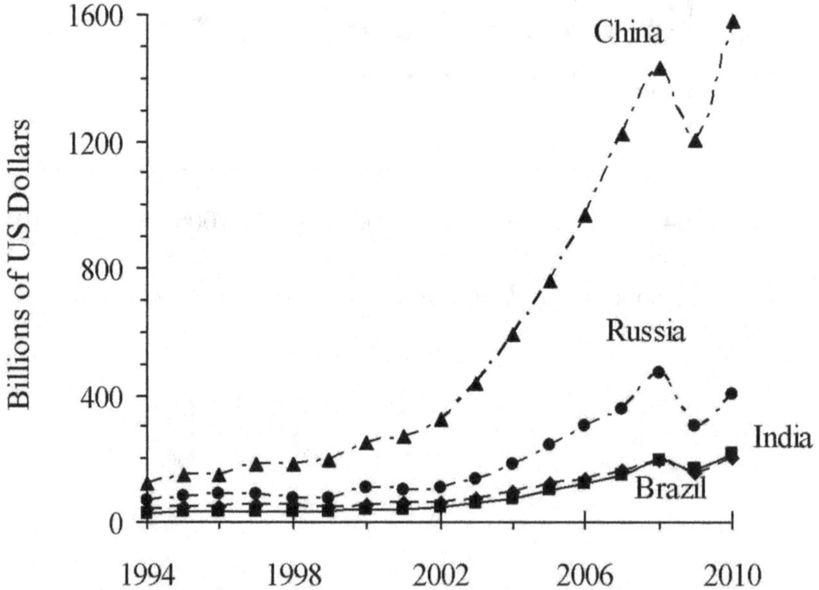

Source: *World Trade Organization*.

Tables 4.1a and 4.2b show the world export market shares of goods and services of selected countries. Up to the 1990s, the United States increased its world export market shares of goods and services nearly every year, but thereafter, during the eight years of the Bush administration, it was losing its share every year. This correlates well with a massive three million job losses in the manufacturing sector during the first five years of the Bush administration (i.e., during 2000–05, as shown in Table 3.1 in the previous chapter). The US share has increased slightly during the Obama administration's first two years, mainly due to the devaluation of the dollar vis-à-vis major currencies. The US dollar has depreciated against other major currencies due to the two rounds of Quantitative Easing (QE) to the tune of trillions of dollars. The United States has a long way to go to reduce its trade deficit. It is worth noting that despite the loss of market shares of goods and services by the United States and other EU nations, Germany has been able to maintain its share, which is mainly because German firms work for their stakeholders and not for shareholders, as discussed at the end of chapter 1.

China is the main beneficiary, as it has increased its world export market shares of goods and services from 3.1 percent in 1997 to 9.4 percent in 2010. Although India is being touted as an emerging economic superpower like China, it has a long way to go. At present India has only 1.7 percent of the world export market shares of goods and services. Due to its massive population and the underdeveloped economy in a number of its states, India will be able to eke out a significant amount of growth rate each year, and its economy may even become third or fourth (in terms of GDP) in the world in the next three to four decades. India needs to strengthen its manufacturing base if it wants to become a global economic power; otherwise it is fast becoming a consumer country like the United States and will remain at the mercy of foreign investors.

Among the BRIC nations, China is clearly the leader right now. In the last twenty years, Japan has lost almost half of its share of the world export market shares of goods and services, which explains why Japan's trade surplus is shrinking every year. A comparison of figures 4.4 and 4.7 clearly shows that free trade policies have favored China the most, while the United States is the loser. As we will see during the discussion on the 1997 Asian Financial Crisis, the 35 percent devaluation of the yuan in 1994 became the turning point for the Chinese economy.

Table 4.1a **World Export Market Shares of Goods and Services
of Selected Countries (1970–2000)**
(percent for total for world)

	1970-9	1980-9	1990-4	1995	1996	1997	1998	1999	2000
US	**12.4**	**12.2**	**13.1**	**12.6**	**13.0**	**13.7**	**13.8**	**14.0**	**14.2**
Japan	6.3	7.9	8.1	7.9	7.2	7.1	6.5	6.7	7.0
Germany	**10.3**	**9.7**	**10.3**	**9.8**	**9.4**	**8.7**	**9.3**	**9.0**	**8.4**
UK	6.0	5.6	5.3	5.0	5.2	5.4	5.6	5.4	5.1
France	7.0	6.6	6.4	5.9	5.5	5.2	5.7	5.5	5.0
Italy	4.4	4.4	4.9	4.8	5.0	4.2	4.8	4.4	3.9
Canada	4.0	3.7	3.4	3.4	3.6	3.6	3.6	4.0	4.2
China	**0.7**	**1.1**	**1.7**	**2.4**	**2.4**	**3.1**	**3.1**	**3.1**	**3.7**
Russia	2.5	2.7	1.5	1.5	1.5	1.5	1.3	1.3	1.5
India	NA	NA	NA	NA	0.6	0.7	0.7	0.7	0.8
Brazil	0.9	1.0	0.8	0.8	0.8	NA	NA	NA	NA
Mexico	0.6	1.0	1.0	1.1	1.2	NA	NA	NA	NA

Source: *World Economic Outlook*, IMF; NA—Data Not Available.

Table 4.1b **World Export Market Shares of Goods and Services
of Selected Countries (2001–10)**
(percent for total for world)

	2001	2002	2003	2004	2005	2006	2007	2008	2009	2010
US	**13.6**	**12.4**	**11.1**	**10.3**	**10.1**	**9.8**	**9.6**	**9.3**	**10.0**	**9.8**
Japan	6.0	5.8	5.7	5.7	5.3	5.0	4.7	4.5	4.3	4.6
Germany	**8.7**	**9.1**	**9.5**	**9.5**	**8.9**	**8.9**	**9.2**	**8.7**	**8.6**	**8.0**
UK	5.1	5.1	4.9	4.8	5.3	4.6	4.3	3.9	3.8	3.5
France	5.0	5.1	5.0	4.8	4.4	4.1	4.0	3.8	3.9	3.5
Italy	4.0	4.0	4.0	3.9	3.7	3.5	3.6	3.4	3.2	2.9
Canada	4.1	3.8	3.6	3.4	3.4	3.1	2.9	2.7	2.4	2.5
China	**4.0**	**4.6**	**5.3**	**5.9**	**6.6**	**7.2**	**7.8**	**8.4**	**8.5**	**9.4**
Russia	1.5	1.5	1.7	1.8	2.1	2.3	2.3	2.7	2.2	2.4
India	0.9	0.9	0.9	1.1	1.2	1.3	1.4	1.4	1.7	1.7
Brazil	NA	NA	0.9	1.0	1.1	1.1	1.1	1.2	1.1	1.2
Mexico	NA	NA	1.3	1.2	1.2	1.8	1.7	1.6	1.6	1.7

Source: *World Economic Outlook*, IMF; NA—Data Not Available.

Figure 4.7 **FOREX Reserve**

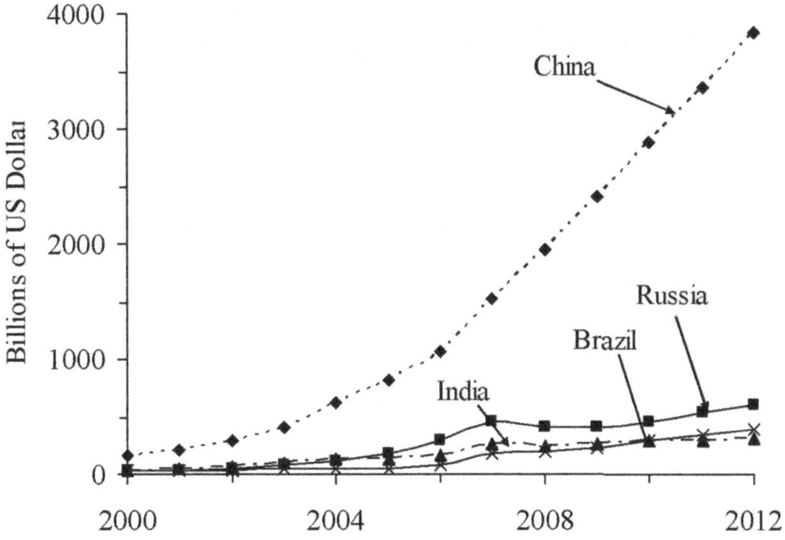

Source: *World Economic Outlook*, IMF (2011 and 2012 are projections)

As shown in Figure 4.7, China and Russia, the two main adversaries of the United States, will continue to amass FOREX at alarming rates. In 2010, China's FOREX increased to $2.85 trillion—20 percent over last year and more than one third of global reserves. By purchasing US debts, China has kept a lid on its currency appreciation. It is worth noting that China and Russia had only $168.9 billion and $24.8 billion FOREX respectively in 2000.[83] In Figure 4.7, FOREX for 20011 and 2012 are projections. Russia had to spend a considerable amount of its FOREX during the peak of the 2008 economic downturn to support the ruble. Also, its FOREX depends on the crude oil price, since oil is its main export. Although India has had trade deficits in the last four years, its FOREX is increasing due to foreign investments and remittances by Indians living overseas.

The US economy now has a serious Catch-22 to deal with. On the one hand, its trade deficit reduced in 2008 and 2009 from its peak in 2006 as Americans are spending less and saving more, creating less demand for foreign goods. On the other hand, this has created record budget deficits for the federal government and a number of states due to a sharp drop in revenues. The sum of the twin deficits—federal budget deficit and trade deficit—is expected to continue to rise in the foreseeable future. All the states, with the exception of Vermont, have a legal requirement to balance their budgets. As legislatures, especially Republicans, do not want to increase taxes, states have to lay off people and reduce services—increase unemployment—in order to balance their budgets.

Table 4.2 **Foreign Exchange Reserves** in December 2010 (in billions of dollars)

Country	FOREX
China	2,876
Japan	1063
Russia	479
Saudi Arabia	445
Taiwan	387
South Korea	291
Brazil	288
India	287
Switzerland	270
Hong Kong	268

Source: The US Central Intelligence Agency's *The World Factbook* at CIA website, August 2011.

If the US economy picks up and consumers start to spend, then the trade deficit will again start to increase. Therefore, in order to somehow keep its Catch-22 at bay, the United States needs a substantial amount of foreign investment in order to keep its interest rates low. This situation cannot go on forever. Countries like China and Russia will not keep financing their rival (i.e., the United States). As discussed earlier, a similar situation led to the collapse of Soviet Union.

A devaluation of the US dollar will also not solve the US trade deficit problem. The dollar was devalued in the 1980s, which helped to reduce the trade deficit, from 3 percent of GDP to 1 percent in two years. At present, however, Americans produce only about 75 percent of the merchandise they purchase, and they import the rest, down from about 90 percent a decade ago. The percentage was even higher in the late 1980s, when the dollar went through a long, managed decline against the German, French, and Japanese currencies. As the dollar fell, domestic manufacturing revived, exports jumped, and the trade deficit shrank.[84] Today, however, any substantial depreciation of the dollar will result in a corresponding increase in consumer goods prices, causing inflation. During the 1980s, a majority of the items sold by large department store chains, such as Wal-Mart and Kmart, was "Made in the USA." Today they sell very few homemade items, and any substantial depreciation in the dollar will only increase the prices of consumer goods.

Due to its nearly double-digit growth rate every year and low debts, China is the new Eldorado of global investors. With its massive FOREX holdings, China will have virtually total control over the US currency. As discussed previously, China has seen the fate of the "bubble economy" of the late 1980s and 1990s in Japan due to the Plaza Accord, and will most likely hesitate to sign a similar accord in relation to the US dollar. China is not just going to accumulate this much of paper of a country "for nothing." At some point the US dollar, therefore, has to give in and collapse. Countries such as India are also becoming like the United States (i.e., consumer countries), and their fates are also going to be similar to that of the United States. At the moment, India's trade deficit with China is increasing every year, and it is exporting minerals to China and importing finished products. Therefore, in the long run this situation is going to lead the global economy into chaos. Hence the current global economy model, where cheap goods and services are produced in China or any Third World country to be sold in other countries, is bound to fail. The 2008 economic downturn was a symptom and warning of its failure.

Table 4.3 **Major Holders of US Treasury Securities**
(in billions of US dollars)

(At the end of year, unless specified)	Japan	China	UK	Oil Exporting Countries[1]	Russia	Hong Kong	Grand Total
2000	317.7	60.3	50.2	47.7	NA	38.6	1015.2
2001	317.9	78.6	45.0	46.8	NA	47.7	1040.1
2002	378.1	118.4	80.8	49.6	NA	47.5	1235.6
2003	550.8	159.0	82.2	42.6	NA	50.0	1523.1
2004	289.9	222.9	95.8	62.1	NA	45.1	1849.3
2005	670.0	310.0	146.0	78.2	NA	40.3	2033.9
2006	622.9	396.9	92.3	110.2	NA	54.0	2103.1
2007	581.2	477.6	158.1	137.9	32.7	51.2	2353.2
2008	626.0	727.4	130.9	186.2	116.4	77.2	3076.9
2009	765.7	894.8	180.3	201.1	141.8	148.7	3685.1
2010	882.3	1160.1	271.6	211.9	151.0	134.2	4437.9
June 2011	911.0	1165.5	349.5	229.6	109.8	118.4	4499.2

[1] Oil exporters include Ecuador, Venezuela, Indonesia, Bahrain, Iran, Iraq, Kuwait, Oman, Qatar, Saudi Arabia, the United Arab Emirates, Algeria, Gabon, Libya and Nigeria.

Source: *U.S. Department of Treasury*; NA—Data Not Available.

Table 4.3 shows the major holders of US Treasury securities. By the end of 2008, China had surpassed Japan as the largest holder of US Treasury securities. The United Kingdom and oil-exporting countries are the third and fourth largest holders of US Treasury securities. Caribbean Banking Centers (Bahamas, Bermuda, Cayman Islands, Netherlands Antilles, and Panama) and Brazil are the fifth and sixth largest holders of US Treasury securities and are not shown in Table 4.3. Hong Kong and Russia are the seventh and eighth largest holders of US Treasury securities. Holding of significant amounts of its Treasury securities by China, Russia, and oil-exporting countries does not bode well for the United States because if those countries start to dump the treasuries, US interest rates will increase drastically.

As mentioned previously, most of the Chinese $3.2 trillion FOREX is in US investment, too. China and Japan had as much as $400 billion and $74.5 billion investments, respectively, in Fannie Mae and Freddie Mac when these two agencies were bailed out by the US government. As US officials were deciding in August 2008 whether to take over Fannie Mae and Freddie Mac, the Treasury Department held informal talks with officials from the People's Bank of China (China's central bank). The Chinese representatives told them they expected the US government to "do whatever is necessary to protect the investments." [85] Russia also cut its investments in these two mortgage giants from $100 billion in early 2008 to $20 billion in November 2008. China is also reducing its stakes in these two after their rescue by the US government.

Unlike the Chinese, who are interested in purchasing high-tech and commodity firms such as 3COM, IBM's laptop division, and Unocal, the Japanese were purchasing trophies like Rockefeller Center, golf courses (such as Pebble Beach, California), prime American hotels, office buildings, and Hollywood studios (such as Columbia Pictures). Had Japan not financed their deficits, interest rates would have skyrocketed, and the US economy, which was based on "Reaganomics" at the time, would have collapsed.

In the last twenty-five to thirty years, the financial sector's share in the profits of US companies has increased from just 5 percent to more than 35 to 40 percent, as shown in Figure 4.8. Most of the financial sector does not add value to the economy. Instead, they are subtracting from the economy. This does not create new value—it squeezes profits out of already created value. When you squeeze the juice out of a fruit, then what remains of the fruit? These days that's what the financial sector is doing with the United States and the global economy. Sectors such as agriculture, industry, trade, and services create new value, whereas the financial sector can create only "profit." These days, banks do not give loans to consumers with the view that those loans should be repaid. Instead, their purpose is to generate perpetual payments in the form of interest and fines. Banks loan so much to people that in the end it forces the loan takers to pay only interests, fines, etc. Apart from this, they come up with new mathematical and statistical algorithms to find ways to create trillions of dollars of investments on paper, some of which have already collapsed.

Reaganomics, or the economic theory of Milton Freidman being practiced by Republicans since the 1980s, does nothing but enrich ultrawealthy people at the cost of the lower and middle economic classes. We will discuss some economic data to prove this point. Although Democrats were criticized for their tax-and-spend policies, they did not mortgage the future of US children and grandchildren. Republicans, however, sold the country to foreigners, especially to China, by their policies of cut taxes and spend. It can be likened to treason. Whenever Republicans were in the White House, they went for massive tax cuts for the wealthy and massive increases in spending on defense, resulting in huge budget deficits. They would advocate small government and balancing the budget only when Democrats brought any spending bill for education, labor, and human resources, which are the very foundations of a country.

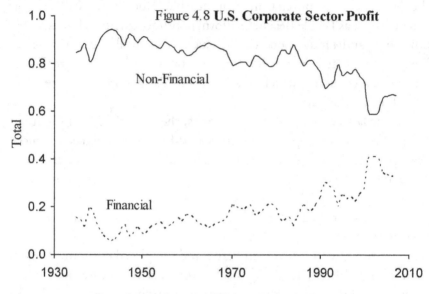

Source: U.S. Bureau of Economic Analysis

As shown in Figure 4.9, productivity has increased at a much faster rate than compensation since the mid-1970s. The profits from the increase in productivity did not go into the pockets of employees but went to stock dividends and Wall Street. On the contrary, benefits such as health insurance and retirement for average workers were reduced in more and more firms over the same period. At the other end of the table, the ratio of CEO to average worker salary increased to a record level, as shown in Figure 4.10.

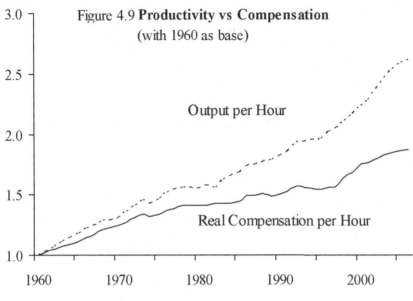

Figure 4.9 **Productivity vs Compensation**
(with 1960 as base)

Source: 2008 Economic Report of the President

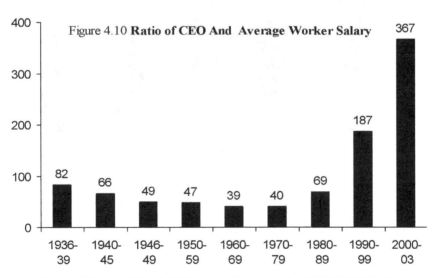

Figure 4.10 **Ratio of CEO And Average Worker Salary**

Source: "Historical Trends in Executive Compensation 1936-2003," Carola
Frydman and Raven E. Saks, 2006,
http://2006.ehameeting.com/schedule/pdfs/session_2c_frydman_and_saks.pdf

The gap between the wages of average workers and the salary and
compensation package of a typical CEO in America is increasing yearly.

Japanese and Taiwanese CEOs make about eleven and fourteen times more than their average employees, respectively, whereas German, French, and Polish CEOs make about twenty, twenty-three, and twenty-five times more, respectively.[86] But the average American CEO earns 262 times more than the average worker—more in one workday (there are 260 in a year) than an average worker earns in fifty-two weeks. In 1965, American CEOs in major companies earned twenty-four times what the average worker earned. This ratio grew to thirty-five in 1978 and to seventy-one in 1989. The ratio surged in the 1990s, and hit three hundred at the end of the recovery in 2000. A fall in the stock market then temporarily reduced CEO stock-related pay, causing it to moderate to 143 times that of the average worker in 2002. Since then it has exploded. By 2005 the average CEO was earning $10,982,000 a year, 262 times the average employee, who received $41, 861.[87]

Figure 4.11a **Real Family Income Growth By Quintile 1947-73**

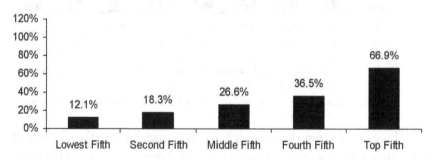

Figure 4.11b **Real Family Income Growth By Quintile 1973-2000**

Figures 4.11a-c show the real family income growth by quintiles during 1947–73, 1973–2000 and 2000–2005. Table 4.4 shows the percentage share of income going to all five income fifths and to the top 5 percent. The mid-1970s seem to be the turning point. Before the mid-1970s, the bottom fifths had more growth in their income than the top fifths every year, but after the mid-1970s they lost the edge to the top fifth, and especially to the top 5 percent, whose income growth was the largest. Although during the Bush Jr. administration all groups had negative income growth, the top fifth lost the least, whereas the lowest fifth lost the most.

Table 4.11c **Real Family Income Growth By Quintile 2000-05**

Source: The State of Working America, Economic Policy Institute, 2006-07

According to a Northeastern University, Boston, study on unemployment during the last quarter of 2009, the unemployment rate among the low-income group was 30.8 percent, almost ten times more than the highest income group. The researchers divided the households into ten groups based on annual household incomes. The unemployment rate among the highest income group, of $150,000 or more, was only 3.2 percent, whereas the unemployment rate among the next highest, with incomes of $100,000 to $149,999, was 4 percent. At the very rear, the unemployment rate of the lowest income group, having household incomes of $12,499 or less, was 30.8 percent, more than 5 percent higher than the overall jobless rate at the height of the 1930s Great Depression. For the next lowest group, having incomes of $12,500 to $20,000, the unemployment rate was 19.1 percent.[88]

In the late 1970s, the cutoff to qualify for the highest-earning one ten-thousandth of households was roughly $2 million in inflation-adjusted, pretax terms. By 2007, it had jumped to $11.5 million. The cutoff to be in the top 1 percent doubled since the late 1970s, to roughly $400,000. By contrast, pay at the median, which was about $50,000 in 2007, rose less than 20 percent. Near the bottom of the income distribution, the increase was about 12 percent. In 2007, the top one ten-thousandth of households took home 6 percent of the nation's income, up from 0.9 percent in 1977. It was the highest level since at least 1913, the first year for which the Internal Revenue Service has data. The top 1 percent of earners took home 23.5 percent of income, up from 9 percent three decades earlier.[89]

Comparison with the US Economy before the onset of the 1930s Great Depression

Table 4.4 **Percentage Share of Income Going to Income Fifths and to Top 5%**

Year	Lowest Fifth	Fourth Fifth	Middle Fifth	Second Fifth	Top Fifth	Top 5 Percent
2005	4.0	9.6	15.3	22.9	48.1	21.1
2000	4.3	9.8	15.4	22.7	47.7	21.1
1989	4.6	10.6	16.5	23.7	44.6	17.9
1984	4.4	10.3	16.4	24.3	44.6	17.0
1981	4.6	10.6	16.7	24.3	43.7	16.5
1979	5.4	11.6	17.5	24.1	41.4	15.3
1973	5.5	11.9	17.5	24.0	41.1	15.5
1970	4.9	10.9	16.4	23.8	44.1	16.1
1960	4.6	10.9	16.4	22.7	45.4	19.6
1950	4.8	10.9	16.1	22.1	46.1	21.4
1947	5.0	11.9	17.0	23.1	43.0	17.5
1946	5.0	11.1	16.0	21.8	46.1	21.3
1941	4.1	9.5	15.3	22.3	48.8	24.0
1935–6	4.1	9.2	14.1	20.9	51.7	26.5
1929	(12.5)		13.8	19.3	54.4	30.0

Source: *The State of Working America*, Economic Policy Institute, 2006–07, p. 59; McElvaine, Robert S., *The Great Depression*, Three Rivers Press, NY, 1993, p. 331.

Table 4.4 also confirms that Reaganomics has skewed the income distribution in favor of the ultrarich. After the 1930s Great Depression, the income share going to the top 5 percent reduced by one-half, from 30 percent to 15 percent, where all others gained. But after the 1980s, the income share going to the top 5 percent increased to 21 percent in 2005, whereas the income share of the other 95 percent has gone down.

According to a 2011 nonpartisan Congressional Budget Office report, the average real after-tax household income for the top 1 percent of the population grew by a whopping 275 percent between 1979 and

2007. On the other hand, the same income for the next-highest 19 percent, the 60 percent of the population in the middle, and the bottom 20 percent, grew by 65 percent, 40 percent, and 18 percent, respectively, over the same period. According to the Internal Revenue Service data, the median compensation in 2010 was just 66 percent of the average income, whereas it was 72 percent in 1980.

At the onset of the 1930s Great Depression, the economic situation in the United States was similar. According to a Brookings Institution study, *America's Capacity to Consume*,[90] the top 0.1 percent of American families in 1929 had a combined income of the bottom 42 percent. In absolute numbers, about 24,000 families had a combined income of more than 11.5 million poor and lower-middle-class families. They also found that income was being distributed with increasing inequality, particularly in the later years of the 1920s. The income of those at the very top increased more rapidly than that of any other group. Toward the end of the 1920s, a larger percentage of the total income was received by the portion of the population having very high incomes than had been the case a decade earlier. Between 1920 and 1929, per capita disposable income for all Americans rose by 9 percent, but the top 1 percent of income recipients enjoyed not less than a 75 percent increase in disposable income. The share of disposable income going to the top 1 percent jumped from 12 percent in 1920 to 19 percent in 1929.[91]

One reason for this inequality was the tax cuts provided by Andrew Mellon, the Treasury secretary from 1921 to 1932, who reduced the top income tax rate from 77 to 25 percent during the 1920s and also reduced federal estate taxes. Mellon was the third-richest person in the country after John D. Rockefeller and Henry Ford. With the onset of the 1930s Great Depression, Franklin Roosevelt increased the top tax rate to 80 percent in 1935. The top tax rate remained at about 70 percent until 1980. At the hands of the Reagan administration it was reduced to 33 percent by 1988. The Clinton administration increased it to nearly 40 percent, but, again, the Bush administration reduced it to 35 percent. Since 1980, tax rates for the top-tier income group have fallen more than the rates for any other group.

In 1929, nearly 80 percent (about 21.5 million families) had no savings, whereas the top 0.1 percent (24,000 families) held 34 percent of all savings. In 1929, the top 0.5 percent of Americans owned 32.4

percent of all the net wealth of individuals. This represented the highest concentration of wealth at any time in American history. One main reason for this growing gap was that due to the introduction of mechanization, productivity was increasing at a faster rate than in any previous era, but wages were not increasing at the same rate. During 1922–29, output per worker in manufacturing increased by 32 percent, whereas the wages increased by a meager 8 percent. With nearly stable prices, the falling production costs resulted in huge profits. In the same period 1923–29, corporate profits increased by 62 percent and dividends by 65 percent.[92]

A 1932 article in *Current History* showed the reason of the 1930s Great Depression:[93]

> We still pray to be given each day our daily bread. Yet there is too much bread, too much wheat and corn, meat and oil and almost every other commodity required by man for his subsistence and material happiness. We are not able to purchase the abundance that modern methods of agriculture, mining and manufacturing make available in such bountiful quantities.

Although the wealthy also purchase consumer goods, they do not purchase in the same proportion of their earnings. For instance, if a family earning $50,000 a year consumes a certain amount of food, buys a car every year, sends their children to college, and buys a house every five years, then a family earning $1 million a year will not be consuming twenty times the food of the first family, twenty cars every year, will not send fifty-plus children to college (usually a family has a maximum of two or three children studying at college level simultaneously) and will not buy twenty houses every five years. Wealthy people buy private jets, yachts, collectibles (valuable items such as rare coins and currencies, paintings, costly villas, etc.); all these are insignificant in terms of consumer market or employment (i.e., these employ very few people). Ultrarich people buy Bernie Madoff's wooden duck worth $2 for $3,000 and Michael Jackson's white glove for $350,000. Therefore, inequality of income distorts the consumer market. If the same amount of money goes to the middle class or lower class, they would buy mass consumer items, by which a large number of people would get employment.

Tax cuts to middle-class people go directly into the general economy, whereas tax cuts to the ultrarich generate economic bubbles.

According to Milton Friedman and Anna Schwartz, the shrinking money supply, due to the large number of bank failures, is to be blamed for the 1930s Great Depression, as it caused less money to be available for businesses. But this can be refuted by the facts that during 1929–31 interest rates declined and so did prices, the latter more sharply than the reduction of the money supply,[94] hence the real money supply was actually growing slightly.

Effects of Stimulus Packages and the Great Depression

The Great Depression, which started in 1929 and ended in 1939 with the start of World War II, was the most severe economic downturn ever experienced by the Western industrialized countries. In the United States, its onset was caused by the collapse of the stock market bubble and the unequal distribution of wealth. Prior to the 1929 stock market crash, the Dow Jones had risen close to 400 percent during the preceding eight years. Initially President Hoover tried to balance the budget in 1931 and 1932 by cutting expenses and raising taxes. Both had adverse effects on the US economy.

Before the 1930s Great Depression, there were recessions in 1797–1800, 1807–14, 1819–24, 1837–43, 1857–60, 1873–79, 1893–96, 1907–8, and 1918–21. The government did not intervene in any of these previous economic recessions and opted to let the economy find its own solutions. But the severity of the 1930s Great Depression displayed the structural defects of the economy, and, for the first time, the government had to intervene by providing massive Keynesian spending in the first half of the 1930s in order to create employment.

Franklin D. Roosevelt became president in 1933, and under his New Deal plan, following Keynesian stimulus spending, the administration created a social welfare system and spent money on development projects such as the Hoover Dam and the Tennessee Valley Authority, which provided employment on a large scale. Several New Deal programs remain active today, with some still operating under the original names, including the Federal Deposit Insurance Corporation (FDIC) and the Federal Housing Administration (FHA). The largest programs still in existence today are the Social Security System, Securities and Exchange Commission (SEC), and Fannie Mae. After watching the hyperinflation of 1921–23 in the Weimar Republic, Germany, Roosevelt was hesitant to commit to massive spending later on.

Due to the stimulus packages, the Roosevelt government was able to reduce unemployment from 25 percent in 1930 to only 15 percent in 1939 at the onset of the Second World War. These numbers were very high according to present standards, as only one member of the family used to generate direct income in those days. The unemployment reduced to a normal level only after the outbreak of World War II when the US economy started churning out arms and armaments. World War II spending on arms and armaments worked as massive Keynesian spending projects. Had there been no world war it might have taken another couple of decades for the country to emerge from the Great Depression.

After the Great Depression, there were recessions in 1953, 1957, 1960–1, 1973–4, early 1980s, early 1990s and early 2000s. These recessions lasted anywhere from one to two years. The recession of 1973–74 was caused by the quadrupling of the price of oil due to an OPEC embargo. The recession of the early 1980s was caused by another rise in the price of oil due to the energy crisis caused by the 1979 Iranian revolution and also due to US monetary policy, high interest rates and inflation. The recession of the early 1990s was due to Reaganomics and the rise in the price of oil in early 1990. The recession in the early 2000s was caused by the collapse of the tech sector bubble and the 9/11 attacks.

During the recessions of the 1980s and 1990s, home values did not collapse all over the country on the scale witnessed in the economic downturn of 2008–09. This recession is different from all the previous ones because unlike previous recessions, the middle class has a big stake in the capital markets through their 401(k)s. The combination of the halving of the values of the 401(k) funds and the drastic reduction in home values leaves these people with no source of funds for major purchases. In past recessions, people were able to use home equity to get cash to buy cars or send their children to college.

The future of home mortgages does not look good, at least for the next several years. Any drop in house prices increases the number of underwater mortgages. At the end of the last quarter of 2010, 27 percent of all mortgages were underwater as compared to 23.2 percent a quarter earlier.[95] In the third quarter of 2010, 23.2 percent of single-family homes were underwater as compared to 21.8 percent in 2009.[96] According to a *Washington Post* analysis, the number of prime mortgages in delinquency exceeded the number of subprime loans in danger of default for the first time in October 2008. At that time, one of every five mortgage holders had a home worth less than the mortgage on it.[97] More job losses result in more defaults on mortgage loans, and this in turn further depresses the housing market and further cuts consumption.

Therefore the government has to provide jobs through stimulus packages (Keynesian stimulus). Had John McCain been elected, his administration would have also had to go for similar stimulus packages, otherwise the country would have faced a Great Depression II immediately. The $1.5 trillion stimulus money of the Obama and Bush administrations has temporarily postponed the Great Depression II. But these stimulus packages have the potential to crash the entire US economy because of massive foreign debt.

By 2019, the cost of servicing the US debt will be $450 billion a year, assuming a low interest rate. But if foreign powers lose their confidence in the US debt, this number will rise rapidly due to the increase in interest rates. Currently, the major entitlements, Social Security and Medicare, constitute about 42 percent of the US federal budget. Hence, after a decade or so, all the revenues will be used for these only.

There is a major difference between the 1930s Great Depression and the coming Great Depression. During the 1930s Great Depression, the Keynesian stimulus (i.e., generating employment by government spending) worked. The 1930s Great Depression ended only after the country entered the Second World War (i.e., when the country started churning out arms and armaments on a massive scale). In fact, only a couple of years after the 1930s Great Depression the living standard in the country had improved in comparison with the pre-Depression period. At present, however, Keynesian stimulus alone will not solve the problem because the country is completely dependent on the import of consumer items, and both the government and its people are in deep debt. Such conditions were not present during the 1930s Great Depression.

According to Lou Crandall, chief economist at Wrightson ICAP, which analyzes Treasury financing trends, "While the current market for [US] Treasuries is booming, it's unclear whether demand for debt can be sustained. There's a time tomb somewhere, but we don't know exactly where on the calendar it's planted."[98] In a similar situation, US and German banks did not help Gorbachev in the late 1980s, which led to the collapse of the USSR.

Both China and the Soviet Union followed communism, but the Soviet Union collapsed, whereas China is on the verge of becoming the most powerful nation in the world. During the Gorbachev years, three major factors distinguished the Soviet Union and China: (1) the USSR had massive foreign debts, whereas China did not, a situation exacerbated by plummeting oil prices, (2) the Soviet economy was urban-based while the Chinese was rural-based, and (3) China was allowed a market in the United States.

Had oil prices increased, like they have during the Putin administration in the first decade of twenty-first century, or had German banks financed Gorbachev's perestroika like Japan financed Reagan's deficits, the USSR and communism would not have collapsed in 1991 at all. It is wrong to claim that that this collapse was due to Reagan's military buildup. Had Japan not financed American deficits in the 1980s, the interest rate would have skyrocketed, resulting in the collapse of both the US economy and capitalism.

The massive spending by the administration may create millions of domestic jobs, but it is not going to solve the trade deficit because of the overvalued dollar. Even if the Obama administration takes a hard-line stance against China and presses for the appreciation of the yuan, American firms will start to import from another country the goods being imported right now from China. On the other hand, if the administration goes for the "Buy American" slogan by raising tariffs, prices will increase drastically, causing inflation.

The economy is going to be in a depressed condition for a significant period of time. Some portion of the United States may have to face an economic situation similar to 1990s Russia after the collapse of the USSR. But unlike Russia, the United States has the latest technology and top scientific talent coupled with a hard-working population. These conditions will allow it to emerge much more powerfully than the 2000

Russia. However, US living standards will not be the same as they were prior to the 2008 recession.

In the end there will be no option for the United States but to restart its domestic manufacturing and service sector units, as the country cannot sustain huge amounts of negative BOP for long, although inflation will go through the roof and the living standard will go down drastically. The sooner this step is taken the better; otherwise the country may witness a 1990s Russian type of economic chaos.

The economic downturn that started in 2008 is the symptom of a structural failure of the global economic model, which is based on the exploitation of cheap labor and commodities in Third World countries in the name of "globalization." This model created a handful of millionaires and billionaires everywhere but is now making everyone a victim. The US economy was booming because of the technology bubble (in the 1990s) and the housing bubble (in the 2000s). It never boomed because of any rise in people's "real income." After the bust of these two bubbles, people have lost their purchasing power (as they lost their quality jobs due to outsourcing). Therefore, the purchasing power of the common people needs to be increased by bringing back jobs and not by just doling out some IRS rebate checks or temporary stimulus funding, which will last for a few months only. Apart from this, it is wrong to put an emphasis on increasing the GDP, which is not a measure of growth at all.

5

•◆•

CASINO CAPITALISM

The advent of Internet technology, and the subsequent integration of national and global economies in the last couple of decades, has given an opportunity for brilliant brains to devise algorithms (i.e., mathematical and statistical methods) to generate money for millionaires and billionaires by moving money from one place to another in any place in the world by the click of a mouse button. This was facilitated by the creation of financial instruments (derivatives, credit default swaps, etc.) that resemble casino games, which create trillions of dollars of investments on paper. Hedge funds play these casino games for extraordinary returns (30 percent to 40 percent each year) for ultrarich people, but when they lose, the taxpayers and common people have to pay for their misdeeds. Until the 2008 economic downturn, Third World countries were the main victims of the hedge funds' casino games. But now Americans, as well as the entire world, are experiencing the effects of these misdeeds.

Wall Street and other financial institutions have become the modern-day Las Vegas and Atlantic City (i.e., casinos where only the ultrawealthy and people working there can win). In traditional casinos most of the games are biased in favor of the owners. Amateur players rarely end up winning. Similarly, on Wall Street and other financial hubs, top executives and hedge funds earn multimillions of dollars. Common people, on the other hand, may think for some time that they are winning, but suddenly due to a financial setback they realize that everything is gone. As most firms have opted out of pension planning, and people are depending on their 401(k)s, heavily invested in stocks, for their retirements, the scenario for the future of retirees in the country is rather bleak.

Phil Angelides is a Democratic member of Congress and is chairman of the bipartisan commission to examine causes of the biggest downturn since the 1930s Great Depression. He says that Goldman Sachs's operation was similar to selling a car with faulty brakes and then selling an insurance policy on that car. Goldman Sachs helped hedge fund manager John Paulson to select securities tied to risky subprime mortgages without telling investors that he was betting against them (i.e., betting that they would fail). Paulson made about $2.7 billion in the process. This type of betting was illegal until 2000 when the Republican-led Congress passed the Commodity Futures Modernization Act of 2000 (CFMA) to make it illegal to regulate these side bets (i.e., without owning the item).

According to a 2009 *New York Times* article, Wall Street has started to pursue securitizations of bundles of life insurances and then selling them to investors. There are $26 trillion life insurance policies in force in the United States, a huge market. The earlier the policyholder dies, the bigger the return—though if people live longer than expected, investors could get poor returns or even lose money. Like the subprime mortgages, it will be difficult to grade an individual life insurance policy, as factors such as race, gender, education, health, and type of health care affect a person's life expectancy. Apart from this, the industry has been plagued by fraud complaints. State insurance regulators, hamstrung by a patchwork of laws and regulations, have criticized life settlement brokers for coercing the ill and elderly to take out policies with the sole purpose of selling them back to the brokers, called "stranger-owned life insurance." According to Steven Weisbart, senior vice president and chief economist for the Insurance Information Institute trade group, "It [securitization of life insurance] is not an investment product, it is a gambling product."[99]

In the United States, many now try to gamble at Wall Street to get maximum return. They may get a high return for some time, but in this gambling, players can also lose everything. People in Japan, on the other hand, have a different mind-set. Japan has the world's second-largest pension market, with assets of $3.47 trillion, after the United States with $15.27 trillion. Japanese pension fund managers like small but stable growth rates of 3 percent to 4 percent a year whereas their counterparts in the United States and Europe look for double-digit growth rates and hence gamble on Wall Street. More than 60 percent of all US pension assets are invested in hedge funds, while 29 percent and only 1.75 percent of all European and Japanese pension assets, respectively, are invested in hedge funds.[100] According to Alicia Munnell, director of the Center for Retirement Research at Boston College, the unfunded state and local pension funds in the United States are more than $1.9 trillion. Most government pension plans assume they will earn 8 percent a year on their investments. This assumption is too optimistic, although some have achieved this return over certain periods.[101]

In this section we will discuss some of the financial deregulation measures and shady mortgages that are blamed for the 2008 Wall Street bank crisis, the effects of Casino Capitalism on small cities, the reason behind the 2008 record oil price rise, and the 1997 Asian financial crisis, which was a precursor to the present US and Euro crises, all as examples of Casino Capitalism.

Deregulation

Although elected leaders in the United States claim to work for the common people, in reality they work for the ultrawealthy people and corporations, as they need money to win elections. The "invisible hand" of Adam Smith is actually the hand of the ultrawealthy and corporations behind the government. This has a self-destructive effect on American capitalism. In this section, we will see how elected leaders formulated rules in favor of financial firms that led to the economic meltdown in

2008, and how casino games played by these firms play havoc with the common people.

Deregulation, the mantra promoted by the Republicans since the 1980s, was behind the 2008 economic meltdown. After numerous bank failures during the Great Depression, the Glass-Steagall Act of 1933 established the Federal Deposit Insurance Corporation (FDIC) and introduced banking reforms such as separation of banking and other financial companies. The 1999 Gramm-Leach-Bliley Act repealed part of the Glass-Steagall Act of 1933, allowing a bank to offer investment, commercial banking, and insurance services. The 1999 Gramm-Leach-Bliley Act allowed firms such as Citigroup and Bank of America to offer investment and insurance services apart from banking after their acquisition and merger with other financial firms, which had been illegal up to then.

In 2004, at the request of big investment banks, the Securities and Exchange Commission (SEC) reduced requirements so that they could pile up debts. At the same time, the SEC was given supervisory power to look into those banks' risky investments, but the SEC assigned only seven people to examine the financial firms—which in 2007 had combined assets of more than $4 trillion. Since March 2007, the office has not had a director. As of October 2008, the office had not completed a single inspection since it was reshuffled more than a year and a half ago. The few problems that examiners' preliminary investigations uncovered about the riskiness of the firms' investments and their increased reliance on debt—clear signs of trouble—were all but ignored.[102]

Derivatives exacerbated the 2008 global economic crisis. Derivatives are financial contracts whose values are derived from the value of something else. A derivative is basically a side bet, (i.e., a bet on loans, bonds, commodities, stocks, residential mortgages, commercial real estate, loans, bonds, interest rates, exchange rates, stock market indices, consumer price index, or even on weather conditions) without owning it. It is similar to the bet a person who is not a player or does not own the team makes with someone on the outcome of a baseball game. If a person is certain that mortgage securities would fail, he would place the bet against them without owning them, making millions and even billions of dollars. For example, a credit default swap (CDS) is a credit derivative contract between two parties. CDS was invented by a JPMorgan Chase team in the mid-1990s.

Brooksley E. Born, the then head of the Commodity Futures Trading Commission, was for regulating the derivative market. However, the wishes of Federal Reserve Chairman Alan Greenspan, Treasury Secretary Robert E. Rubin, and Securities and Exchange Commission Chairman Arthur Levitt Jr. prevailed. Ms. Born left the CFTC in June 1999. The Commodity Futures Modernization Act of 2000 made it illegal to regulate the derivative market. Derivatives are modern financial casino games. After the 2008 Wall Street banking crisis, in his congressional testimony Alan Greenspan said that he was wrong in his support of deregulating the derivative market.

Warren Buffett famously described derivatives bought speculatively as "financial weapons of mass destruction." George Soros avoids using them "because we don't really understand how they work." Felix G. Rohatyn, the investment banker who saved New York from financial catastrophe in the 1970s, described derivatives as potential "hydrogen bombs."[103] For instance, in October 2008, trading in Gulf Bank, one of the largest lenders in Kuwait, was halted after a major customer defaulted on a currency derivative contract, a bet on the euro that dived against the dollar in the previous ten days. It was reported that losses were as much as 200 million dinars or nearly $750 million.[104]

By mid-2008 the global derivatives market was close to $530 trillion. The global CDS market increased from $900 billion in 2000 to $62 trillion in 2008. According to Eric Dinallo, the insurance superintendent for New York State, about 80 percent of these $62 trillion in credit default swaps outstanding were speculative. In comparison, the value of the New York Stock Exchange was $30 trillion at the end of 2007 before the start of the 2008 crash.

American International Group (AIG), the world's largest private insurance company, had sold $440 billion in credit-default swaps tied to mortgage securities. When the housing bubble burst the CDSs tied to mortgage securities began to send shock waves throughout the global market. To prevent a chain reaction, the US government had to rescue AIG. When AIG and several others were running out of money after being downgraded by credit-rating agencies because of mounting losses, a $700 billion fund was established by the US Congress to bail out Wall

Street firms. This triggered a clause in its credit-default swap contracts to post billions in collateral. AIG is considered "too big to fail," so the US government had to save it. The failure of AIG would send a shockwave through the finance industry, as it had insured assets of financial firms all over the world.

Shady Mortgages

The 2008 Wall Street crisis was triggered by the defaults of record numbers of subprime mortgages. Investment banks were securitizing the mortgages, including the subprime mortgages, and selling them all over the world (i.e., the mortgages were sold as securities to investors). Typically, a bundle of say one hundred home mortgages was sold as securities to investors.

In finance, a security is an instrument representing financial value. When the subprime mortgage market started to collapse in 2007, the investment banks that had sold these securities started to lose money. Although the mortgage-based securities affected by the subprime crisis was said to be less than $2 trillion, the collapse of the US housing sector affected non-subprime mortgages too, leading to further losses in mortgage-based securities. Bank officials were under pressure from their higher-ups to give mortgages, and, in turn, they as well as the top officials were getting huge year-end bonuses. At investment banks also, officials were putting pressure on workers to churn out securities that packaged mortgages and other forms of debt into bundles for resale to investors all over the world. The officials, including the CEOs at these investment banks, were making millions of dollars in bonuses due to the profit related to the sale of these securities. These officials were taking huge risks for their bonuses to show short-term gains for their financial institutions, and many of those gains turned out to be huge losses.

During the 1990s and early 2000s, low interest rates and large foreign investments created a housing sector boom in the United States. The percent of home ownership in the United States increased from a consistent 63 percent to 64 percent from the 1960s to early 1990s to a record 69 percent in 2005. During this housing boom period, banks were giving housing loans to people whose income was not sufficient to pay the monthly mortgage. However, as home prices were rising every year at a record pace, people were making money by selling homes to each other. When home prices started to collapse, not only people having subprime mortgages but people with prime mortgages found it difficult to pay their mortgages too.

According to a Brookings Institution study, prime mortgages dropped to 64 percent of the total in 2004, 56 percent in 2005, and 52 percent in 2006.[105] According to Credit Suisse, 29 percent of new mortgages in 2005 allowed borrowers to pay interest only—not principal—or pay less than the interest due and add the cost to the principal. It was up from 1 percent in 2001. In 2006, half of new mortgages required no or minimal documentation of household income. According to the National Association of Realtors, the average down payment for the first-time home buyers was 10 percent, whereas in 2007, it was only 2 percent. Suppose you have $20,000 cash. In 2006, you could get a 5 percent down mortgage to buy a $400,000 home whereas a 10 percent mortgage will limit you to buy only a $200,000 home.[106]

According to John D. Parsons, a supervisor at a Washington Mutual mortgage processing center, almost all were granted mortgage loans irrespective of their real incomes. Parsons said that it was normal to see babysitters claiming salaries worthy of college presidents, and school teachers with incomes rivaling stockbrokers. Interviews with two dozen employees, mortgage brokers, real estate agents, and appraisers revealed the relentless pressure to churn out loans.[107]

Credit Rating Agencies like Moody's and Standard & Poor's also played dubious roles by first assigning investment-grade ratings to these subprime mortgage-related securities. Both these agencies were getting substantial amounts of money by grading these products. But when subprime mortgages started to collapse, they suddenly downgraded the mortgage-related securities to junk ratings. According to the Nobel Prize economist Joseph Stiglitz, "I view the ratings agencies as one of the key culprits. They were the party that performed that alchemy that converted the securities from F-rated to A-rated. The banks could not have done what they did without the complicity of the ratings agencies."[108]

Despite having mortgage-related losses, top executives at Wall Street were getting huge bonuses. In 2007, Wall Street firms paid $33.2 billion in bonuses. Seven of Wall Street's biggest firms (Merrill Lynch,

Citigroup, Bear Stearns, Morgan Stanley, JPMorgan Chase, Lehman Brothers, and Goldman Sachs) paid a combined total of $122 billion in total compensation and benefits, up 10 percent since 2006, despite seeing their net revenue collectively fall 6 percent. On the other hand, in the same year mortgage-related losses reported by the seven firms totaled $55 billion and wiped out more than $200 billion in shareholder value, which was nearly half the value of their holdings. Three of those firms suffered their biggest losses ever in the final months of 2007. Employee compensation at those firms was equal to 47 percent of net revenue in 2007, compared with 40 percent the year before.[109]

In 2006, Merrill Lynch had record earnings of $7.5 billion, and the firm gave $5 billion to $6 billion in bonuses in that year. A twenty-something analyst with a base salary of $130,000 received a bonus of $250,000, and a thirty-something trader with a $180,000 salary got $5 million. Dow Kim, executive vice president, received a $35 million bonus, whereas his salary was only $350,000. Since then, the company lost three times the money in mortgage-related investments, leading to the company, founded in 1914, being sold to Bank of America in late 2008. In 2006, more than fifty people at Goldman Sachs were paid more than $20 million in bonuses. At Wall Street firms, bonuses are based on short-term profits, which encourage people to take risks like gamblers in a casino.[110]

When home prices started to collapse, not only did people with subprime mortgages find it difficult to make their mortgage payments, people with prime mortgages had difficulties too. Bear Stearns, founded in 1923 and one of the largest global investment banks and securities trading and brokerage firms, collapsed in early 2008 because of the subprime mortgage crisis and was sold to JP Morgan Chase for as low as ten dollars per share, a price far below the fifty-two-week high of $133.20 per share, traded before the crisis. The federal takeover of Fannie Mae and Freddie Mac in September 2008 cost taxpayers about $400 billion. By the first half of 2008, the value of bad loans of Washington Mutual had reached $11.5 billion.[111] Due to its mortgage-related crisis and subsequent withdrawal of $16.4 billion in deposits, during a ten-day bank run in June 2008, Washington Mutual, a hundred-year-old bank, was seized by the FDIC and finally sold to JP Morgan Chase for $1.9 billion in September 2008.

In September 2008, after the failure of Lehman Brothers and the emergency rescue of AIG, Henry Paulson, then US Treasury secretary, warned of an economic calamity greater than the 1930s Great Depression when President Bush and congressional Democratic leaders agreed to the $700 billion bailout. Government officials have acknowledged difficulties in tracking this $700 billion bailout fund because, apart from providing lending to customers and other banks, banks have leeway to use the money for other things, such as buying other banks, paying dividends to investors, or even bonuses to executives. Most of this money is being paid to the parties who won the bet on the derivatives. AIG, which had a record $62 billion loss in the last quarter of 2008, received about $170 billion as an emergency loan from the Fed until March 2009, and it paid $75 billion of this loan in the final months of 2008 to several domestic and foreign banks (such as Goldman Sachs, Merrill Lynch, Morgan Stanley, Bank of America, Societe Generale, Deutsche Bank, and Barclays), as well as to several US municipalities. Most of this money was paid due to the collapse of mortgage-based securities.

Although banks, investment firms, and a majority of hedge funds lost huge amounts of money due to the collapse of the housing sector and the ensuing stock market collapse, some hedge funds made millions, even billions, by betting on the collapse of the housing sector in 2008. For instance, John Paulson, the New York hedge fund manager, made $3.7 billion in 2007 by placing his bet on the collapse of the mortgage market. George Soros and James Simons made $2.9 billion and $2.8 billion, respectively, in 2007. At the beginning of 2007, Paulson's hedge fund had $6 billion, and by the end of December 2007, his fund assets were worth $28 billion. A few years ago, individual income reaching into billions of dollars was unfathomable. In 2002, the first year Alpha Magazine tracked hedge fund compensation; the top twenty-five managers earned $2.8 billion combined. Hedge funds are pools of private money, largely generated from wealthy individuals, pension funds, and endowments, used for a wide range of investments. Usually 80 percent of any gains are given to such investors, while the fund manager takes 20 percent, plus an annual fee for his or her services.[112] Apart from this, these hedge fund managers claim their incomes as capital gains and pay only 15 percent federal taxes rather than the regular income tax rates, at least twice as high. On the other hand, several states are running out of money in this economic downturn, laying off school teachers and cutting back on essential services.

In 1978, the tax on capital gains and dividends was 35 percent. Due to a series of reductions since 1978, this tax is only 15 percent right now. The top 0.1 percent of the nation's earners—about 315,000 individuals out of 315 million—makes about half of all capital gains on the sale of shares or property after one year, and these capital gains make up 60 percent of the income as defined by the Forbes 400. According to the Congressional Budget Office, more than 80 percent of the increase in income inequality is the result of an increase in the share of household income from capital gains.[113]

In short, banks gave home loans to people based on fictitious paper. Bank officers as well as investment bankers made hundreds of millions of dollars in salaries and bonuses because of them. Later on, common people lost money in shares, but hedge funds made a lot of money bringing down the shares of these banks. It all boils down to the fact that the whole mechanism, or dynamics, if you like, created a domino effect leading taxpayers to pay trillions of dollars for the bankers' misdeeds and exacerbating the economic recession of the country as well as that of the entire world.

Effects of Casino Capitalism on Small Cities

We will discuss the cases of two cities, one in the United States and another in Europe, to see how the lives of common people have been affected for the next several years by the games played at Wall Street's casinos.

Jefferson County, Alabama's largest county with 659,000 residents, is on the verge of bankruptcy because of losing bets on interest rates. Since mid-2008, the county is fighting to stave off what would be the largest municipal bankruptcy in the country over its $3.2 billion debt. JPMorgan Chase persuaded the county to convert its debt from fixed interest rates to adjustable rates. They also recommended that the county use interest-rate swaps that would protect it if interest rates rose. Larry P. Langford, the local official who signed off on the deals, said in a deposition in June 2008, "I still don't understand 99 percent of it." The county paid JPMorgan Chase, Bank of America, Bear Sterns, and Lehman Brothers Holdings Inc. $120 million in fees—six times the prevailing fees for the amount of the county's debt for interest rate swaps. During the last few years, Jefferson County entered into a series of complex transactions, called swaps, worth a staggering $5.4 billion. Of eleven swaps and similar contracts that Jefferson County went into from 2001 to 2003, eight were with JPMorgan Chase. JPMorgan, Bank of America, Bear Stearns, and Lehman Brothers Holdings Inc. charged Jefferson County about $50 million above prevailing prices for eleven of the interest-rate swaps the county bought between 2001 and 2004. None of the fees were disclosed to the commissioners, records show. Porter, White & Co., the Birmingham-based financial advisory firm later hired by the county to analyze its swaps, said the banks raked in as much as $100 million in excessive fees on all seventeen of its swaps. The swaps are contracts in which the county and the banks agreed to exchange periodic payments based on the size of the outstanding debt and changes in prevailing lending rates. [114]

The worst came when Jefferson County's two bond issuers, Financial Guaranty Insurance Co. and XL Capital Assurance Inc., suffered hundreds of millions of dollars in losses on securities tied to home loans. This led to the downgrading of credit ratings of these two by Standard & Poor's and Moody's Investors Service. When a bond insurer is downgraded, so are the bonds it has guaranteed. Hence the interest rate of the $3.2 billion Jefferson County debt increased to 10 percent in February and March 2009 from 3 percent in January 2009. The monthly debt payment increased to $23 million from $10 million. The county is paying this extra money (i.e., taxpayers' money) to the banks instead of building schools, hospitals, public housing, or hiring police officers. To pay for this ill-fated deal, the residents' sewer rates have quadrupled. [115] Several cities in Massachusetts have been facing situations similar to that of Jefferson County. In mid-2009, the Securities and Exchange Commission (SEC) decided to take action against JPMorgan Chase for the violation of rules created by the Municipal Securities Rulemaking Board, the main regulator for the municipal bond market.

The Jefferson County story can be described in this way: the county was recommended to gamble, or bet, on the interest rate rather than get the loan at a fixed rate. They entered into an agreement with banks in which periodically complex mathematical and statistical equations, involving several factors beyond the control of the county, would churn out a number for the interest rate for the massive debt. It can only be likened to the situation where an amateur playing poker in a casino has no idea about the next deck of card.

The second case relates to eight municipalities in Norway who lost almost all their money due to global casino capitalism. Four of these small cities—Narvik, Rana, Hemnes, and Hattfjelldal in the far north of Norway—lost heavily in US credit derivatives in 2008. The funds were sold by Terra Securities, an investment firm owned partially by Terra Group, a union of seventy-eight Norwegian savings banks, while the products were delivered by Citigroup, the world's largest bank based in the United States.

Narvik is a close-knit community of 18,000. As a consequence of the losses the people of Narvik experienced loss of local services such as kindergartens, nursing homes, and cultural institutions.[116] Town halls in several of the communities lowered the temperature to cut back on heating bills during the frigid Norwegian winter. Streetlights were turned off during the long, dark Arctic night. In the aftermath budgets were scaled back so much that the elderly at a local retirement home were left to sleep in hallways.

The invested money was borrowed on revenue anticipated from electricity sales over the coming decade. Terra Securities told city officials that it was a low-risk investment, tied to municipal bonds but cleverly insulated by several layers of funds to hedge against further losses. In fact, as events showed before the end of the year, the risks were high—far higher than people in these towns understood. It was unclear whether those risks were ever communicated. Some town council members suggested that Terra Securities, in translating the Citigroup material into Norwegian, may have left out the parts that raised doubts. The fact is, they explained, the cities had been working with Terra representatives for several years and felt inclined to accept their advice. It was like buying a Volvo: You don't inspect the new car carefully; you rely on Volvo's reputation. Terra, the Norwegian securities firm that was the go-between with Citigroup, was forced into bankruptcy in late 2007.

In August 2009 on its behalf, a prominent Oslo lawyer, Jon Skjorshammer, filed a case against Citigroup in US District Court for the

Southern District of New York seeking over $200 million for violations of the United States securities laws. Skjorshammer said, however, that the Terra brokers probably did not understand the scheme themselves. Citigroup's oral and written descriptions inadequately portrayed the risk, he charged; they had used a faulty mathematical demonstration to prove how one fund would hedge against losses by the other. Moreover, he said, the way the instrument was constructed called on the Norwegian towns to provide additional funds if Citigroup's tactics lost money, in effect insuring Citigroup against losses of its own.[117]

One important point to note was that by investing through the complex system of derivatives, these cities were getting only marginally better return than traditional investments. But in this gamble, they lost almost their entire investments.

These examples show that the multimillion-dollar bonuses of executives at Wall Street and other financial institutions are mostly taxpayers' money. One has to just connect the missing dots. If a doctor would have done a similar thing (e.g., prescribed a medicine with such a disastrous effect), then not only he would have lost his entire wealth, he would have been in prison for several years also. But nobody on Wall Street or in any financial institution has been prosecuted for the 2008 Great Recession.

The 2008 Record Oil Price Rise

It is a general misconception that the record oil price rise in the first half of 2008 was due to the increase in oil consumption by growing economies such as China and India. It is not true at all. According to the US Department of Energy, the worldwide supply of oil actually went up from the last quarter of 2007 until the second quarter of 2008, whereas the worldwide demand went down, and hence the price of oil should have gone down instead of going up. Instead, the price of oil reached record levels.[118] According to the November 2008 International Energy Agency forecast for global oil demand in 2009, the world will need an average of 86.5 million barrels of oil a day in 2009, compared with 86.2 million in 2008, a growth of just less than half a percent.[119] This forecast was done before the onset of the 2008 global economic recession.

According to Michael Masters, a hedge fund manager, the investor demand for commodities, and oil futures in particular, was created on Wall Street by hedge funds and the big Wall Street investment banks such as Morgan Stanley, Goldman Sachs, Barclays, and J.P. Morgan, which made billions investing hundreds of billions of dollars of their clients' money.[120] In his US Senate testimony in May 2008, Michael Masters said, "Assets allocated to commodity index trading strategies have risen from $13 billion at the end of 2003 to $260 billion as of March 2008 and the prices of the 25 commodities that compose these indices have risen by an average of 183% in those five years." Masters claimed that in the last five years, speculators' demand for petroleum futures had increased by 848 million barrels, and that was nearly equal to the increase in demand of China (920 million barrels). These speculators have now stockpiled, via the futures market, the equivalent of 1.1 billion barrels of petroleum, effectively adding eight times as much oil to their own stockpile as the United States has added to the Strategic Petroleum Reserve over the last five years. These investors have purchased over two billion bushels of corn futures in the last five years. Right now, Index Speculators have stockpiled enough corn futures to potentially fuel the entire United States ethanol industry at full capacity for a year. That's equivalent to producing 5.3 billion gallons of ethanol, which would make America the world's largest ethanol producer. In 2007 Americans consumed 2.22 bushels of wheat per capita. At 1.3 billion bushels, the current wheat futures stockpile of Index Speculators is enough to supply every American citizen with all the bread, pasta, and baked goods they can eat for the next two years. Commodities futures markets are much smaller than the capital markets, so multibillion-dollar allocations to commodities markets will have a far greater impact on prices. In 2004, the total value of futures contracts outstanding for all twenty-five index commodities amounted to only about $180 billion. Compare that with worldwide equity markets, which totaled $44 trillion, or over 240 times bigger. In 2008, index speculators poured $25 billion into these markets, an amount equivalent to 14 percent of the total market.[121] These types of transactions are not between producers and consumers and have no real economic value.

According to Dan Gilligan, "Approximately 60 to 70 percent of the oil contracts in the futures markets are now held by speculative entities. Not by companies that need oil, not by the airlines, not by the oil companies. But by investors that are looking to make money from their speculative positions." Gilligan is the president of the Petroleum Marketers Association, representing more than eight thousand retail and wholesale suppliers. He says his members in the home heating oil business, such as Sean Cota of Bellows Falls, Vt., were the first to notice the effects a few years ago when prices seemed to disconnect from the basic fundamentals of supply and demand. Cota says there were plenty of products at the supply terminals, but the prices kept going up and up. "We've had three price changes during the day where we pick up products, actually don't know what we paid for it and we'll go out and we'll sell that to the retail customer guessing at what the price was," Cota remembered. The volatility is being driven by the huge amounts of money and the huge amounts of leverage going into these markets. In a five-year period, Michael Masters said, the amount of money institutional investors, hedge funds, and the big Wall Street banks had placed in the commodities markets went from $13 billion to $300 billion. Last year, twenty-seven barrels of crude were being traded every day on the New York Mercantile Exchange for every one barrel of oil that was actually being consumed in the United States.[122]

In 2000, Congress effectively deregulated the futures market, granting exemptions for complicated derivative investments called oil swaps, as well as electronic trading on private exchanges. Michael Greenberger, a former director of the Division of Trading and Markets at the Commodity Futures Trading Commission, said, "This was when Enron was riding high. And what Enron wanted, Enron got. When Enron failed, we learned that Enron, and its conspirators who used their trading engine, were able to drive the price of electricity up, some say, by as much as 300 percent on the West Coast." The oil bubble began to deflate early last fall when Congress threatened new regulations, and federal agencies announced they were beginning major investigations. It finally popped with the bankruptcy of Lehman Brothers and the near collapse of AIG, both heavily invested in the oil markets. With hedge funds and investment houses facing margin calls, the speculators headed for the exits. "From July 15th until the end of November, roughly $70 billion came out of commodities futures from these index funds," Masters explained. "In fact, gasoline demand went down by roughly five percent over that same period of time. Yet the price of crude oil dropped more than $100 a barrel. It dropped 75 percent."[123]

A June 2008 Massachusetts Institute of Technology study, which analyzed world oil production and consumption, also concluded that the basic fundamentals of supply and demand could not have been responsible for the 2008 run-up in oil prices. The study concluded, "The oil price is a speculative bubble."[124]

US authorities are suing three companies and two individuals for repeatedly manipulating the crude oil market in early 2008, when the world oil price was setting records. According to the Commodity Futures Trading Commission, they first bought large quantities of oil in the market, pushing oil prices higher. Then they dumped their holding of physical oil, most of it in the course of just one day. At the same time, they also bought short positions in the futures market, making a huge profit, as their dumping of oil lowered the oil price.[125]

Petroleum exporting countries such as Russia, Saudi Arabia, and Venezuela, several of them being anti-US, reaped the benefits of record oil price and made hundreds of billions of dollars. Russia now has the third-largest FOREX (Foreign Exchange Reserve) in the world. On the other hand, four-dollar-a-gallon gas prices created havoc in the US economy. The best-selling gas-guzzling SUV market dropped drastically, causing auto manufacturers such as GM, Ford, and Chrysler to close down their manufacturing plants and showrooms and lay off tens of thousands of workers. This is one of the factors that drove these car giants close to bankruptcy. While oil companies were raking in record tens of billions of dollars in profits each quarter, higher gas prices were causing a rise in transportation costs and raising the price of all food products in supermarkets. This increased inflation. It affected the sales of supermarkets such Wal-Mart and Kmart as higher food and gas prices left fewer dollars in the pockets of lower-income people to spare. All over the world, hundreds of millions of people fell below the poverty line because of double-digit inflation due to rising food costs. Oil-importing countries such as India had to spend up to 2 to 3 percent of its GNP as a subsidy on gasoline, as a substantial rise in gasoline price would have destabilized the entire country. Several countries had double-digit inflation for several months because of the rise in fuel costs. According to the World Bank, more than one hundred million people have been pushed into poverty because of rising food prices due to oil price increases.

When you squeeze the juice out of a fruit, then what remains in the fruit? That's what the hedge funds have done with the US and the global economy.

The 1997 Asian Financial Crisis

The 1997 Asian Financial Crisis was a financial crisis that engulfed most of Asia, barring countries such as China and India, which started in July 1997 in Thailand and raised fears of a worldwide economic meltdown. In this crisis, hedge funds and investment banks made tens of billions of dollars at the expense of tens of millions of Asians who lost their jobs. Affected countries lost several years of economic progress. Countries such as China and India, whose currencies were not fully convertible, were not affected by this financial crisis. This crisis was a precursor to the present US and Euro crises.

Fifty years ago, East Asian countries were in very bad shape, but they reduced their poverty significantly by achieving universal literacy and improving their economies using domestic funds, something they were able to do because of saving rates close to 40 percent.

At the end of the Korean War, the South Korean economy was in worse shape than the Indian economy, but in the next thirty-five years it achieved phenomenal economic growth and joined the ranks of the developed countries. In the early years of its transformation, the South Korean government did not allow Korean industry to borrow from abroad. This policy was dropped after the United States applied pressure.

Following the 1985 Plaza Accord, the yen gained against the dollar, and the Japanese started shifting their production units to low-cost East Asian countries. Between 1991 and 1995, annual Japanese manufacturing investment in East Asia almost tripled, from $2.9 billion to $8.1 billion. Japanese exporters supplied the region with vastly stepped-up quantities of capital and intermediate goods as they increased the share of Japanese exports going to East Asia by 40 to 50 percent in the same short period.[126]

In order to increase its exports, China devalued its currency, the yuan, by 35 percent in 1994. Japan then had to devalue its yen to maintain its export level. Other Asian countries delayed devaluation until 1997. This caused a sharp fall in their exports while China's 1997 exports increased by 20 percent. Japan also had a trade surplus of $91 billion that year.

After years of large trade surpluses, South Korea's imports began to exceed its exports. In 1996, its trade deficit was $23.7 billion. Its foreign exchange reserves at the end of 1997 were only $8.87 billion, compared to $29.4 billion at the end of 1996. Thailand's 1997 trade deficit was about $10 billion. Taiwan's trade surplus that year fell 44 percent to $7.6 billion—its lowest since 1984. In December, it had a trade deficit of $40 million, quite rare for that country.

China's trade surplus with the United States, in turn, had been increasing exponentially year by year, and in 1997 reached about $40 billion. Chinese exports in 1996 were valued at $150 billion, which was almost equal to the total value of the exports of Indonesia, Malaysia, Philippines, and Thailand combined. China's foreign exchange reserves (FOREX) at the end of 1997 were about $142 billion, second highest after Japan's.

At the same time, foreign investment had been flooding other Asian countries with dollars despite trade deficits. Thailand had the weakest economy in the region because of its high debts, which were about 38 percent of GDP. When currency traders, notably billionaire investor George Soros, saw the vulnerability of the Thai economy, they bought several forward contracts worth more than $15 billion and flooded the international market by selling bahts, the Thai currency, in May 1997. This was a speculative attack on the baht, believing that it would devalue. Thailand at first tried to prop up its currency by selling dollars and buying bahts, but when its FOREX reserve dropped into the danger level, it had to unpeg the baht from the dollar on July 2, 1997, resulting in a free fall for the Thai currency. Due to free convertibility, Thais also moved their money out of the country by converting it into dollars, depleting the nation's foreign reserves further. According to Thailand's central bank, it spent more than $16 billion in its failed attempt to prop up its currency. (Speculative currency traders sell a currency at a value they consider to be high on the expectation that it will depreciate so that they can buy the currency back for much less than they sold it for. The difference in price is the trader's profit.).

The crash of the baht created a domino effect and resulted in the crash of all other currencies and stock markets in the region one by one. Malaysian Prime Minister Dr. Mahathir Mohamad called Soros "a moron" and blamed him for the Asian crash. He also blasted Western economic powers for attempting to exploit and dominate the developing world. Indonesian president Suharto compared the currency traders to "gamblers." He said, "We have 30 years' experience of building a strong foundation. Then, in six months it collapses, not because of an internal crisis, but because there is manipulation of our currency."

To bail out the economies of Thailand, Indonesia, and South Korea, the International Monetary Fund arranged $17 billion, $43 billion, and $57 billion, respectively, in loans. This money was used to repay loans to Western banks/creditors. These countries also had to swallow the bitter pills prescribed by the IMF or the US Treasury Department—higher interest rates, privatization of state companies and services, devaluation of currencies, and slashed public expenditures for subsidies. Prior to the crisis, these countries had modest budget surpluses, and inflation was low; many of the draconian measures prescribed were entirely irrelevant to its causes.

In 1998, GDP in Indonesia fell by 13.1 percent, in South Korea by 6.7 percent, and in Thailand by 10.8 percent. The stock markets of these countries also dropped, by 50 to 84 percent. In a ripple effect, currencies and stock markets in Latin America, including Chile, Brazil, Argentina, and Venezuela, dropped 20 to 30 percent.

Due to the steep devaluation of Asian currencies, prices of essential items in these countries increased by significant amounts. For example, in Indonesia the price of rice increased by about 36 percent, electricity by 200 percent, milk by 50 percent, and cooking oil by 40 percent. It was poor people who suffered the most. They also faced layoffs due to the closure of massive infrastructure projects. For the average person, the real meaning of the IMF was indeed "I'M Finished" and not the International Monetary Fund.

India and China escaped the crisis because of capital controls. Malaysia avoided the fate of Thailand, Indonesia, and South Korea because it went for tight money controls. Some Wall Street economists, the IMF, and US Treasury Secretary Robert Rubin criticized Malaysia for its money controls, predicting that it would scare off investors. They were proven wrong. In addition, while all other developing countries' economies shrank, China and India saw sizable growth (about 8 and 5 percent, respectively), even with capital controls.

The crisis also exposed unfair lending practices by Western institutions. If a creditor loans to a foreign firm at 7 percent, and the firm thinks that it can make 15 percent yearly from this money, but the firm goes bankrupt, it should be a problem for the creditor and not the whole nation or the IMF. It needs to be considered as a bad loan. Before providing the loan, the creditor needs to check the lender's creditworthiness. This is standard practice, and the possibility of bankruptcy is always considered a part of any loan. Contrary to standard practice, however, the IMF intervened in East Asia and issued loans there after the crash so that Western creditors could recover their money. In the case of Thailand, people invested a lot of money in real estate, but since there were not enough buyers, the real estate market crashed. It was due to Thailand's real estate sector that most East Asian economies eventually suffered, but currency speculators made a lot of money.

It was after watching the IMF at work during this crisis that Joseph E. Stiglitz, the 2001 winner of the Nobel Prize in economics and chief economist at the World Bank from 1996 to 1999, expressed how appalled he was by the way the IMF and the US Treasury Department had responded (as quoted in the introduction of this book). "The IMF may not have become the bill collector of the G-7, but it clearly worked hard (though not always successfully) to make sure that the G-7 lenders got repaid," Stiglitz wrote.[127] It was perhaps he who described the crisis best:

The IMF first told countries in Asia to open up their markets to hot short-term capital [It is worth noting that European countries avoided full convertibility until the 1970s.]. The countries did it and money flooded in, but just as suddenly flowed out. The IMF then said interest rates should be raised and there should be a fiscal contraction, and a deep recession was induced. As asset prices plummeted, the IMF urged affected countries to sell their assets even at bargain basement prices. It said the companies needed solid foreign management (conveniently ignoring that these companies had a most enviable record of growth over the preceding decades, hard to reconcile with bad management), and that this would happen only if the companies were sold to foreigners—not just managed by them. The sales were handled by the same foreign financial institutions that had pulled out their capital, precipitating the crisis. These banks then got large commissions from their work selling the troubled companies or splitting them up, just as they had got large commissions when they had originally guided the money into the countries in the first place. As the events unfolded, cynicism grew even greater: some of these American and other financial companies didn't do much restructuring; they just held the assets until the economy recovered, making profits from buying at fire sale prices and selling at more normal prices.[128]

In his book *Globalization and Its Discontents*, Stiglitz, who was also a member of the Council of Economic Advisers under President Clinton, described meetings where President Clinton was frustrated because an increase of one-quarter to one-half percentage point in the interest rate by Federal Reserve Bank Chairman Alan Greenspan might destroy "his" nascent economic recovery.[129] A comparison here with the actions of the IMF during the East Asian debacle is instructive: There, the IMF forced interest rates to raise by 25 percentage points—fifty times the interest rate Clinton complained about—for economies going into recession. The IMF argument for this enormous increase was that higher rates would make a country more attractive for investors. In reality, it made the situation even worse. Generally, a crisis starts due to Western creditors' refusal to roll over short-term loans out of concern about firms' potential inability to repay their loans on account of high indebtedness. A large increase in interest rates, however, makes matters worse for these firms. An increase in interest rates increases the number of ailing firms, causing an increase in nonperforming loans. Therefore, an increase of 25 points in interest rate is enormous and will thus have more catastrophic consequences.

The 1997 crisis in turn triggered an oil-price slump, causing Russia's

1998 crisis owing to nonpayment of taxes by its oil and energy sectors. The Clinton administration subsequently organized $22.6 billion in IMF and World Bank loans for Russia in July 1998 over concerns about destabilizing a country with nuclear capabilities, which could potentially cause political if not military problems for the United States, but most of this money was siphoned out of the country. The Russian ruble collapsed within a couple of months. An increase in crude oil prices on international markets the next year helped Russia recover, however.

6

•◆•

COLLAPSE OF THE AMERICAN
ECONOMY AND ITS EFFECTS

The 2008 economic downturn was the result of the unraveling of the 1944 Bretton Woods Accord, due to which the US economy had thrived since the 1980s, as well as the greedy Wall Street bankers and investors who have turned the global economy into a gambling den. The downturn has proved that the US economy is not an exceptional economy. It is, however, exceptional in that it may print its currency as much as it wants to fund its twin deficits—budget and trade deficits. Even under the Paul Ryan plan, which drastically cuts welfare programs, the public debt will increase by $6 trillion. In 2011, the unemployment situation improved slightly due to the government stimulus. Now the government is not in a position to spend similar large amounts in stimulus, as it will certainly cause a rating downgrade of the Treasury bills by the rating agencies in the very near future. For the last several years, the increase in private sector jobs has been very minimal, and it will remain that way. It is almost a certainty that the unemployment rate is going to increase, which will increase the budget deficits at all the levels—federal, state, and local—increasing the public debt. The increase in public debt will cause the rating agencies to further downgrade the public debt at all the three levels, creating a vicious cycle.

The Nikkei average went up to about 39,000 in December 1989, but after the crash it hovered around 15,000 during the lost decade of the 1990s. In the last several years it has hovered around 9,000. Several economists, including Nobel Prize winner Paul Krugman, fear a similar lost decade for the US economy, too, which would cause the Dow Jones to hover around 4,000, leading 401(k) to become 101(k). As a majority of firms have stopped pension options, the future for the entire country seems very bleak, especially because of the unsustainable debt of the government. The federal debt has exploded to a level where in the very near future the government will have problem in funding the Social Security System, Medicare, and Medicaid. While making comments on the Tea Party's claim of President Obama being a socialist, MSNBC news anchor Chris Matthews said that we have the largest socialist programs, such as the Social Security System, Medicare, and Medicaid, in the world, and nobody, even Republicans or Tea Party members, wants to touch any of these. He further said that if we do not have these programs, then our cities would be like the slums of Calcutta.

If Dow Jones tanks to 4,000, making 401(k) become 101(k) for retirees, then the last three decades of Reaganomics will show its true colors (i.e., by reducing the size of government, they have destroyed the only source people might have in their hours of need).

Apart from the public debt crisis, the cumulative US trade deficits are also not sustainable. China's FOREX is increasing at an alarming rate. Also, China is holding a substantial amount of US debts. It is almost certain that China is going to bring down the economic superpower status of the United States. It is just a question of when the United States will witness its own Suez fiasco, which brought down the United Kingdom's superpower status. Once a country loses its economic superpower status, it loses its military superpower status also.

Europe is also witnessing a grave economic crisis. They can temporarily solve it by the creation of common euro zone bonds, denominated in euro, for all the euro countries. In the end, they are going to face a situation like the 1930s Great Depression, which will engulf the entire global economy.

After an economic collapse in the United States, consumer prices will skyrocket as goods formerly manufactured in other countries will have to be manufactured domestically owing to the crash of the dollar and its uselessness as a medium of foreign exchange. Domestic manufacturing firms will have to be restarted, and common people will be hit hard by the price shocks. After the 2008 Great Recession, police forces are being downsized all over the United States due to the sharp reduction of revenues collected by the local administration. When the economy collapses, the strength of the police force, which will be downsized further, may be insufficient to control the ensuing skyrocketing level of violence. Due to nonrestrictions on the purchase of guns, incidents of violence will be much deadlier than ever witnessed in the history of the country. Ultrarich people may be forced to organize local militias to safeguard themselves and their properties, as is witnessed in places like Karachi, Pakistan. We may see food riots in several parts of the country. It is then that people will try to find answers for their misfortune. A time is coming when Presidents Reagan and Bush Jr. will be considered worse than President Hoover. Apart from increasing the nation's debt, the Reagan and Bush Jr. administrations made budget cuts in education, labor, and human resources, which are the very foundation of a country. In the run-up to the Iraq attack, when the US media just followed the administration's policy like a religion, almost all the major US media, including CNBC, were making bullish market statements for several years before the stock market crash even though there were several indications to the contrary. Once the US economy collapses, this same media will become a part of the ensuing upheavals and play a major role in bringing about fundamental changes in the US political and economic system.

As discussed in chapter 1, the present crisis in the global economy is going to lead to a complete collapse of the present system of global trade. The only solution is to implement the Keynesian proposals during the deliberation for the 1944 Bretton Woods Accord (i.e., a global currency and a limit on trade deficit and trade surplus).

For several years after the collapse of its economy, the US economy will be like 1990s Russia, and the living standards will nosedive. But unlike Russia, the United States has the latest technologies and scientific top talents hand in hand with a hard-working population. Hence it will emerge much more powerful than the 2000s Russia. For some time, however, its living standards will not be the same as the present, as it will have to restart its manufacturing units at home to produce most of the consumer items that right now it is getting cheaply from outside due to the strong US dollar, which is highly overvalued.

After the collapse of the USSR in 1991, Russia's superpower status evaporated immediately. No one, not even its neighbors, had any more fear of the once-mighty Soviet army. Soviet submarines and aircraft carriers were found rusting in dockyards. Only a few of them avoided going to junkyards. Both the Ottoman Empire and the British Empire also collapsed due to their debts. Similarly, the economic crises in the United States and among its Western allies will severely restrict their influence in the turmoil in the Middle East and North African Islamic countries. In 2011 we were already witnessing it as the United States and its allies had very limited power to influence the Arab Spring, which is spreading like wildfire throughout the Middle East and North Africa. This would lead to the overthrow of regimes friendly to the West in countries such as Jordan, Lebanon, Saudi Arabia, Pakistan, and Kuwait by Islamic fundamentalists. History has already given us a telling example of this kind of developmental logic in the first half of the last century: it was the 1929 stock market crash and subsequent Great Depression that gave rise to Hitler. In the next chapter, we will discuss how a US economic collapse would lead to drastic political changes in the world, especially in the Islamic world, leading to the modernization of Islam. If China plays its cards carefully, after the end of the global economic crisis it could emerge as the strongest country in the world though slightly bruised.

As Germany was not solely responsible for starting World War I, it was with great difficulty that Germans swallowed the Treaty of Versailles. They put the entire blame for the treaty on the political leaders of their fledgling democracy. By 1922, more than four hundred political assassinations had been carried out in Germany, mostly by right-wing political extremists. Treaty signatory Matthias Erzberger was one of the leaders assassinated. The reparation clause in the Treaty of Versailles and the 1930s Great Depression are generally recognized as causes of Hitler's rise. In 1921, Germany paid the first installment of 1 billion marks as reparations. It did so by printing paper Deutsche marks and selling them in the open market. This caused horrendous inflation of the German currency.

Hitler's Nazi Party became popular only after the 1929 stock market crash and the subsequent 1930s Great Depression. In the 1930 German elections, the Nazis and Communists received 18 and 13 percent of the vote, respectively; 37 and 15 percent in July 1932; and 33 and 17 percent in November 1932. Nazi Party membership increased from 170,000 in 1929 to 1,378,000 in 1932. Due to the economic depression and ensuing political chaos, the eighty-four-year-old Paul von Hindenburg, the then president, finally appointed Hitler as chancellor. Eventually, on August 2, 1934, after the death of Hindenburg, Hitler became president. Hitler tried to establish a thousand years of the Third Reich, but instead paved the way for thriving democracies in most of Europe and the decolonization of Asia and Africa.

Until the early 1900s, nobody was predicting that democracy would replace kingdoms in most of Western Europe, or that Asian and African countries would gain independence within five to six decades. In order to give birth to a beautiful child, a woman has to go through the pains of labor. Europe went through a similar crisis in the first half of the last century. World Wars I and II were necessary in order to change the global socioeconomic and political environments of those times, in Europe in particular. Had those wars not occurred, much of Europe might still be ruled as kingdoms, and most Asian and African countries might still be awaiting independence from their colonial masters.

World War II had a profound effect on the colonial powers, as it completely destroyed their economies. Although Hitler committed crimes against humanity, I give him—and not Gandhi—credit for India's independence immediately after World War II. Hitler destroyed the economies of Britain and France to such an extent that they were no longer able to financially maintain their military forces, and they became incapable of containing the burgeoning freedom movements in their colonies. It is worth noting that Britain was in such bad shape that it received about one-fourth of the total aid given under the US Marshall Plan. Regardless of Gandhi or any other charismatic leader, Britain would have left India in 1947 purely for financial reasons, due to its wholly collapsed economy. After World War II, Britain left not only India but nearly all its other holdings, including Jordan in 1946, Palestine in 1947, Sri Lanka in 1948, Myanmar in 1948, and Egypt in 1952. For the same reason, France also had to grant independence to Laos in 1949 and Cambodia in 1953, and had to leave Vietnam in 1954. Had there been no Hitler and no World War II, it most probably would have taken another thirty or more years for India and some of the other colonies to achieve independence.

Large-scale unemployment and acute poverty in the general population along with corruption in high places give rise to militancy. This previously led to the rise of socialist and communist movements and leaders in Third World nations such as India, Vietnam, Chile, Nicaragua, and Angola, and several Islamic nations, including Egypt (Gamal Abdel Nasser), Iran (Mohammad Mossadegh), Iraq (Abdul Karim Qassim and later on the Baath Party), Syria (Baath Party), Algeria (Ben Bella and Boumédienne), Tunisia (Democratic Constitutional Rally party, previously known as the Socialist Destourian Party), South Yemen (Yemeni Socialist Party), Libya (Muammar al-Gaddafi), and Somalia (Siad Barre), as well as various factions of the PLO. Nowadays, the unemployed and poor are swayed to militancy in the name of religion: the Hindu parties Shiva Sena and Bajrang Dal in India, the Islamic Salvation Front in Algeria, Hamas in Palestine, Hezbollah in Lebanon, and the Mehdi militia in Iraq.

History may repeat itself in the twenty-first century. What we are in fact witnessing in the Middle East and elsewhere is not Samuel Huntington's clash of civilizations—but the modernization of Islam. Islam is the only major religion being imposed by government fiat anywhere in the world, and as such is a throwback to medieval values. Today Islamic civilization is going through what Europe went through between World Wars I and II. The creation, first, of Israel in 1948, and the invasion of Iraq in 2003 have catalyzed deep changes that will result in its modernization. As discussed in my book *The Modernization Islam and the Creation of a Multipolar World Order* (Booksurge, 2008), along with the explosive circumstances developing in several Islamic nations, the collapse of the American economy will also play a role in the changes to come. At the end of this crisis, Islam will cease to be the guiding force where it now leads, and the majority of Islamic nations will become secular and democratic, much as Turkey. Until World War I, Turkey, whose population is 99 percent Muslim, had been the seat of the Ottoman Empire (1299–1922) and the Islamic caliphate. Since 1923 it has been a secular, democratic nation. In addition to undergoing secularization, Muslims worldwide will start to follow the spiritual aspects of Islam more than its social and militant aspects and sharia. Religions such as Christianity and Hinduism went through this transformation several centuries ago. Now it is time for Islam to do the same.

7

•—◆—•

EFFECTS OF US INTERVENTION
IN AFGHANISTAN (1980–89)

The border region between Pakistan and Afghanistan is the epicenter of
Islamic terrorism. In this chapter we will study the history of the origin
of Islamic terrorism in these two countries.

With the dismantling of the Berlin Wall in 1989, the Cold War
between the world's two superpowers ended. During the Cold War,
the United States and the Soviet Union never met directly in military
confrontations due to fear of Mutually Assured Destruction (MAD).
Instead, they fought proxy wars in the Third World. Those wars left
behind millions of victims worldwide.

Both the United States and the USSR used any underhanded tactics
available to defeat the other during the Cold War. The Johnson, Nixon,
and Ford administrations did not hesitate to send American troops in
support of Third World dictators, regardless of their human rights records.
Only one point mattered, and that was the dictators' unquestionable
support for US interests. It was only the Carter administration that

openly objected to the human rights violations perpetrated by earlier American-supported dictatorships.

Following World War II, the United States spent $12 billion under the Marshall Plan for the reconstruction of war-torn Europe. Participating countries included Austria, Belgium, Denmark, France, West Germany, Great Britain, Greece, Iceland, Italy, Luxembourg, the Netherlands, Norway, Sweden, Switzerland, and Turkey. A main purpose of the Marshall Plan was to contain the spread of communism in Western Europe, particularly in France and Italy.

In the 1990s, when the Soviet Union became economically bankrupt and collapsed, the United States should have provided the victims of the Cold War assistance similar to that under the Marshall Plan, purely on humanitarian grounds. Providing such aid could have helped prevent countries like Afghanistan from becoming a breeding ground for Islamic militants. Today, perhaps as a direct consequence of its neglect, the United States has to increase its defense spending by hundreds of billions of dollars in order to fight the militancy that has arisen there. The Iraq War alone will cost American taxpayers trillions of dollars. Apart from this, in order to fight the Taliban and Al Qaeda in Pakistan and Afghanistan, the United States has been providing billions of dollars in aid to Pakistan every year since the 9/11 attacks. If the Clinton administration had opted to provide badly needed funds to Afghanistan after the Soviets left, it would have greatly checked the growth of Islamic terrorism, which arose as a direct result of the desperate economic plight of the Afghan people. Therefore, I wrote in a 1996 article:

The end of the Cold War has found the Russian economy in ruins; it is in no position to alleviate the sufferings of Third World countries brought about by superpower proxy wars. Hence, it is up to the United States to contribute a significant amount for economic improvement and alleviation of suffering in these countries. This year [1995–96] the US budget contains $256.6 billion for defense expenditures. This was $11.2 billion more than the Pentagon demanded. The US does not hesitate to use several million dollars worth of Cruise missiles against Saddam Hussein. But it has completely forgotten the victims of the Cold War ... It would be good for the US too if it helps bring peace to Afghanistan. Afghanistan was a Waterloo for the USSR but it might become a Frankenstein for the US.[130]

Although several nations are victims of Soviet intervention, this is not the subject of this book. It can be stated, however, that Soviet dictator Joseph Stalin and Chinese dictator Mao Zedong themselves were responsible for killing millions of their own countrymen. From 1936 to 1938, Stalin conducted a campaign of terror and killed more than one million Soviet citizens, sending about seven million to labor camps, where an additional two million died. More than ten million Chinese were persecuted and one million were killed during the 1966–69 Mao-led Cultural Revolution.

When the Soviets sent troops into Afghanistan, the Reagan administration proceeded to fund, train, and provide the latest weaponry to the Afghan resistance. The United States, instead of sending American troops to Afghanistan, gave more than $5 billion worth of the most modern weaponry to the Afghan mujahideen ("strugglers") to fight against the Soviets. Saudi Arabia gave a similar amount. Other Islamic countries, such as Iran, helped the mujahideen both in monetary as well as military terms. Shoulder-fired antiaircraft missiles such as the Stinger worked wonders, and Afghanistan became the Soviet Waterloo.

Tragically, once the Cold War was over, the United States revealed itself as completely indifferent to the sufferings of the war-torn Afghan nation. In 1995–96, the United States pledged only about $308,000 for Afghan reconstruction, out of a total of $35.6 million in humanitarian aid to the Afghans offered by the rest of the international community. It is worth noting that the US defense budget for the year 1995–96 was $256.6 billion. On the other hand, after the collapse of the Soviet empire, the United States gave monetary support to Russian president Boris Yeltsin, helping Russia get a three-year loan for more than $10 billion from the IMF. This was one of the largest loans from the IMF to any country. Apart from this, the United States also spent more than $7 billion for the removal and disposal of nuclear warheads from former Soviet republics such as Ukraine, Kazakhstan, and Belarus, and on the destruction of hundreds of missiles.

Although the Cold War destroyed the economies and lives of

millions of people in countries such as Afghanistan, Vietnam, Laos, Cambodia, Chile, Angola, Argentina, and East Timor, Afghanistan suffered the most because of three factors:

(1) Unlike other countries, Soviet troops were directly involved, and hence the United States used all its resources (money as well as the latest weaponry) to defeat the Soviets.

(2) In order to fight the Soviets, the United States along with the Saudis termed the war against the Soviets as the war against infidels, and in this process they started the culture of "mujahideens," which was not there previously. Muslims all over the world came to Afghanistan to fight against infidel Soviets. After the withdrawal of Soviet troops, the training centers for the mujahideens kept churning out mujahideens to fight at other Islamic hotspots worldwide, such as Bosnia, Kashmir, Egypt, Algeria, and Saudi Arabia. It is worth noting that the Saudi government did not fund the Afghan mujahideens directly. Instead, Saudi businessmen financed them. Because of the Saudi involvement, the Pakistan army, its ISI (intelligence service), and mujahideens were indoctrinated into Wahhabism, the radical form of Islam followed by the Saudis. After the withdrawal of the Soviets, Afghanistan exported Saudi Wahhabism to other Islamic countries once the mujahideens started to return to their own countries and other Islamic hot spots. It is worth noting that the Taliban government, which ruled in Afghanistan from 1996 till late 2001 (when they were overthrown by the US-led coalition forces), was recognized by only three countries: Pakistan, Saudi Arabia, and the United Arab Emirates.

(3) Its neighbor Pakistan. The US administration did not give money to or train Afghan mujahideens directly but instead funded and trained them via Pakistan's ISI and Pakistan's army. After the Soviets left Afghanistan, Pakistan used the training facilities of Afghan mujahideens for training Kashmir militants. Apart from this, in order to gain control

of Afghanistan, Pakistan's ISI created the Taliban in 1996. Less than a year from its establishment, the Taliban were able to capture almost all of Afghanistan with the help of the Pakistani army.

After the collapse of the Soviet-backed Najibullah regime in 1992, dozens of mujahideen groups fought amongst themselves for power, and Kabul became a fierce battleground. Common people started saying that life during the Soviet-backed regime had been better.

Afghanistan became a battleground for proxy wars among several countries. Pakistan was actively supporting the Taliban, while Iran, Russia, and India were supporting other groups in their fights against the Taliban. It was during these years that the country became a training ground for mujahideen fighting internationally, including in Bosnia, India (Kashmir), Egypt, Algeria, and Saudi Arabia.

Aside from warfare, life in Afghanistan had been at a standstill for more than a decade until the Taliban took over. Schools and colleges in most places were closed. Children grew up knowing only the Kalashnikov culture. It was normal to see even young boys carrying AK-47s in the countryside. After his visit to Kabul in 1994, Russell Gordon wrote,

Most of the fighters in the conflict are very young. Whereas the civilians and older soldiers seemed tired of the war, the young fighters were still enthusiastic. "Many have been fighting since they were eight years old," a former teacher said. "Now, 14 years later, they're 22 and the Kalashnikov is the only rule they've ever known.[131]

Gordon further wrote:

There was little incentive for the fighters to lay down arms. As soldiers, they get food, clothes, $21 a month, and all the ammunition they want. Each man is his own mini-emperor with, to paraphrase China's Mao Zedong, the power that grows out of the barrel of a gun. In fact, there were few other options for young people in Kabul. Many neighborhoods have been leveled, with the schools both wrecked and looted. The intellectuals having fled long ago, the next generation is growing up armed and illiterate. When money runs low, it's not unheard of to have entire units bought out by their opponents.[132]

Until the emergence of the Taliban in 1996, out of a population of fifteen million in 1979, about one million Afghans had been killed, two million were displaced within Afghanistan, and more than three million filled refugee camps in Pakistan and Iran. According to one estimate, about two million people were disabled. In fighting among various tribal factions, the civilian death toll in Kabul between 1992 and 1996 was estimated at thirty thousand to forty thousand—more than twice the number killed during the forty-month siege of Sarajevo.[133]

In February 1996, Afghanistan's foreign minister, Najibullah Lafraie, whose government was overthrown the same year by the Taliban, said, "We fought against the country that Ronald Reagan called the evil empire, and it was as a result of our sacrifices that the evil empire collapsed. But afterwards we were forgotten."[134] Lafraie's statement indicates the complete negligence of the United States toward countries it used to win wars against the Soviet Union. The United States has therefore itself to blame for the rise of Islamic militancy and terrorism based on how it used Afghans to fight the Soviets. Based on the analysis of the social, political, and religion environments in the Middle East, I wrote in a 1995 article:

> The US has sowed the seeds of the next Cold War by employing the low-cost war strategy in Afghanistan. Although a rise in Islamic fundamentalist movements world-wide was inevitable, US involvement in Afghanistan only hastened the process.[135]

In the 1980s the United States spent millions of dollars to supply Afghan schoolchildren with textbooks filled with violent images and militant teachings from the Quran. It was part of a covert attempt to spur resistance against the Soviet occupation. When the Taliban came to power, they continued using these American-produced books, though they scratched out human faces in keeping with their strict fundamentalist rules. Published in the dominant Afghan languages of Dari and Pashtu, the textbooks were developed in the early 1980s under a US Agency for International Development (AID) grant to the University of Nebraska-Omaha and its Center for Afghanistan Studies. During the period 1984 to 1994, the agency spent $51 million on the university's education programs in Afghanistan.[136] The following was the introduction to the Persian alphabet in a first-grade language arts book:

Alif [is for] Allah.
Allah is one.
Bi [is for] Father (*baba*).
Father goes to the mosque …
Pi [is for] Five (*panj*).
Islam has five pillars …
Ti [is for] Rifle (*tufang*).
Javad obtains rifles for the Mujahidin …
Jim [is for] Jihad.
Jihad is an obligation. My mom went to the jihad. Our brother gave water to the Mujahidin …
Dal [is for] Religion (*din*).
Our religion is Islam. The Russians are the enemies of the religion of Islam …
Zhi [is for] Good news (*muzhdih*).
The Mujahidin missiles rain down like dew on the Russians. My brother gave me good news that the Russians in our country taste defeat …
Shin [is for] *Shakir*.
Shakir conducts jihad with the sword. God becomes happy with the defeat of the Russians …
Zal [is for] Oppression (*zulm*).
Oppression is forbidden. The Russians are oppressors. We perform jihad against the oppressors …
Vav [is for] Nation (*vatn*).
Our nation is Afghanistan … The Mujahidin made our country famous … Our Muslim people are defeating the communists.

The Mujahidin are making our dear
country free.[137]

In the textbooks, children were taught to count with illustrations showing tanks, missiles, and land mines. Even after the AID stopped funding this program in 1994, the textbooks continued to circulate in various versions, even after the Taliban seized power in 1996. One page showed a resistance fighter with a bandolier and a Kalashnikov slung from his shoulder. Above the soldier is a verse from the Quran. Below is a Pashtu tribute to the mujahideen, who are described as obedient to Allah. Such men will sacrifice their wealth and life itself to impose Islamic law on the government, the text says.[138] Some of the math problems in third- and fourth-grade textbooks were as follows:

(1) "A Kalashnikov bullet travels at 800 meters per second. A mujahed has the forehead of a Russian in his sights 3,200 meters away. How many seconds will it take the bullet to hit the Russian's forehead?" [139]

(2) "A group of mujahedin kills 178 out of 3,560 enemy soldiers in battle. What percentage of the enemy have they killed?"[140]

(3) "One group of mujahedin attacks 50 Russian soldiers. In that attack 20 Russians were killed. How many Russians fled?"[141]

8

•◆•

HISTORY OF ISLAM AND ISLAMIC EMPIRES

In this chapter we will look at the history of Islam, Islamic scriptures, origins of some controversial Islamic tenets (such as Jihad, place of women in Islam, polygamy, circumcision), Islam's relationship with other religions, and Islamic empires. The majority of these controversial tenets were prevalent in pre-Islamic Arabia. I have discussed these in detail in my book *The Modernization Islam and the Creation of a Multipolar World Order* (Booksurge, 2008).

Even though we watch with disbelief as Islamic fighters behead and mutilate hostages and soldiers in Iraq and elsewhere, actually Prophet Muhammad did all these things—practices prevalent in seventh-century Arabia—himself, and they are recorded in the Quran. We should not blame Muhammad for this, but we should blame those who are following these seventh-century practices today. Excluding the divinity aspects of the Muhammad's revelations the Quran is just the social practices of seventh-century Arabia. The coming Great Depression is going to drastically affect Islam as a religion.

Islam is a monotheistic religion like Judaism and Christianity. In Arabic, Islam means "submission," or total surrender to God. It was founded by Prophet Muhammad, who performed no miracles, unlike central figures in other religions, in the seventh century. Unlike Moses, who claimed the Jewish Torah, which means "law" or "teaching" in Hebrew, was revealed to him by God in a single session, Muhammad claimed that he received messages from God over the last twenty-three years of his life. These messages have been collected in the Quran, which is the foundation of Islam. The prophets of ancient Israel were the first to preach the unity of God. Zoroastrianism, Christianity, and Islam later taught the same thing.

Unlike Christ in Christianity, Muhammad is not worshipped in Islam. Islam deems worshipping anyone except God a *shirk*, or polytheism, a sin. According to Muhammad, Islam is a divinely revealed religion like Judaism and Christianity, but because there were errors in their scriptures, Allah sent him as the "Reminder." He also claimed that Abraham was the first Muslim, and he himself the last messenger, or the Islam: "seal" (*khatimah*). He did not claim to bring a new religion: "[God] has established for you [the Arabs] the same religions enjoined on Noah, on Abraham, on Moses, and on Jesus (Quran 42:13)."[142]

Quran

"Quran" in Arabic means "the Recitation." Officially it is not to be translated into any other language, since God said to Muhammad: "We have revealed unto thee an Arabic Quran." A convert to Islam generally takes an Arabic name.

The Quran is regarded by Muslims as God's revelation to Muhammad. According to Islam, Quran was revealed to Muhammad by the angel Jibrīl (Gabriel) from 610 to his death in 632. It is said that while meditating in a cave in 610, he received his first divine revelation, when he was forty. Almost all the revelations occurred when there was an important event in Muhammad's life, for example before a battle, after victory or defeat in a battle, or a problem in his family. On several occasions God was providing the solutions to the problems faced by Muhammad through the revelations.

After Mohammad's death, Muslims started quarrelling among

themselves about the true contents of the Quran, since Muhammad had left no official version. Eventually, the third caliph, Uthman, asked Zayd, aide to Mohammad, to compile an official version. This was completed in 657, twenty-five years after Muhammad's death. After declaring it to be official, Uthman ordered all other versions destroyed.

The Quran consists of 114 suras (meaning series or chapters), which vary in length from three verses ("al-Nasr" and "al-Kawthar") to 287 ("al-Baqarah"). The verses within the suras are also of unequal length: Some are of two words and some are one-half page. Each sura has a title, usually a word mentioned within the chapter itself. Longer chapters generally appear earlier in the Quran and shorter chapters later. They are not arranged in the sequence of revelation.

Sharia

The sharia is Islamic law, which is based mainly on the *hadith*, or sayings of Muhammad. For the first few decades, hadith were circulated by the companions of Muhammad. Later, people began fabricating them to suit their own purposes.

An effort was started to collect hadith and eliminate dubious ones using certain verification processes in the seventh century. Sunni Muslims consider there to be six major collections. Out of these six, the *Sahih* (The Verified) of al-Bukhari is considered most reliable.

Al-Bukhari was born in Bukhara, present-day Uzbekistan, in year 194 of the Hejira (AD 816) and died in year 248 of the Hejira (AD 870). An eminent scholar, he traveled throughout the Islamic world to Syria, Iraq, Egypt, and the Hijaz, a region west of Saudi Arabia having Mecca and Medina. He was able to interview 1,080 persons and to collect six hundred thousand hadith. [143] Out of some two hundred thousand, not counting additional thousands that he rejected without examination, he selected only seventy-three hundred as authentic. His works consist of 97 books divided by subject of interest into 3,450 chapters. Even so, Muslims kept many of the rejected hadith in circulation. They eventually boiled down to 2,762 in all. [144]

Muhammad continued most pre-Islamic Arabian traditions. Shahrastani (d. 1153), a twelfth-century historian, in his *Al Milal wal-Nihal*, documents interesting traditions with respect to monotheism, resurrection, and certain specific rituals of pre-Islamic Arabia that were identical to those of the Islamic period. The customs of proclaiming divorce thrice to end a marriage, of washing after sexual intercourse, of *ghusl* (washing the cadaver before burial), and of the general cleaning of the body were all practiced in pre-Islamic Arabia.[145]

Muhammad also perpetuated the old legal system—"an eye for an eye." Because there was no police or prison system, the only punishment given to a criminal was equivalent to the crime he committed. Nevertheless, Muhammad did foster the individualism that was beginning to appear in Arabia; thus, the Quran decrees that a murdered man's relatives can punish only his murderer, not just any member of his tribe, as in the old system.[146]

Madhahib: Jurisprudence

Madhahib, Islamic schools of thought (sing. *madhhab*), wrote the *sunnah* (Muhammad's way of life) for followers to emulate. There are four madhahib: Hanafite, Malikite, Shafi'I, and Hanbalite.

(1) *Hanafite*: This is the oldest and the most liberal of the four Sunni schools of legal thought. It was developed in Iraq by Abu Hanifah (699–767) and put more emphasis on *ra'y*—private opinion or human reason. It is dominant in Turkey, Albania, Central Asia, Afghanistan, the Indian subcontinent, and Iraq.

(2) *Malikite:* This school is based on the works of a judge of Medina, Malik ibn Anas (715–795). Apart from the hadith and *ijma* (consensus of the scholars), it used citizens of Medina as a source also. It is dominant in North and West Africa.

(3) *Shafi'i:* The third important school was that founded by Muhammad ibn Idris ash-Shafi'i (767–820), who was a disciple of Malik. It is more conservative than the Hanafite and Malikite schools. Although it accepts the authority of four sources of jurisprudence (the Quran, hadith, ijma, and *qiyas*, or analogy), it downgraded provisions for ra'y, private

judgment. It is dominant in Egypt, some parts of India, Somalia, Yemen, Indonesia, Thailand, Sri Lanka, Maldives, and Malaysia.

(4) *Hanbalite:* This school, founded by Ahmad ibn-Hanbal (780–855), is the most conservative of the four. It accepts only those traditions that are in accordance with the Quran and hadith, and insists on following religious duties and responsibilities as defined by the sharia. It was dominant in Iraq and Syria in the fourteenth century, and was revived again in the eighteenth century with the rise of Wahhabism in Arabia.

Wahhabism, founded by Muhammad ibn Abd-al-Wahhab (1703–92), is based on the teachings of Ahmad ibn Hanbal, founder of the Hanbalite school, and Ibn Taymiyya (1263–1328). He advocated observing the original teachings of the Quran and hadith, and was against any innovations. Because of his views, he was forced out of his birthplace, the ancient oasis town of Uyaynah, now part of Saudi Arabia. He then settled in Dir'iyah, capital of Najd (present-day Saudi Arabia), ruled by Muhammad ibn Sa'ud, who converted to Wahhabism. Ibn Hanbal opposed worshipping saints and the construction of shrines and mausoleums, and considered these acts worthy of the death penalty.

As part of the evolution of Islam, special schools, called *madrassas* in Arabic, began to be established in the eleventh century to teach legal studies or a particular madhhab. A madrassa usually consisted of a building for study, residences for teachers and students, and a library. The Quran and hadith were common subjects in all madrassas. Muhammad ibn Mūsā al-Khwārizmī (780–850 AD), the father of algebra, studied and taught at the madrasas at Bukhara and Khiva in Central Asia, and was also a member of the House of Wisdom in Baghdad during the rule of Caliph al-Ma'mun. His book *Al-Kitab al-Jabr wa-l-Muqabala* provided symbolic operations for the systematic solution of linear and quadratic equations. The word "algebra" is derived from al-Jabr. The Latin translation of his book on the Indian numerals introduced the decimal and zero to the Western world in the twelfth century. The word "algorithm" (a definite list of well-defined instructions for completing a task) is a corrupted form of his name, which is derived from algoritmi, the Latinization of his name.

Saudi Arabia follows Wahhabism, which is the original form of Islam and is based on Islamic principles formulated by the cleric Muhammad ibn Abd-al-Wahhab. It is trying to export Wahhabism to other countries by opening schools all over the world.

In 2001, the Taliban destroyed two ancient, colossal images of Buddha in Bamiyan Province, about 150 miles from the capital of Kabul, using explosives, tanks, and anti-aircraft weapons, claiming that Islam forbids the construction of images of humans and animals. This was not unique on their part, however. They were only following in the footsteps of the Saudis, who have destroyed almost all buildings related to the founder of Islam. Today there are fewer than twenty structures remaining in Mecca that date back to the time of the Prophet fourteen hundred years ago. The litany of this lost history includes the house of Khadijah, the wife of the Prophet, demolished to make way for public lavatories; the house of Abu Bakr, the Prophet's companion, father of Ai'sha (Muhammad's favorite wife), and first caliph, now the site of the local Hilton hotel; the house of Ali-Oraid, the grandson of the Prophet, and the mosque of Abu Qubais, now the location of the king's palace in Mecca.[147]

Jihad

Jihad in Arabic means "struggle," or "striving." In the Quran, it usually means "striving on the path of God" and is of two types: Greater Jihad and Lesser Jihad. Examples of Greater Jihad are moral striving and fighting against one's lower tendencies, whereas Lesser Jihad is to fight the enemies of Islam. A place where Muslim law prevails is known as "Abode of Islam" (*dar al-Islam*), while the rest of world is known as "Abode of Unbelief/Idolatry/War" (*dar al-kufr/shirk/harb*), or generally simply "House of War," *dar al-harb*. The presumption is that the duty of jihad will continue, interrupted only by truces, until all the world either adopts the Muslim faith or submits to Muslim rule. Those who fight in the jihad qualify for rewards in both worlds—booty in this one, paradise in the next.[148]

Women in Islam

In pre-Islamic Arabia, the condition of women was terrible. The Quran elevated the status and rights of women in seventh-century Arabia, but these seem too restrictive now, in the twenty-first century. In the ancient environment, where women were so devalued that female infanticide was a common and tolerated practice, the Quran introduced reforms that prohibited it, permitted women to inherit, restricted the practice of polygamy, curbed abuses of divorce by husbands, and gave women the ownership of the dowry, which had previously been paid to the bride's father. As the thrust of the Quranic reforms regarding women's status was an ameliorative one, it seems reasonable to conclude, as did Fazlur Rahman, an eminent liberal scholar of Islam, that "the principle aim of the Quran was the removal of certain abuses to which women were subjected."[149]

For some modern Islamic militants, the enrolment of women in a traditional profession such as teaching is too much. However, Iranian cleric Ayatollah Khomeini, in his sermons and writing both before and after the 1979 Islamic Revolution, spoke with great anger of the inevitable immorality that, he said, would result from women teaching adolescent boys.[150] The most quoted hadith against woman is recorded by al-Bukhari: According to 'Abdallah Ibn 'Umar, the Prophet said, "I took a look at paradise, and I noted that the majority of the people there were poor people. I took a look at hell, and I noted that there women were the majority."[151]

Turkey's Kemal Ataturk took exactly the opposite view. In a series of speeches delivered in the early 1920s, he argued eloquently for the full emancipation of women in the Turkish state and society. Their most urgent present task, he repeatedly told his people, was to catch up with the modern world; they would not catch up if they only modernized half of their population.[152]

Women's Right of Inheritance

In the pre-Islamic tradition, women had no assured right of inheritance, which in any case was a matter between men, the men of the husband's clan or her own relations:

Before Islam, when a man lost his father, brother, or son, and that person left a widow, the heir, taking advantage of the privileges of the dowry paid by the dead man, hastened to the widow, covered her with his cloak, and thus arrogated to himself the exclusive right to marry her. When he married her, he deprived her of her right to the part of the inheritance constituted by the dowry. But if the widow succeeded in getting to her own clan before the arrival of the heir, he lost his rights over her in favor of her own clan.[153]

In Arabia, it was customary for a man to give a *mahl*, a dowry, to his bride. This had usually been absorbed by the woman's male relatives. In Islam, the dowry is to be given directly to the woman herself, so in the event of divorce, a man is not allowed to reclaim the mahl, and a woman's security is assured (suras 2:225–40; 65:1–70).[154]

Inequality was evident in the laws of inheritance also, derived by the sharia from the Quran. A man is allowed to bequeath not more than one-third of his property as he wishes to persons or purposes that would not otherwise inherit from him. The remainder must be divided according to strict rules. His wife will receive at most one-third. If he leaves sons and daughters, a daughter would inherit only half the share of a son; if he leaves only daughters, each would receive a certain proportion of his property, but the remainder would go to his male relations. (This is Sunni law; in Shiite law, daughters inherit everything if there are no sons.) The provision, that daughters receive only half as much as sons, echoes another stipulation of the sharia: In a legal case, the testimony of a woman has only half the weight of a man's.[155]

In questions of heritage, the Quran tells us that male children should inherit twice the portion of female children:

A male shall inherit twice as much as a female. If there be more than two girls, they shall have two-thirds of the inheritance, but if there be one only, she shall inherit the half. Parents shall inherit a sixth each, if the deceased have a child; but if he leaves no children and his parents are his heirs, his mother shall have a third. If he has brothers, his mother shall have a sixth after payment of any legacy he may have bequeathed or any debt he may have owed (Quran 4:11–12).[156]

To justify this inequality, Muslim authors lean heavily on the fact that a woman receives a dowry and has the right to maintenance from her husband.[157]

Polygamy

Ancient Arabia probably suffered a shortage of men because of frequent tribal warfare, leaving a surplus of unmarried women, who were often badly exploited. The Quran is most concerned about this problem and resorted to polygamy as a way of dealing with it.[158]

The sharia, basing itself upon the Quran and the example of the Prophet, allowed a man to have more than one wife, to a limit of four provided he could treat them all with justice and did not neglect his conjugal duty to any of them. He could also have slave concubines to any number, without their having any rights over him.[159] Of note, these particular codes were revealed after the loss of several Muslim men in the battle of Uhud.

Those who have referred to Muhammad's plural marriages as evidence of his sensual nature make little mention of the fact that in the prime of his youth and adult years, Muhammad remained thoroughly devoted to Khadija, his wife, and would have no one else as his consort. This was in an age that looked upon plural marriages with favor and in a society that in prebiblical and postbiblical days considered polygamy an essential feature of social existence.[160] The Bible also records polygamy: King David had six wives and numerous concubines; King Solomon was said to have had as many as seven hundred wives and three hundred concubines; and Solomon's son Rehoboam had eighteen wives and sixty concubines.[161]

A woman was unable to divorce her husband in pre-Islamic Arabia, but the Quran gave her this right under limited conditions. According to the sharia, while a wife can divorce her husband only for good reason (impotence, madness, denial of her rights) and only by recourse to a qadi (judge) or by mutual consent, a husband can repudiate his wife without giving any reason by a simple formula uttered three times in the presence of witnesses. A marriage contract can provide some protection against this if it stipulates that part of the dowry, the so-called "postponed" part, should be paid by the husband only if and when he repudiates his wife. A wife can also hope for support from her male relations, and if repudiated she can return with her property to her family home. She will have custody of the children and the duty of bringing them up until they reach a certain age, defined differently in the various legal codes; after that, the father or the ex-husband's family obtains custody.[162] The custom of proclaiming divorce thrice to end a marriage was, incidentally, practiced in pre-Islamic Arabia, and is not original to Islam.[163]

Women—Unfit to Govern

There is a famous hadith frequently used by Muslim men to debar women from positions of power. During the Battle of the Camel between A'isha and 'Ali, A'isha contacted a wealthy companion of Prophet Muhammad in Basra, Abu Bakra, to help her. A'isha was the favorite wife of Muhammad. Abu Bakra told her that he was against civil war. After the battle, he is supposed to have said to her:

> It is true that you are our *umm* [mother, alluding to her title of "Mother of Believers," which the Prophet bestowed on his wives]; it is true that as such you have rights over us. But I heard the Prophet say: "Those who entrust power [*mulk*] to a woman will never know prosperity."[164]

This was reported in al-'Asqalani's thirteenth volume, where he quotes al-Bukhari's *Sahih*, which contains the traditions that al-Bukhari classified as authentic after a rigorous process of selection, verification, and counterverification.[165]

Women have recently become political leaders in Muslim-majority countries: Benazir Bhutto in Pakistan, Sheikh Hashina and Khaleda Zia in Bangladesh, and Megawati Sukarnoputri in Indonesia. A fundamentalist nation like Saudi Arabia, however, uses hadith to debar women from politics and even refuses them the voting rights. In 2011, the king of Saudi Arabia declared to give women voting rights and allow them to run in the 2015 local elections, but still women cannot vote or be elected to high political positions.

Circumcision

Feminists frequently condemn Islam for the custom of female circumcision. This is despite the fact that it is really an African practice. It is never mentioned in the Quran, is not prescribed by three of the four main schools of Islamic jurisprudence, and was only absorbed into the fourth school in North Africa, where it was a fact of life.[166]

Islam and Other Religions

On the eve of the Arab-Muslim conquest, the clash of two great empires—Sassanian Persia and Byzantium—had spread war throughout Asia Minor, where Christianity was emerging from paganism by fire and sword. Under ecclesiastical pressure, a considerable amount of discrimination affecting Jews was introduced into Byzantine law. Jews were killed periodically, and synagogues were expropriated or burned down.[167]

In Visigoth Spain, after King Reccared converted from Arianism to Catholicism in 587, the state gave force of law to the anti-Jewish canons of the Councils of Toledo from 613 to 694. In 613 and again in 633 and 638, Jews were subject to expulsion or baptism. The twelfth Council of Toledo (680) adopted King Erwige's edicts that Jews renounce Judaism within a year, that forced baptism be administered on pain of confiscation of property, and that those resisting be punished by head-shaving, accompanied by one hundred strokes of the rod and exile.[168] This anti-Jewish policy, which was opposed by some members of the clergy and the nobility, pushed King Egica (687–702) to impose his authority by hardening his stance. The sixteenth Council of Toledo (693) ordered that the property of Jews be confiscated and their taxes increased. A proclamation by the seventeenth council (694) ordered all Jews to be made slaves and dispersed over the kingdom; their families were to be broken up and their children from the age of seven taken from them and brought up in the Christian faith.[169]

Pope Gregory IX added the following decrees in 1227: Muslims and

Jews must wear distinctive clothing; they must not appear on the streets during Christian festivals or hold public office in Christian countries; and the *muezzin* was forbidden to offend Christian ears by summoning the Muslims to prayer in the traditional way.[170]

Muhammad thus lived in an era of violent interreligious clashes and forcible conversions. We therefore see similar provisions in the Quran for how Muslims should treat non-Muslims, and many of these are in effect today. Until early last century, Jews in Yemen were forced to wear clothes and shoes of a particular color. In Afghanistan, fundamentalist Talibans forced Hindus to put a two-meter yellow cloth on their houses. In the Ottoman Empire, Christians and Jews paid personal taxes (jizya) while Muslims did not on a regular basis.[171] In the Mughal Empire, fundamentalist Muslim rulers like Aurangzeb forced only Hindus to pay personal taxes.

The Quran discusses rules and laws in the House of Islam (Dar al-Islam), but is silent on how Muslims should live where non-Muslim infidels rule or how they should live in the House of War (Dar al-Harb). The presumption is that it is the duty of Muslims to continue fighting infidels in the House of War, interrupted only by truces, until all the world either adopts the Muslim faith or submits to Muslim rule.

In Islamic law, conversion from Islam is apostasy, a capital offense for both the one who is misled and the one who misleads him. On this question, the law is clear and unequivocal. If a Muslim renounces Islam, even if a new convert reverts to his previous faith, the penalty is death. In modern times, the concept and practice of *takfir*, recognizing and denouncing apostasy, has been greatly widened. It is not unusual in extremist and fundamentalist circles to decree that some policy, action, or even utterance by a professing Muslim is tantamount to apostasy, and to pronounce a death sentence on the offender. This was the principle invoked in the *fatwas* (religious decrees) against Salman Rushdie, in the murder of Egypt's President Sadat, and against many others.[172]

Islamic Empires

Muhammad's life can be divided into three distinct parts. In Mecca, he attacked polytheism and preached monotheism. But when he felt threatened, he went to Medina. In Medina he fought against the enemies of Islam and delineated Islamic principles for dealing with military conflict and other religions. Finally, after victory over the Meccans, he became head of state and formed the nucleus of the Islamic Empire.

Within a very short time, Muslim armed forces conquered the Arabian Peninsula and the Persian Empire, and created a caliphate. They then conquered Christian Syria, Palestine, Egypt, and North Africa, and later on the southern part of Europe, including Spain, Portugal, and southern Italy. While Islam was enjoying its golden age from the seventh to the fourteenth centuries, Europe was struggling through its Dark Ages after the breakup of the Roman Empire and also because of massive raids by several groups of barbarians, principally the Vikings. At the end of this period, in the fourteenth century, the bubonic plague, or "Black Death," ravaged the entire continent, killing anywhere from one-quarter to one-half of the population.

During the fifteenth and sixteenth centuries, Islam comprised three empires: the Ottoman (eastern Europe, western Asia, and most of the Maghrib, the region of North Africa bordering the Mediterranean Sea), the Safavid (Persia, or modern Iran), and the Mughal (the Indian subcontinent). During this period, the Ottomans formed alliances with European nations against common enemies. For example, they entered into a military alliance with France, England, and the Netherlands against Hapsburg Spain and Hapsburg Austria, and they granted France the right of trade within their empire. In addition, the major European powers established embassies and consulates in the empire, and the Ottomans eventually sent missions to those countries.

Until the middle of the eighteenth century, the Ottoman army was in a position to defeat any European country in war. But after the rise of European naval power and the introduction of new industrial technology beginning in the eighteenth century, the empire declined vis-à-vis the Europeans. European economies were thriving, and a few European countries, especially Britain, France, and the Netherlands, colonized parts of Asia and Africa. The new technology and new wealth from their colonies allowed Europe to surpass the Ottomans, who lagged behind in technology. As a result, their military power became weaker in relative terms as well. In 1798, Napoleon occupied Egypt for three years. Although he was ousted after this time, the Ottomans could accomplish this only through an alliance with the British. This was the first incident when they had to take the help of a European power to oust someone from a Muslim state.

During the first half of the nineteenth century, the population of Europe increased by about 50 percent. By 1850 London was the world's largest city with a population of two and a half million. Other European capital cities grew too, and a new kind of industrial urbanization emerged dominated by offices and factories. At this time more than half the population of England was urban. This concentration in cities provided manpower for industry and the military, as well as a growing domestic market for the products of factories. Between the 1830s and the 1860s, regular steamship lines connected ports of the southern and eastern Mediterranean like Marseille and Trieste with London and Liverpool. Textiles and metal goods found a wide and growing market, and British exports to the eastern Mediterranean increased 800 percent in value between 1815 and 1850. By that time even Bedouin nomads in the Syrian desert were wearing shirts made of Lancashire cotton. Simultaneously, Europe's need for raw materials for the factories and food for the population that worked in them encouraged the production of crops for sale and export. The export of grain continued, although it became less important as Russian grain exports grew. Tunisian olive oil was in demand for the making of soap, Lebanese silk for the factories of Lyon, and, above all, Egyptian cotton for the mills of Lancashire.[173]

On the other hand, the economies as well as the populations of Arab countries were stagnant. They had not yet entered the railway age, except for minor startups in Egypt and Algeria. Internal communications were bad and famine could still occur. Populations changed little in size during the first half of the nineteenth century. Although Egypt's population increased from four million in 1800 to 5.5 million in 1860, in most other countries it remained inert, and in Algeria, for special reasons, it went down considerably, from three million in 1830 to 2.5 million in 1860. Some of the coastal ports grew in size, particularly Alexandria, the main port for the export of Egyptian cotton, which increased from some ten thousand persons in 1800 to one hundred thousand by 1850. Otherwise, most cities' populations remained roughly the same size. Apart from areas that produced crops for export, agricultural production remained at subsistence level and was insufficient to lead to an accumulation of capital for productive investment.[174]

From the 1850s onwards, because of the need for money for the army, the administration, and public works, the Ottoman government started borrowing from European banks, which had come into being as institutions with the purpose of investing accumulated European capital globally. Between 1854 and 1879, the Ottoman government borrowed on a large scale and on unfavorable terms. Of a nominal amount of 256 million Turkish pounds it received only 139 million, the remainder being discounted. By 1875, it was unable to carry the burden of interest and repayment, and in 1881 a Public Debt Administration representing foreign creditors was set up. It was given control of a large part of the revenues, and in that way had virtual control over acts of government that had financial implications. Between 1862 and 1873, Egypt borrowed 68 million British pounds but received only two-thirds of that, the rest being discounted. In spite of efforts to increase its resources, including the sale of its shares in the Suez Canal—built in 1869 mainly with French and Egyptian capital and Egyptian labor—to the British government, by 1876 it was unable to meet its obligations. A few years later Anglo-French financial control was imposed. Then the British invaded and occupied Egypt in 1882.[175]

European occupation of Muslim areas was initiated by France, which occupied Algiers in 1830 and made Algeria a French colony. In 1839, the British occupied the port of Aden in the Arab Peninsula.

During World War I, the Ottoman Empire fought alongside Germany and Austria and lost to Britain, France, and the United States. After the war, the empire was dissolved in 1920 under the Treaty of Sèvres. This treaty was rejected, however, by the Turkish National Movement, led by Mustafa Kemal, a military commander. Kemal led the movement to victory over occupying Greek, Italian, and French forces, and signed the Treaty of Lausanne in 1923 for the establishment of the Republic of Turkey, which brought the Ottoman Empire to an end.

At the height of its power the Ottoman Empire (1299–1922, based in the present-day Turkey) ruled on three continents: Southeastern Europe, North Africa, and the Middle East. It was also a religious empire, based on Islam. In the sixteenth century, the Ottoman ruler started using the title "Caliph." After their defeat, Muslim leaders as far away as the Indian subcontinent launched movements to influence the British government to protect the caliphate, a spiritual and political leadership system that started after the death of Prophet Muhammad in 632. Even Mahatma Gandhi and his Congress Party made an alliance with Muslim leaders, who had formed the All India Khilafat Committee, to actively participate with them in the Khilafat Movement (1919–24) to pressure the British government in this direction. It is an irony that Muhammad Ali Jinnah, who later became instrumental in partitioning India along communal lines into India and Pakistan, dismissed this campaign as "religious frenzy."

9

•◆•

PRESENT SITUATION IN ISLAMIC COUNTRIES

AN INVENTORY OF ISLAMIC NATIONS

Of an estimated 2009 world population of 6.8 billion, Muslims represent 23 percent: 1.57 billion. More than 60 percent of the global Muslim population is in Asia, and about 20 percent is in the Middle East and North Africa. However, the Middle East-North Africa region has the highest percentage of Muslim-majority countries. More than one-fifth of the world's Muslim population (three hundred million people) lives in countries where Islam is not the majority religion.[176]

Muslims are a majority in 47 countries. These are the following, according to their form of government, percent Muslim population, and other data (from the US Central Intelligence Agency's *The World Factbook* at CIA website, September 2011):

(i) Democracy:

Country	Muslim (% of Population)	Area (sq km)	Population	Religion and State
Bangladesh	89%	143,998	158,570,535	State Religion
Senegal	94%	196,722	12,643,799	Secular
Sierra Leone	60%	71,740	5,363,669	-
Turkey	99%	783,562	78,785,548	Secular
Iraq	97%	438,317	30,399,572	Secular

(ii) Emerging Democracy:

Albania	70%	28,748	2,994,667	NA
Gambia	90%	11,295	1,797,860	Secular
Indonesia	86%	1,904,569	245,613,043	-
Lebanon	60%	10,400	4,143,101	-
Niger	80%	1,267,000	16,468,886	Secular
Nigeria	50%	923,768	155,215,573	Secular

Casino Capitalism

(iii) Limited Democracy:

Algeria	99%	2,381,741	34,994,937	State Religion
Azerbaijan	93%	86,600	8,372,373	Secular
Burkina Faso	60%	274,200	16,751,455	Secular
Chad	53%	1,284,000	10,758,945	Secular
Djibouti	94%	23,200	757,074	Secular
Egypt	90%	1,001,450	82,079,636	State Religion
Guinea	85%	245,857	10,601,009	Secular
Kazakhstan	47%	2,724,900	15,522,373	Secular
Kyrgyzstan	75%	199,951	5,587,443	Secular
Malaysia	60%	329,847	28,728,607	State Religion
Maldives	NA	298	394,999	State Religion
Mali	90%	1,240,192	14,159,904	Secular
Mauritania	100%	1,030,700	3,281,634	Islamic State
Tajikistan	90%	143,100	7,627,200	State Religion
Tunisia	98%	163,610	10,629,186	State Religion
Turkmenistan	89%	488,100	4,997,503	Secular
Uzbekistan	88%	447,400	28,128,600	Secular
Yemen	NA	527,968	24,133,492	Islamic State

(iv) Authoritarian:

Libya	97%	1,759,540	6,597,960	-
Syria	90%	185,180	22,517,750	State Religion

(v) Monarchy:

Bahrain	81%	760	1,214,705	State Religion
Brunei	67%	5,765	401,890	State Religion
Jordan	92%	92,342	6,508,271	State Religion
Kuwait	85%	17,818	2,595,628	State Religion
Morocco	99%	446,550	31,968,361	State Religion
Oman	NA	309,500	3,027,959	State Religion
Qatar	78%	11,586	848,016	State Religion
Saudi Arabia	100%	2,149,690	26,131,703	Islamic State
UAE	96%	83,600	5,148,664	State Religion

(vi) Theocracy:

Iran	98%	1,648,195	77,891,220	Islamic State

(vii) Transitional:

Comoros	98%	2,235	794,683	State Religion
Eritrea	NA	117,600	5,939,484	-
Pakistan	95%	796,095	187,342,721	Islamic State
Somalia	NA	637,657	9,925,640	Islamic State
Sudan	NA	1,861,484	45,047,502	-

(viii) No Functional Government:

Afghanistan	99%	652,230	29,835,392	Islamic State

Countries with the Largest Number of Muslims

	Estimated 2009 Muslim Population	Percentage of Population that is Muslim	Percentage of World Muslim Population
Indonesia	202,867,000	88.2%	12.9%
Pakistan	174,082,000	96.3%	11.1%
India	160,945,000	13.4%	10.3%
Bangladesh	145,312,000	89.6%	9.3%
Egypt	78,513,000	94.6%	5.0%
Nigeria	78,056,000	50.4%	5.0%
Iran	73,777,000	99.4%	4.7%
Turkey	73,619,000	98.0%	4.7%
Algeria	34,199,000	98.0%	2.2%
Morocco	31,993,000	99.0%	2.0%

Source: Mapping the global Muslim population: A report on the size and distribution of the world's Muslim population, PewResearch Center, October 2009.

Countries with the Largest Number of Muslims Living as Minorities

	Estimated 2009 Muslim Population	Percentage of Population that is Muslim	Percentage of World Muslim Population
India	160,945,000	13.4%	10.3%
Ethiopia	28,063,000	33.9%	1.8%
China	21,667,000	1.6%	1.4%
Russia	16,482,000	11.7%	1.0%
Tanzania	13,218,000	30.2%	0.8%
Ivory Coast	7,745,000	36.7%	0.5%
Mozambique	5,224,000	22.8%	0.3%
Philippines	4,654,000	5.1%	0.3%
Germany	4,026,000	5.0%	1.0%
Uganda	3,958,000	12.1%	0.3%

Source: Mapping the global Muslim population: A report on the size and distribution of the world's Muslim population, PewResearch Center, October 2009.

MIDDLE EAST AND NORTH AFRICAN ISLAMIC COUNTRIES

Following the dissolution of the Islam-centered Ottoman Empire after World War I, the leading colonial powers, Britain and France, carved up the Middle East and North Africa, creating most of the nations we know there today, now about forty in number, for administrative reasons.

Saudi Arabia is home to the two holiest places in Islam, Mecca and Medina. The Saudi dynasty originated in 1744, when Muhammad bin Saud, the ruler of the town of Al-Dir'iyyah, near Riyadh, joined forces with a cleric, Muhammad ibn Abd-al-Wahhab. The present Saudi Arabia was founded by Abdul Aziz Ibn Saud in 1902, when he defeated the rival Al-Rashid family at Riyadh, then captured adjoining areas by defeating other opponents. In 1927, the British signed the Treaty of Jedda with Abdul Aziz, recognizing his kingdom. It is a monarchy ruled by the sons and grandsons of the king. Saudi Arabia is the world's leading petroleum exporter. It is the only producer country that has the capacity to increase its production by millions of barrels a day.

We need to study the situation in Saudi Arabia in detail, as in most of the Islamic hot spots worldwide, Islamic militants are trying to enforce Wahhabism, the most radical and original form of Islam, followed by Saudi Arabia. This is the direct results of Saudi businessmen's funding of Afghan mujahideens' struggle against the infidel Soviets in Afghanistan during the 1980s. It is worth noting that fifteen out of nineteen hijackers in the September 9, 2001, attacks were from Saudi Arabia.

According to Wahhabism, the Quran is the constitution, and all laws must follow Islamic law. No other religion is allowed. Although American troops stationed in Saudi Arabia are there only to protect the kingdom from outside threat, US soldiers who wear a cross or Star of David must keep the symbols hidden, and they must worship in private. In November 2005, a Saudi court sentenced a teacher to forty months in prison and 750 lashes for "mocking religion" for having discussed the Bible and praised Jews.[177]

In Saudi schools, up to one-third of every child's schooling is on religious topics. In the early years the curriculum focuses on simple things such as rules for prayer. By the time Saudi students reach high school, they have at least one period in six devoted to study of religious topics, including interpreting the holy texts and ways of keeping their faith pure. A student cannot move on to the next grade if he flunks a religious class, unlike other subjects. Learning is by rote, questions are discouraged.[178]

Eleventh-graders at the elite Islamic Saudi Academy in northern Virginia study energy and matter in physics, differential equations in precalculus, and stories about slavery and the Puritans in English. In their Islamic studies class, however, textbooks tell them that the Day of Judgment cannot come until Jesus Christ returns to Earth, breaks the cross and converts everyone to Islam, and Muslims start attacking Jews.[179]

King Fahd Academy, a Saudi-run school, was opened in 1995 near Bonn, Germany, with a $20 million donation from Saudi King Fahd bin Abdul Aziz Al Saud. It was established so that Saudi diplomats' children could be educated in conformance with their culture. Later on, conservative German Muslims began sending their children to this school because of its orthodox education and low tuition. The academy came to prominence in 2003 when a television news show secretly taped a teacher's sermon in its mosque. He said children must learn "to throw a spear, swim and ride, to be strong and brave, so they will be willing to join the jihad," according to a transcript of the sermon.[180]

Following this, the local government launched an investigation. It obtained copies of class schedules and found the Saudi embassy and school routinely understated the time devoted to religion and overstated the time devoted to math, science, and academics. The government also commissioned a study of the school's textbooks. The findings shocked local leaders: Two-thirds of the textbooks taught students to hate non-Muslims, while one in five praised martyrdom, urged violence against non-Muslims, or threatened hell for infractions against Muslim ritual.[181]

Saudi Arabia's religious police, also known as *muttawa*, are employed by the Commission for the Propagation of Virtue and the Prevention of Vice to patrol public places. They ensure that women are covered in black cloaks, that the sexes do not mix in public, that shops close five times a day for prayers, and that men go to the mosque for worship. The Taliban, when they ruled Afghanistan, had a similar governmental office called the Department for the Promotion of Virtue and Prevention of Vice.

The death of innocents is no obstacle to the enforcement of these codes. In a tragic fire at a Mecca girls school in March 2002, fifteen girls died. The building lacked basic safety precautions and was locked from the outside. Some newspapers reported that the muttawa barred male rescuers from entering the burning building and stopped fleeing girls from leaving because the girls did not wear veils.[182]

In the last fifteen years, there have been several terrorist attacks inside Saudi Arabia to protest the presence of the Americans. In the 1996 Khobar Towers attack in Saudi Arabia, nineteen US servicemen were killed and 372 foreigners were wounded. Khobar Towers housed US Air Force personnel. In May 2003, four car bombs detonated simultaneously in various Western enclaves in the Saudi capital, Riyadh, killing at least thirty-five people. In May 2004, four Islamic terrorists raided a housing complex in Khobar, taking more than fifty hostages and killing twenty-two of them. In April 2007, authorities arrested 172 Islamic extremists, claiming that they were planning air attacks on Saudi oil installations, jail raids to free Islamic militants, and suicide attacks on government officials.

After its independence in 1962, Algeria has been under either military rule or one-party government. In 1991–92 the first multiparty elections were held in Algeria, but with the blessings of Western nations the military intervened when Islamic political leaders won. About two hundred thousand people have died in the ensuing fifteen-year-old civil war, and, according to Human Rights Watch, seven thousand or more people disappeared at the hands of security forces in the 1990s.[183] In the 1999 presidential elections, the candidate supported by the military won, but only after six rivals dropped out claiming fraud. In the most recent elections, in May 2007, voters had the option of choosing only from a list of candidates cleared by the military. In recent years there have been a number of bombings as well as suicide bombings by Islamic militants at government buildings and UN offices in Algeria.

Bahrain is a constitutional monarchy headed by a king. Sunni Muslims are in power in Bahrain even though Shiites constitute a majority. The majority of cabinet members are from the royal family. Bahrain has a bicameral legislature with a lower house, elected by universal suffrage, and an upper house, appointed by the king. In February 2002, the king announced a new constitution that gave women the right to vote and run for office. In the 2006 parliamentary elections, one woman won by default, whereas the Islamists won the majority. Bahrain is home to the administrative headquarters of the US Navy's Fifth Fleet.

Since its independence in 1954, Egypt was under either military rule or one-party government until 2005. The last fifteen years have seen several deadly attacks on foreigners in Egypt aimed at disrupting the tourist industry, which brings in several billions in currency to the Egyptian economy. The Muslim Brotherhood, an Islamic fundamentalist organization, was founded by an Egyptian schoolteacher, Hassan al-Banna, in 1928 in Egypt. Its goal is to convert secular Egypt into an Islamic society based on the Quran and Sunnah. It has branches in other Middle East countries also. It was banned in 1948. After being accused of assassinating Nasser, thousands of its members were tortured in the 1960s. President Anwar Sadat eventually freed most of its members, however, claiming that he would implement sharia as Egyptian law. When its members assassinated Sadat in 1981, the Egyptian government again cracked down. The Brotherhood, nevertheless, won eighty-eight out of 454 seats in the 2005 parliamentary elections, with President Hosni Mubarak's ruling National Democratic Party obtaining a majority of 314 seats, ninety fewer than in the 2000 elections. It is worth noting that in order not to antagonize the ruling party, Brotherhood candidates ran from only 150 constituencies (out of a total of 454). It is widely believed that Brotherhood is going to win the elections to be held after the overthrow of Hosni Mubarak.

Iran is a theocratic country. Shiite is Iran's official religion. The Supreme Leader, who is a cleric, is commander-in-chief of the armed forces, controls the military intelligence and security operations, and has sole power to declare war. The country also has a president, who is elected by universal suffrage for a term of four years. Presidential candidates must be approved by the Council of Guardians, a group of clerics, most selected by the Supreme Leader, prior to running for office in order to ensure their allegiance to the ideals of the Islamic revolution. Unlike the president, the Supreme Leader is not an elected official. He has final say in all matters.

Unlike other Middle East countries, Iran poses a threat to US interests in the region. According to the International Atomic Energy Agency in May 2007, Iran was three to eight years away from building a nuclear bomb.[184] It may be able to accomplish this faster, however, because nuclear bomb technology is freely available now, and if the United States could make a nuclear bomb from scratch in less than five years in the 1940s, certainly Iran can do better with the technology available now.

Because of the fear of an Iranian nuclear bomb, the United States, Israel, or both can strike at Iranian nuclear installations, just as Israeli jets bombed the French-built Osirak nuclear reactor near Baghdad in 1981.

If the United States and/or Israel attack Iran, Iran can do the following:

(1) It can block the vital Strait of Hormuz, through which pass much of the world's oil supplies, by sinking several ships.

(2) It can launch missiles against Israel.

(3) It can create problems for pro-US/Western Islamic regimes, especially for tens of thousands of US troops deployed in the region.

Iran currently has three types of missiles: Shahab-1 (range two hundred miles), Shahab-2 (range three hundred miles), and Shahab-3 (range 806 to 930 miles). The Shahab-3 can reach Israel as well as American troops stationed in Saudi Arabia and Iraq. The first two missile types are based on Russian Scud missiles, and Shahab-3 is on a North Korean model. Shahab means "shooting star" in Farsi, the main language of Iran. According to US intelligence sources, Iran keeps its Scud missiles in several deep tunnels along its coastline, including on some of its islands in the Strait of Hormuz. This gives Iran the capacity to block the strait, which is a conduit for more than one-third of the world's oil. Another Middle East crisis involving Iran will cause the price of oil, which is already high, to go through the roof.

In 2010, Iran obtained four S-300 surface-to-air missile systems, two from Belarus and two others from another unspecified source.

Russia signed a 2007 contract to sell the S-300s but has not delivered so far. The S-300 is capable of shooting down aircraft, cruise missiles, and ballistic missile warheads at ranges of over ninety miles and at altitudes of about ninety thousand feet.

Jordan is a constitutional monarchy. Although there is a parliament, and parliamentary elections are held regularly, the king has the real executive authority. The armed forces are also under his control. Palestinians are about half of its population of approximately six million. Jordanian intelligence agencies vet the appointment of every university professor, ambassador, and important editor even though the country is one of the region's most liberal. Its secret police eavesdrop with the help of perhaps thousands of Jordanians on its payroll, similar to the informant networks in the former Soviet Bloc.[185] In November 2005 there were three simultaneous Islamic terrorist bombings at hotels in the capital, Amman. At least fifty-seven people died and 115 were wounded.

In the post–World War II world, Lebanon was known as the Arab banking capital and the "Switzerland of the Middle East." Its capital, Beirut, was visited by a large number of tourists, and was known as the "Paris of the Middle East" until the Lebanese Civil War (1975–90) left it in ruins. After 1990, it enjoyed peace and invested in rebuilding its infrastructure until the 2006 Israeli invasion, which caused large-scale damage.

The Islamic organization Hezbollah was founded in 1982 in Lebanon by Lebanese Shiites in response to the Israeli invasion of southern Lebanon. Its charter is to create an Islamic state in Lebanon. It provides schools, hospitals, and agricultural services in the south of the country. Hezbollah's leader frequently condemns al-Qaeda. It plays an important role in Lebanese politics. Some Western countries, including the United States, regard it as a terrorist organization like Hamas. It gets financial and military support from both Syria and Iran.

In February 2005, Rafik Hariri, former prime minister and billionaire, was assassinated in a car bomb in Beirut. This led to several days of protests in Lebanon. It also led to the UN Security Council, with the United States and France playing an instrumental role, passing Resolution 1559, which called for Syrian withdrawal from Lebanon and disarming Hezbollah. Syria subsequently pulled its fourteen thousand troops out of the country, and in the 2005 parliamentary elections after this withdrawal, an anti-Syrian alliance won and formed a coalition government.

When Hezbollah kidnapped two Israeli soldiers on July 12, 2006, Israel launched a full-fledged attack on Lebanon that lasted for thirty-three days and destroyed much of its infrastructure. More than one thousand Lebanese civilians and forty-four Israelis were killed.

Libya gained full independence in 1951 as a constitutional and hereditary monarchy under King Idris. In 1969, Muammar Abu Minyar al-Gaddafi, an army officer, staged a coup and ousted the king. Gaddafi was ousted in 2011. In 1988, on its way from London to New York, Pan Am Flight 103 exploded over Lockerbie, Scotland, killing all 259 people on board, including several Americans and eleven people on the ground. The UN Security Council subsequently imposed sanctions against Libya in 1992, barring all air travel and military sales until it turned over two suspects in the bombing. One of the two suspects was convicted of murder by a panel of three Scottish judges and was sentenced to twenty-seven years in prison in 2001, and the other was acquitted.

Morocco gained independence in 1956. It is a constitutional monarchy with an elected parliament. The king of Morocco has the real executive powers. He can dissolve the government and deploy the military. In the last six to seven years there have been several cases of suicide bombings in Casablanca, Morocco's largest city, killing several dozen people and injuring several hundreds.

Qatar is half the size of New Jersey. It has natural gas reserves of ninety trillion cubic feet, the second-largest in the world after those of Russia.[186] After the dissolution of the Ottoman Empire, it was a British protectorate, and gained independence in 1971. In 1995, the present king deposed his own father when he was on vacation in Switzerland. He has introduced a new constitution, which gives voting rights to women. Qatar is the headquarters of Al Jazeera, the Arabic-language satellite television news channel.

Israel is the only democratic country in the entire Middle East and is based on Jewish religion. Historically, Jews have been mistreated by Muslim rulers in the Middle East until as late as the first half of the twentieth century. The Ottoman Empire ruled Palestine from 1517 to 1917–18, and, due to Islamic laws, Jews were forbidden to bear arms, were permitted to ride asses only, not camels or horses, and only sidesaddle rather than astride; and were obliged to wear a distinct garb.[187] Hence it was natural that some Jewish leaders and groups would want to take revenge against Muslims.

It is true that Israel is a small country surrounded by enemies and hence needs security. Israel is now, however, the strongest military power in the Middle East. Apart from its superiority in conventional weapons, it is the only country in the region with nuclear weapons, about two hundred of them. It has the fourth-largest army in the world with about seven hundred thousand army personnel available within twenty-four hours in case of war, and it has the fourth-largest air force in the world. Apart from this, the United States is always there to airlift any armaments needed.

It has been estimated that more than six million Jews were murdered in the World War II Holocaust. It was one of the main reasons why Western countries helped Jews in creating the homeland of Israel that Jews had lost two thousand years ago. At that time, first Romans and then Muslims drove them from the region by force, and hence the creation of Israel became a healing process for them. Because of so much suffering, it was natural for the founding fathers and leaders of Israel to act disproportionately while taking revenge against their enemies. Their Arab neighbors had to get the full measure of their anger. There is a limit to everything, however. In 1995, when commenting on the plight of the suffering Palestinians, Ehud Barak, the highest-ranking military officer at that time and future prime minister of Israel, said that had he been born a Palestinian instead of an Israeli, he probably would have joined a "terrorist" organization.[188]

In September 2008, Ehud Omert, the then Israeli prime minister, also said that Israel must withdraw from nearly all of the territory seized during the Six-Day War in 1967 (i.e., all of the West Bank as well as East Jerusalem) to attain peace with the Palestinians and that any occupied land it held on to would have to be exchanged for the same quantity of Israeli territory.

Israel's settlements in the occupied territories are illegal, according to international laws. Not only the UN and European allies of the United States consider these settlements illegal, even the US State Department legal adviser found, in response to an inquiry from the Congress in 1979, these settlements to be inconsistent with international law. Despite the passage of time, this legal opinion has never been revoked or revised.[189] Immediately after the 1967 Arab-Israeli war, the legal counsel of the Israeli foreign ministry, Theodor Meron, was asked whether international law allowed settlement in the newly conquered land. In a memo marked "Top Secret," Mr. Meron wrote in no uncertain terms, "My conclusion is that civilian settlement in the administered territories contravenes the explicit provisions of the Fourth Geneva Convention [to which Israel was a signatory]." He also wrote that a military decree issued on the third day of the war in June said that military courts must apply the Geneva Conventions in the West Bank.[190] The 1949 Fourth Geneva Convention is meant to protect people under occupation from torture and unnecessary hardship, and to guarantee basic services such as education, health care, and other services. Article 49 of this Convention clearly states, "The Occupying Power shall not deport or transfer parts of its own civilian population into the territory it occupies."

Israel's numerous illegal settlements in territories occupied in the 1967 war are one of the main obstacles to peace with the Palestinians. In March 2006, Jimmy Carter wrote in the Tel Aviv newspaper *Haaretz* that Israel's "colonization of Palestine" through expanding Jewish settlements is the single greatest obstacle to resolution of the conflict. He also said Israel was insincere at peace negotiations during the 1990s when it offered to withdraw only a small proportion of the 225,000 settlers living in the West Bank:

> The best official offer to the Palestinians was to withdraw 20% of them, leaving 180,000 [Israelis] in 209 settlements, covering about 5% of the occupied land. The 5% figure is grossly misreading, with surrounding areas taken or earmarked for expansion, roadways joining settlements with each other and to Jerusalem, and wide arterial swaths providing water, sewage, electricity and communications. This intricate honeycomb divides the entire West Bank into multiple fragments, often uninhabitable or even unreachable.[191]

It is only the United States that is saving Israel at the UN. Without the United States, there would have been several dozen UN Security Council resolutions against Israel in the last three to four decades. The total number of vetoes used by the United States to stop Security Council resolutions critical of Israel is greater than the total of vetoes cast by the four other nations on the Security Council having veto power combined. In the UN General Assembly, Israel can muster the support of only four or five nations (out of more than 150+ countries) for the numerous resolutions against her.

Right now the strong pro-Israeli lobby groups, such as the American Israel Public Affairs Committee (AIPAC), are dictating the US Middle East policy. Pro-Israeli groups like AIPAC are founded by first generation American Jews who have strong bonds with Israel. Like the Cuban Americans, Israel may not expect the same bonding from the next generations of American Jews. The five-decade-old US economic embargo against Cuba was mainly due the first generation Cuban Americans who migrated to the United States after the 1959 Communist takeover in Cuba and their fierce opposition to Cuba's Communist government. Now the United States has started to lift economic embargoes against Cuba because the post-Communist-revolution Cuban American generations do not fiercely oppose the Communist government in Cuba as much as their previous generations. A similar mentality is emerging among American Jews, with the establishment of a new Israeli lobby group called J Street.

The overthrow of Mubakar in Egypt is a major blow for Israel, as Mubarak was pro-Israel and solidly behind the US policy in that region. Now the post-Mubarak Egypt is taking several measures that show its anti-Israel stance. In February 2011, it allowed the passage of two Iranian warships through the Suez Canal to the Mediterranean for the first time since the 1979 Iranian Revolution and lifted the blockade of the Gaza Strip. It will be a disaster for Israel if Egypt unilaterally withdraws from the 1978 Camp David Accords. After the killing of Turkish citizens in the 2010 Gaza aid flotilla in a raid by the Israeli navy, the Islamist government in Turkey has hardened its stance on Israel. After the refusal of Israel to apologize for the killing of its citizens, Turkey has suspended all defense ties with Israel, and its prime minister is trying to build a coalition against Israel.

Also, with the collapse of the US economy, the focus of the United

States will turn inwards, and the decline of its international influence will affect Israel adversely. In October 2004, in a confidential ten-year forecast, the Israeli foreign ministry's Center for Political Research also said Israel is set on a collision course with the European Union and could turn into a pariah state, on a par with South Africa during the apartheid years, if the conflict with the Palestinians is not resolved. According to the forecast, the EU is pushing to become a major global player in the next decade, and as a result the United States, Israel's main ally, could lose international influence.[192]

Apart from this, with time the range and accuracy of Hamas's (as well as Hezbollah's) missiles will increase and will penetrate deeper and deeper inside Israel, threatening more and more Israelis (we are talking about decades and not years). In 2010, Hezbollah had forty thousand rockets, twice what it had in 2006, and also these rockets have long range, with more accuracy than previous models. Hence in any future conflict with Israel these rockets will reach all over Israeli territory. Israel does not have an option but to come up with a solution at the earliest possible time. The more Israel delays the two-state solution, the more it increases the probability of one state for the entire region, which does not bode well for the present Jewish population in Israel because then most of them will end up migrating to the United States.

President Mohamed Siad Barre ruled as a dictator in Somalia from 1969 to 1991. Somalia has had no recognized central government since warlords ousted him in 1991. After his ouster, a civil war erupted that resulted in a disruption in agriculture and food distribution. This caused a famine in the country. Therefore, in 1992 and again in 1993, the UN Security Council authorized a peacekeeping force for the conduct of humanitarian operations in the country. Nineteen American troops and more than one thousand Somalis were killed in October 1993 in the capital, Mogadishu, in fighting between UN troops and Somali warlord Mohamed Farrah Aidid. Aidid was killed in 1996.

Syria gained independence in 1946. Between 1946 and 1956, it had about twenty different governments and four different constitutions. Finally, leftist army officers, who were members of the Baath Party, engineered a coup and captured power in 1963. Hafez al-Assad, minister of defense and father of the present president, ousted the civilian party leadership and declared himself president in 1970. He was a secular, brutal dictator. In 1982, the Syrian army sealed off the city of Hama after the armed uprising of the Muslim Brotherhood and massacred close to ten thousand people.

The current President Assad is Alawite, a Muslim minority regarded by orthodox Sunni Muslims as heretical and disparagingly referred to as "little Christians": indeed, some scholars believe their liturgy to be partly Christian in origin. Mr. Assad's father, Hafez al-Assad, who was president from 1971 until his death in 2000, kept himself in power by forming what was in effect a coalition of Syria's religious minorities, through which he was able to counterbalance the weight of the Sunni majority. In the Assads' Syria, Christians have done particularly well: in his final years, five of Hafez's seven closest advisers were Christians. Christians are fearful that if the Assad regime should fall, their last real haven in the Middle East will disappear and be replaced by yet another fundamentalist government, as may be the case in Iraq.[193]

Syria poses no serious threat to the United States, and its main enemy is Israel. Syria wants the Golan Heights back, which Israel won in the 1967 war, and this is the main reason behind its funding of Hezbollah and Hamas. During the Bush administration Syria was vilified as an axis of evil, but the Obama administration has shown willingness to talk with Syria. The prime objective of the Syrians is to get the Golan Heights. With the Benjamin Netanyahu as prime minister in Israel, it will be difficult for Syrians to achieve this goal.

Turkey is the only Muslim-majority NATO member and has the second-largest army in NATO after the United States, with a combined strength of more than one million uniformed personnel. It is a democratic, secular country established in 1923 under the leadership of Mustafa Kemal Atatürk in the aftermath of World War I. Before that war, Turkey had been the seat of the Ottoman Empire (1299–1922), which at the height of its power ruled in three continents (southeastern Europe, North Africa, and the Middle East).

The secularization of Turkey is so established that in 1999 Merve Kavakci, a female member of Parliament, was ousted from the assembly after she appeared wearing a type of headscarf worn by more conservative Muslim women—wearing such a headscarf in public places is illegal. If Turkey is admitted into the European Union, its secular democratic principles would gain strength.

The Constitutional Court of Turkey can strip the public financing of political parties that it deems antisecular or separatist, or ban their existence altogether. In 1997, the popular Welfare Party was banned on the grounds of threatening the secular nature of the state. When the leaders of the banned party formed the Virtue Party (Fazilet Partisi), this too was found unconstitutional on the same grounds and was banned in 1999. In 2001, however, they formed the Justice and Development Party, which received the most votes in the 2002 parliamentary elections, allowing it to form the government. The Islamic party is popular among the middle and lower classes.

The Turkish army has ousted four governments in the past fifty years (1960, 1971, 1980, and 1997) in order to maintain the secular status of the country. The first pro-Islamic prime minister, Necmettin Erbakan, was one of its targets, in 1997.

When, in a 1997 speech, the current prime minister, Recep Tayyip Erdogan (at that time mayor of Istanbul), recited a poem that included the line, "The mosques are our barracks, the minarets our bayonets, the domes our helmets and the believers soldiers," he was arrested and convicted of "inciting public enmity and hatred." At his sentencing he received ten months in prison, was stripped of his office, and was barred from politics for life. He only served four months, however, and in 2001 the political ban was lifted in a general amnesty.[194]

Although the present Turkish government of Justice and Development Party, an Islamic party, is trying to get rid of the secular laws, the country will not turn back the clock and become an Islamic country like Saudi Arabia or Pakistan because the majority of its population will not accept it.

Yemen is an Islamic state with all its laws based on the Quran. It is considered another Afghanistan, a breeding ground for Islamic militants. It is one of the poorest countries in the Middle East. Instead of crushing opponents, President Ali Abdullah Saleh (in office from 1990 to 2011) survived by sharing authority with tribal leaders, religious figures, and military chieftains, many of whom are quick to register their displeasure with a show of arms. Yemen's military is dotted with so-called Afghan Arabs, mujahideen warriors who fought with Osama bin Laden against the Soviets in Afghanistan and later helped northern Yemen defeat the socialists of the south in 1990 and 1994. In the rugged countryside, where President Saleh's reach is nearly theoretical, a phalanx of tribal warlords stands as proxies for government rule. According to Sheda Mohammed, a female lawyer in Sana, "Everybody here has a Kalashnikov and a few grenades in their closet."[195]

Al-Iman University in Sana, which has attracted hundreds of non-Yemini students to its courses in Islamic law, science, and economics, has long been considered by Western officials to be a factory for producing Islamic extremists. John Walker Lindh, the American captured with Taliban fighters in Afghanistan, was a product of this university. It was built with help from the Yemini government, private donors in the Persian Gulf region, and Turkey's now-banned Welfare Party.[196]

OTHER ISLAMIC COUNTRIES AND HOT SPOTS

During my Indian Administrative Service training in the mid-1980s, I, along with my dozen colleagues, spent about a week with the Indian army along the Indo-Pakistan border, also called the Line of Control (LOC), in Jammu and Kashmir. During the one-week training, we were briefed by senior army officials about the history and situation in the region. Several senior army officials were blaming Jawahar Lal Nehru, first prime minister of India, for the Kashmir crisis. When the British left India in 1947, British-controlled states, also called British India, were divided between India and Pakistan in a plebiscite along religious lines. Under the Indian Independence Act of 1947, the paramountcy of the British over about six hundred princely states lapsed, and these states were free to join India or Pakistan or become sovereign. Despite insistence from the Indian National Congress (the ruling party before and after the independence of India), it was Muhammad Ali Jinnah, the founder of Pakistan, and his Muslim League party, who had insisted against having a plebiscite clause for the princely states in the Indian Independence Act of 1947. Jammu and Kashmir was one of these princely states. Jinnah thought that after the lapse of paramountcy many princely states would stay out of India.

Had Jammu and Kashmir been part of British India, it would have gone to Pakistan, since Muslims constituted about 77 percent of the state's population. After the lapse of the paramountcy in August

1947, the maharaja of Jammu and Kashmir, Maharaja Hari Singh, was uninterested in joining either country. But within a week of the independence, Pakistan's army along with five thousand tribesmen attacked J&K. When they were just five kilometers from his capital, Maharaja Hari Singh signed the Instrument of Accession, becoming part of India, in a panic. India conducted a massive airlift of army personnel to Jammu and Kashmir the following day and captured major parts of Jammu and Kashmir within two weeks. The intruders were on the run, and the Indian army would have captured the entire Jammu and Kashmir territory, but, against the advice of his cabinet members, Prime Minister Nehru took matters to the UN Security Council on January 1, 1948. There, India accused Pakistan of sending both regular troops and tribesmen into Jammu and Kashmir. This led to the establishment of the UN Commission in India and Pakistan (UNCIP) by the Security Council to assess the claims and counterclaims of the two countries. The chairman of the UNCIP was Dr. Josef Korbel, father of former US secretary of state Madeline Albright. On August 13, 1948, the UNCIP passed a resolution asking Pakistan to withdraw its troops and tribesmen from Jammu and Kashmir. "Once Pakistan withdraws them, the administration by the local authorities needs to be restored, India will reduce its troops to the barest minimum and then a plebiscite will be held to ascertain the wishes of the people of the state." The cease-fire went into effect on January 1, 1949, and the cease-fire line became the Line of Control.

It was in fact wrong on the part of Nehru to take the Kashmir issue to the UN. It is said that had he given a few more days to the army, all of Jammu and Kashmir would have been recaptured. Sixty years later, India is still paying the price for his blunder. By taking the matter to the UN, Nehru internationalized the issue and made Pakistan a party in the issue. By signing the Instrument of Accession, however, Maharaja Hari Singh had made Jammu and Kashmir part of India. This was completely legal under the Indian Independence Act of 1947, signed by both India and Pakistan, which gave sovereignty of the state to Maharaja Hari Singh after the lapse of British paramountcy. The act contained no provision for ascertaining the wishes of the people of the princely states through plebiscite. This understanding was confirmed on February 4, 1948, by the US representative, Warren Austin, who said in the Security Council, "With the accession of J&K to India, this foreign sovereignty (of Jammu and Kashmir) went over to India." In addition, Justice Owen Dixon of Australia stated in his September 15, 1950, report to the Security Council that Pakistan had violated international law by crossing into Jammu and Kashmir territory. It was thus completely wrong on the part of Nehru to agree to a plebiscite in a territory that was a legal part of India. Nevertheless, the plebiscite was conditional upon Pakistan withdrawing its troops and tribesmen from the state and restoration of the administration to the local authorities. In the last sixty years, Pakistan has not fulfilled the first two conditions, and hence, according to the UN resolution, Pakistan is responsible for the stalemate.

India and Pakistan have fought three wars—in 1947–48, 1965, and 1971. Two of these were over Kashmir. In addition, India has been fighting a covert war in Kashmir since 1989. Currently, India, Pakistan, and China control 45 percent, 35 percent, and 20 percent, respectively, of the original Jammu and Kashmir territory (i.e., during preindependence period). China received about thirty-five thousand square kilometers in Aksai Chin in the 1962 war with India and another five thousand square kilometers in Balistan ceded by Pakistan under a treaty signed in March 1963. Indian Kashmir has three regions: Kashmir Valley, Jammu, and Ladakh. The Indian-controlled Kashmir Valley (IKV), Jammu, and Ladakh have Muslim, Hindu, and Buddhist, respectively, majorities. Pakistan-Administered Kashmir (PAK) has a Muslim majority. The bone of contention is just IKV, a one-hundred-mile-long valley, which is about 9 percent of the original J&K territory.

After watching the defeat of a superpower, the USSR, by Afghan mujahideens, Pakistan's dictator General Zia started the same kind of low-cost war by sending trained Islamic militants into Kashmir in the late 1980s to bleed India after it had become clear that Pakistan would never be able to defeat India in direct war. For centuries, Kashmir had been a place noted for its adherence to the gentle Sufi form of Islam. It was the only place where no communal riots and killing took place during the partition of India. In the early 1990s, militants killed Hindus in the Kashmir Valley (IKV), causing Hindus to flee. No Hindus live there now. In late 1990s, Pakistan's Inter-Services Intelligence (ISI) started infiltrating the valley with Islamic fundamentalists trained in

Afghanistan's terrorist universities. According to American officials, the ISI even used al-Qaeda camps in Afghanistan to train covert operatives for use in a war of terror against India.[197] Terrorist training camps that had been closed after the September 11 attacks on the United States have been reactivated again in Pakistan-controlled Kashmir.

Countries such as Israel (occupied lands in the 1967 Arab-Israeli War) and China (Tibet and Xinjiang) are changing the demography of their disputed territories, but the demography of India-controlled Kashmir cannot be changed due to Article 370 of the Indian Constitution, according to which Indian citizens from other states and Kashmiri women who marry men from other states cannot purchase land or property in Jammu and Kashmir. On the other hand, in Pakistan-Administered Kashmir (PAK), the demography has changed drastically since 1948 as the original Kashmiris are now a minority in PAK because of immigration of non-Kashmiris. Due to sizable Muslim votes in several states of India, political leaders will never be able to amend or repeal Article 370 of the constitution. All national political parties, except Hindu fundamentalist Bhartiya Janata Party (BJP), are against amending or repealing Article 370 of the Indian Constitution. Therefore it is difficult to amend or repeal this article, as an amendment to the Indian constitution needs not only to be passed by India's parliament by a special majority, it must also be ratified by at least half of the state legislatures by a special majority.

Although India has the third-largest Muslim population in the world after Indonesia and Pakistan, a section of Muslim political leaders in Kashmir Valley (IKV) kept raising the issue of implementation of the UN Security Council resolution (i.e., a plebiscite to garner Muslim votes). After the entry of "mujahideens," Kashmir Valley (IKV) has become an albatross for India. Not only is more than half of India's regular army stationed in J&K; India is spending several billion dollars each year in fighting Muslim militants there. This money could well be spent on development works elsewhere in India. Apart from this, the Kashmir issue is a single-point agenda in all of Pakistan in its fight against India. Therefore, India will have no option but to leave Kashmir Valley (IKV), where Muslims are in the majority. In the case of the division of Pakistan, discussed in the next chapter, we may have an independent Kashmir, a country after the merger of Pakistan-

Administered Kashmir (PAK) and Indian-controlled Kashmir Valley
(IKV). India will not simply give the Kashmir Valley (i.e., IKV) to
Pakistan because it would not like to lose face internationally. Also,
no Indian political party would survive if its government takes this
decision. Apart from this, the majority of people (Muslims) in Indian-
controlled Kashmir (IKV) do not want to join Pakistan (it is confirmed
by recent Gallup polls) because they enjoy far better conditions than
their counterparts in PAK. Therefore, India would like to see either
an independent or self-administered Kashmir after the merger of the
two Kashmirs (IKV and PAK). But it will sound the death knell for
Pakistan, as it will give fresh impetus to separatist movements in Sindh,
Balochistan, and the North-West Frontier. All three states already have
strong separatist movements.

When the British left India in 1947, Bangladesh was part of
Pakistan and was called East Pakistan. Due to the atrocities committed
by the West Pakistani army, however, it was liberated by India in the
1971 Indo-Pak War. Four years after its independence, the country
witnessed a series of military coups. Since 1991 it had seen peaceful
transitions of power according to democratic procedures. On August
17, 2005, about five hundred small bombs exploded at about three
hundred locations in sixty-three of Bangladesh's sixty-four districts.
An Islamic group, Jama'atul Mujahideen, claimed responsibility for the
bombings, and leaflets were found at the bomb sites advocating Islamic
rule for Bangladesh. Pakistan's Inter-Services Intelligence (ISI) is said to
outsource terrorist activities to Bangladesh's intelligence agencies.

Malaysia gained independence from the British in 1957. It is now
a federation of thirteen states formed in 1963. Originally Singapore
was also part of Malaysia but left the federation in 1965. Malaysia has
a constitutional elective monarchy: the king is elected from among
the nine hereditary sultans of the Malay states for a five-year term; the
other four states, which have titular governors, do not participate. Out
of the country's twenty-three million people, Muslims comprise about
60 percent, and it has substantial Chinese and Indian minorities. Islam
is the official religion, and Muslims are obliged to follow the sharia
courts. Couples are detained for holding hands in public, and Muslims
are fined if they fail to fast.

M. Moorthy, a thirty-six-year-old Indian-origin Hindu, became a national hero by being the first Malaysian to climb Mount Everest. When he died in 2005, he was buried as a Muslim despite his widow's appeal in Malaysia's High Court that he never converted to Islam. Before his death he was in a coma for a few days. As soon as he died, the sharia court declared that Moorthy had converted to Islam before his death and hence should be buried as a Muslim. Evidence from his military colleagues, who were Muslims, was admitted as conclusive proof, while his wife and other relatives were not given a hearing because "they were not Muslims." The High Court ruled that it had no jurisdiction in religious matters.

Indonesia is the world's fourth-most-populous country and has the world's largest Muslim population. Islam was introduced here by traders, and today 90 percent of the population is Muslim. Officially it is a secular country and a republic with an elected parliament and president. During his more than three decades in office, General Suharto suppressed Islamic groups and their influence using force. After nearly facing financial collapse during the 1997–98 East Asian economic crisis, Suharto had to resign, which led to both political and economic reforms.

In 1972, Abu Bakar Bashir cofounded "Al Mukmin," an Islamic boarding school, or *pesantren*, which is like a Pakistani *madrassa*. Pesantrens are mostly private schools offering Quranic education, although some of the larger pesantrens also offer the official curriculum that enables students to take the university entrance examination. In 1982, Mr. Bashir was put on trial for advocating the creation of an Islamic state by President Suharto's government. He was sentenced to nine years in prison but was released in 1985, when he fled to Malaysia. After the fall of Suharto in 1998, he returned to Indonesia. Asmar Latin Sani, the suicide bomber responsible for the attack on Jakata's J. W. Marriott Hotel on August 5, 2003, was a graduate of al Mukmin. Apart from Asmar, 11 others died in the attack.

It is claimed that Mr. Bashir is the spiritual head of Jemaah Islamiyah, a militant Southeast Asian Islamic organization that has the goal of establishing an Islamic state comprising Indonesia, Malaysia, the southern Philippines, Singapore, and Brunei, although he denies any relationship with this organization. In 2002, a US governmental demand that Bashir be turned over to the Americans was refused by the Indonesian government. The Indonesian government did, however, charge Bashir with treason in 2004 and again with terrorism in 2005. He was found guilty on a lesser charge of immigration violations in 2004 but was found guilty of conspiracy in the 2002 Bali bombing. He was sentenced to three years of prison in 2004 and two and a half years in 2005 but was released in June 2006.

More than five thousand people have died since 1999 in clashes between Muslims and Christians in Indonesia's Maluku Islands. In 2000, a Muslim paramilitary organization, Lashkar Jihad, was formed in West Java and sent its forces to the Malukus to fight along with Muslims against Christians.

On October 12, 2002, two bombs killed 202 people and injured several hundred, mostly foreigners, near a nightclub on the tourist island of Bali. On October 1, 2005, three bomb explosions killed at least twenty-five people and wounded more than one hundred, also on Bali. These bombs targeted popular seafood restaurants frequented by foreign tourists. Bali is a Hindu-majority island in a Muslim-majority country.

Jemaah Islamiyah has, however, suffered serious setbacks as many of its suspected members were arrested after the 2002 attack. In addition, its mastermind, Riudan Ismuddin, also known as Hambali, was captured by the CIA in 2003.

After being part of the Soviet Union, the majority of Muslims in Central Asia in ex-Soviet republics, such as in Uzbekistan, Kyrgyzstan, and Tajikistan, are secular in nature. Hizb ut-Tahrir al-Islamiyya (The Islamic Party of Liberation), founded 1953 by Shaykh Taqiuddin al-Nabhani in Jordanian-ruled East Jerusalem, is a radical Islamic movement in this region that advocates the creation of a caliphate by peaceful means. Recently there are reports of Islamic militants trained in Pakistan engaging in violent activities in these countries.

Russia has been fighting Islamic separatists in Chechnya since 1991. Neighboring regions Dagestan and Ingushetia in Russia also witnessed bombings by Islamic militants. After the 1999 massive army action by Russian president Putin on Chechnya to drive out the Chechen, the region was relatively quiet. Recently Chechnya, Dagestan, and Ingushetia have witnessed several bombings, which include suicide bombings, by Islamic militants, resulting in the killing of several hundred people. Bombings and shootings have become daily occurrences in the region.

Following the dissolution of the USSR and the creation of Islamic countries along China's border, Xinjiang Muslims began a bloody separatist movement in the 1990s. Unrest in the late 1990s resulted in a surge of executions. Amnesty International reported that at least 190 people, an average of nearly two a week, were executed in Xinjiang from January 1997 to April 1999. China claims that several hundred Ulghurs have received training from the Taliban in Afghanistan, and several Ulghurs were among the Taliban fighters captured during the 2001 Afghanistan War. The number of serious separatists inside China is still believed to be small.[198] Because of the Islamic militants in Xianjiang province, China cooperates with the United States, India, Russia, and other countries in fighting Islamic militancy.

Out of seventy-six million people in the Philippines, only about 5 percent are Muslim. They live in the deep south of the country, where Muslim separatists have been fighting for a homeland for more than a century. At present, two rebel groups operate in this region: the Moro Islamic Liberation Front, and Abu Sayyaf, which is smaller but more extreme. Two of the three terrorists convicted for the 1993 World Trade Center bombing, Ramzi Yousef and Abdul Hakim Murad, lived in Manila between 1994 and 1995. They were also accused of planning to bomb eleven jet planes over the Pacific.

Thailand also has a small Islamic separatist movement, on its southern border with Malaysia.

Pakistan

Pakistan is the world's main breeding ground for Islamic militants. These militants get support from the local administration (i.e., from the country's intelligence service, ISI). Pakistan is linked directly or indirectly to most terrorist activities that occur. Hence, it is important to study Pakistan in detail. Here are some examples of terrorist activities linked to Pakistan:

(1) Before he boarded American Airlines Flight 93 in Paris in December 2001, "shoe bomber" Richard Colvin Reid was receiving orders via e-mails from Pakistan.[199]

(2) The financier of the 9/11 attacks in the United States was finally traced by the FBI to Karachi, Pakistan.

(3) All the top al-Qaeda leaders, such as Ayman al- Zawahiri, are hiding in Pakistan.

(4) In the past, several top al-Qaeda leaders (such as Abu Zubaydah in 2002 and Khalid Sheikh Mohammed in 2003) were caught in Pakistan.

(5) Ramzi Yousef, one of the planners of the 1993 World Trade Center attack in New York City, which killed six and injured 1,042, was caught in 1995 in Pakistan.

(6) In 1998, eight young Muslim men were caught in Yemen and convicted of bombing British targets in that country. Six of them were of Pakistani origin.

(7) Four British men convicted in April 2004 of planning fertilizer-bomb attacks around London also trained in Pakistani camps, according to court papers in the case, known as Operation Crevice.[200]

(8) In late July 2005, two militants told a Pakistani journalist working on contract for the *New York Times* that they met one of the 2005 London bombing suspects, Shehzad Tanweer, on a trip to a militant training camp in the Mansehra district in northwest Pakistan.[201]

(9) Three of the four dead July 7, 2005, London bombers were middle-class Britons of Pakistani origin, and all three had traveled to Pakistan in the past. Just before the bombings, they had been in constant contact with Pakistan.

(10)The imprisoned would-be bombers who on July 21, 2005, had tried to blow up three trains and a bus in London, were

East African refugees and ex-convicts, and had travelled to Pakistan months before the attacks.[202]

(11) In September 2007, American authorities helped Danish and German security officials thwart bombing plots by Islamic militants; electronic intercepts from Pakistan led to their capture. The militants had also received terrorist training at camps in Pakistan. According to German officials, they learned to prepare chemical explosives and military-grade detonators that they intended to use to build three car bombs.[203]

(12) In September 2006, Islamic militant Omar Khayam, an accused leader of seven men charged in 2004 with stockpiling half a ton of explosives in an al-Qaeda-linked bombing plot, said during his trial in a British court, "The ISI [of Pakistan] has had words with my family in Pakistan regarding what I have been saying. I think they are worried I might end up revealing more about them, and right now the priority has to be the safety of my family there. I am not going to discuss anything related to the ISI anymore or my evidence."[204]

(13) On May 2, 2011, Osama bin Laden was shot and killed in a private residential compound in Abbottabad, Pakistan, by US Navy SEALs. Abbottabad, just a few hours drive from Islamabad, has Pakistan's most prestigious military institution, less than a mile from the compound where bin Laden was killed.

(14) An Indonesian militant accused in the 2002 Bali bombings was caught in Pakistan in early 2011. The United States had offered $1 million reward for information leading to his capture.

(15) China blamed Muslim militants, trained in Pakistan, for killing eleven people in the Xinjiang region in 2011.

According to British counterterrorism officials, most major terrorist plots in the United Kingdom in recent years, including the July 7, 2005, public transit bombings in London, can be traced back to al-Qaeda operatives in Pakistan.[205]

According to European and US antiterrorism officials, as Al Qaeda regains strength in the badlands of the Pakistani-Afghan border, an increasing number of militants from mainland Europe are traveling to Pakistan to train and to plot attacks on the West. According to a French intelligence official, "Unlike Iraq, where foreign fighters plunge quickly into combat, recruits in Pakistan are more likely to be groomed for missions in the West. Aspiring holy warriors drawn to the Pakistani-Afghan border region today include European converts and militants from Arab, Turkish and North African backgrounds."[206]

According to the 2008 RAND Corp. study "Counterinsurgency in Afghanistan," "NATO officials have uncovered several instances of Pakistani intelligence agents providing information to Taliban fighters, even "tipping off Taliban forces about the location and movement of Afghan and coalition forces, which undermined several US and NATO anti-Taliban military operations."[207] The ISI of Pakistan is supporting the Afghan insurgents because it does not want to lose its leverage in the region to countries such as India and Iran once the Western forces led by the United States leave the region.

Pakistan was created by Muslim leaders such as Muhammad Ali Jinnah and Liaquat Ali Khan, who were originally from the Hindu majority states in undivided India. Once these top leaders were gone (Jinnah died in 1948, and Khan was assassinated in 1951), Pakistan became leaderless politically, and Pakistani army generals took over the country. The United States supported these dictators and hence democracy could not take deep roots in the country. In all wars it has fought, the United States has claimed to be fighting for freedom and democracy. However, in all its Cold War battles it did not hesitate to deal repeatedly with military dictators instead of democratically elected leaders, as the latter inevitably tend towards a socialist or participatory style of government.

Pakistan's armed forces became proponents of Islamic holy war during General Zia-ul-Haq's rule in the 1980s. The 1979 Soviet intervention in Afghanistan and subsequent US funding of the Afghan mujahideen via the ISI made the Pakistani army holy warriors in the name of Islam, since it was the Pakistani army that was training the mujahideen. At the entrance to the Pakistan Military Academy, an Arabic-lettered sign proclaims: "Victory Awaits Those Who Have Faith in God." The curriculum includes a six-month course in Islamic studies. The official motto of the army is: "Faith, Piety and Jihad in the Way of Allah."[208] It is worth noting that it was Pakistan's army that created and supported the Taliban government in Afghanistan in the mid-1990s.

According to Seymour M. Hersh, a veteran journalist, the militancy and the influence of fundamentalist Islam has grown by leaps and bounds. In the past, military officers, politicians, and journalists routinely served Johnnie Walker Black during their talks, and drank it themselves. But now, even the most senior retired army generals offered him only juice or tea, even in their own homes. Officials and journalists said that soldiers and middle-level officers are increasingly attracted to the preaching of Zaid Hamid, who joined the mujahideen and fought for nine years in Afghanistan. On CDs and on television, Hamid exhorts soldiers to think of themselves as Muslims first and Pakistanis second.[209]

The Pakistani government had no control over the terrorist training camps, as they were run by ISI, Pakistan's equivalent of the CIA. The ISI works independently of the government and gets several billion dollars every year from illegal drugs, using poppy cultivated along the Pak-Afghan border. Under pressure from the United States, the Pakistani government tried to bring the ISI under civilian control in 2008, but they were forced by the army to withdraw this decision.

As discussed previously, the Saudi government did not fund the Afghan mujahideens directly in their war against the Soviets; instead, Saudi businessmen financed them. Because of the Saudis' involvement, the Pakistani army and its ISI were indoctrinated into Wahhabism, the radical form of Islam followed by Saudis. Apart from this, the US administration also funded or trained mujahideens via Pakistan's ISI and Pakistan's army. Therefore after the Soviets left Afghanistan, Pakistan used the training facilities of Afghan mujahideens for training Kashmir militants.

It is very difficult for any Pakistani government to control the Islamic militants and the army, as anti-India culture runs deep in Pakistan. In general, they blame India for the dismemberment of Pakistan in 1971 when India liberated East Pakistan in a war lasting just two weeks. From

March to December 1971, the West Pakistani Muslim army massacred more than three million Bengali-speaking East Pakistani Muslims. This genocide was brought to a halt only when India invaded East Pakistan and liberated it from the West Pakistani military dictators, resulting in the formation of the new nation called Bangladesh. Because of the genocide, India had more than ten million refugees from East Pakistan.

The ISI had an indirect, longstanding relationship with al-Qaeda. They even used al-Qaeda camps in Afghanistan to train their own covert operatives to serve as terrorists against India. In 2000, due to American anxiety over the link between the ISI and various militant groups in Kashmir as well as with the Taliban, President Clinton was surrounded by extraordinary security on his trip to Pakistan in 2000.[210] Air Force One arrived in Pakistan empty while another small unmarked plane, carrying the president, arrived separately, after which his motorcade stopped under an overpass, and Clinton changed cars.[211]

The ISI has created several militant groups, such as Jaish-e-Mohammad and Lashkar-e-Taiba, in order to fight a low-cost war in Indian-held Kashmir. The membership of Lashkar-e-Taiba, an anti-India Islamic militant group, extends to about 150,000 people, according to a midlevel officer in ISI. Together with another jihadi group, Jaish-e-Muhammad, the Lashkar loyalists could put Pakistan "up in flames," the officer admitted. According to Bruce Riedel, who led President Obama's review of Afghanistan and Pakistan policy in 2009, "Lashkar-e-Taiba and Al Qaeda are allies in the global Islamic jihad. They share the same target list, and their operatives often work and hide together."[212]

ISI is now outsourcing terrorist activities to Bangladesh's intelligence agencies. According to Startfor, a US intelligence news and analysis agency, the ISI is working with Bangladesh's intelligence agencies to facilitate cooperation between northeast India's militant groups and other jihadist outfits in South Asia.[213]

Pakistan, which had served as a conduit for billions of dollars in arms from the US government to the mujahideen, has today become a victim of its own complicity. While the Soviet-backed Najibullah government did indeed collapse in 1992, modern American weaponry pervades Pakistani cities such as Karachi and Lahore, making them battlegrounds for gang wars. Poor Afghans sold this weaponry, including rapid-fire rifles, AK-47s, grenades, land mines, rockets, rocket launchers, and rocket-propelled grenades to the indigenous, independent tribals living along the Afghan-Pakistan border. The United States made no attempt to collect these weapons, and so both Afghanistan and Pakistan were deluged with them. As a retired Pakistani army lieutenant general said, "Pakistan developed a sort of Kalashnikov culture. Weapons became a power symbol for politicians and others."[214]

In a September 2001 interview, Haji Ahmad Khan Kukikhel, chief of the one-hundred-thousand-strong Kikikhel tribe in the North-West Frontier Province, said, "The Americans are to blame for all these weapons of terror. We used to have single shot rifles. Now we have automatics and 10,000 people have died in the tribal areas as a result. In this province we can get everything except the atomic bomb."[215]

Pakistan's dismal education system is blamed for the growth of the madrassas, the breeding ground for the suicide bombers. Pakistan spends only about 2 percent of its GNP on public education, one of the lowest rates in the world and just behind Congo in UN Development Program rankings. Government-run schools are generally considered horrendous. They often lack teachers, books, electricity, running water, and even roofs.[216] The Islamic madrassas are two-room ramshackle huts with tin roofs and run usually on alms provided by affluent members of Pakistani society. Besides being free, the madrassas provide two meals a day, and two sets of clothes and a pair of shoes every year.[217]

Madrassa students are expected to memorize the entire Quran—hundreds of pages—a task that on average takes students about three years. There is little time for other studies. A 1995 study by the government found that only 5 percent of elementary school children could pass a basic quiz in reading, writing, and arithmetic. About 1.5 to 1.8 million boys attend these schools. Many reach fifteen years of age having learned nothing but the Quran.[218] In Gujar Khan, a town thirty-five miles from Islamabad, for example, about fifty madrassas are functional, compared with fewer than ten government educational institutions.[219]

Larger madrassas, however, underwent a dramatic change after the Soviet invasion of Afghanistan, when policy planners in Islamabad, Saudi Arabia, and Washington realized the schools could provide good foot soldiers to fight the Russians. In the 1980s, madrassas received millions of dollars in aid from Western and wealthy Arab nations, and some of them blossomed into huge complexes. Teachers at the schools, earlier too poor to buy bicycles, were seen driving expensive cars and in the company of armed bodyguards. They got a further boost in the mid-1990s, when the madrassa-educated Taliban took control of 90 percent of neighboring Afghanistan.[220]

Pakistan has its own share of people like Rush Limbaugh, Glenn Beck, and other Christian televangelists, in the form of Amir Liaquat Hussain and Hamid Mir. According to Mr. Mir, Pakistan can become a superpower and even place a man on the moon within five years if left unmolested by the United States, Jewish Israel, and Hindu India. He advocates for the conquest of India by Pakistan. He also reminds them about their glorious past of having thousands of years of Islamic empires that ruled on three continents as well as in South Asia.

Recently there is a sea change in the Islamic militancy in Pakistan, which does not bode well for its own existence. According to Pakistani investigators, despite a crackdown on al-Qaeda's command structure, which has yielded significant arrests, the terrorist organization is finding new recruits in the middle class and is forming smaller cells. Terrorist cells "are multiplying with the crackdown on al-Qaeda," said Tarid Jamil, Karachi chief of police. Educated, middle-class Pakistanis run many of these new groups, rather than the madrassa students who have been associated with Islamic extremism in Pakistan in the past. Militant groups have regularly recruited from seminaries inside Pakistan's tribal areas, but traditionally have had less success in Pakistani cities.[221]

Talibanization of Pakistan is already under way. A large area near the Pakistan-Afghanistan border is already under the Taliban's control, and they are also trying to impose sharia rules in major cities of Pakistan. The number of suicide attacks in Pakistan exploded in 2007, going from four in 2005 and seven in 2006 to fifty-six in 2007. In 2007, suicide bombers killed 759 people, including 230 security personnel, and injured 1,685.[222] In the first eight months of 2008, there were twenty-eight suicide bombings in Pakistan, killing more than 471 people. By comparison Iraq saw forty-two such attacks and 463 deaths; Afghanistan had thirty-six incidents and 436 casualties.[223] In 2009, there were eighty suicide attacks in Pakistan, killing 1,217 people and injuring 2,305. Although the number of suicide attacks reduced to fifty-two in 2010, a total of 1,224 people were killed and 2,157 were injured in these attacks.[224]

The brazen attack by a group of highly trained militants with night vision equipment on a heavily guarded naval base in Karachi, Pakistan, in 2011, close to a facility where some of Pakistan's nuclear weapons are stored, raises a big question as to how long it will take for militants to get hold of nuclear weapons. In their attack, they destroyed two antisubmarine and maritime surveillance-capable P-3C Orion aircrafts received from the United States.

There is a growing danger that Pakistan's nuclear bombs or technology for manufacturing a dirty bomb may fall into Islamic militant hands. China originally transferred nuclear weapons and missile technologies to Pakistan because it wanted to keep India tied down in its own subcontinent. In response to five Indian nuclear tests in early May 1998, Pakistan announced that it had successfully conducted five nuclear tests the same month. Pakistan had no indigenous missile program, but in the early 1990s it acquired the short-range M-11 from China. Then, in the late 1990s, it received the medium-range *No Dong* from North Korea, renaming it the *Gauri*, and in exchange provided nuclear bomb technology to North Korea.

Because Pakistan's civilian government is doing whatever the United States wants, most probably Pakistan's nuclear bombs are under US control, and if there is any chance for Pakistan to fall to Islamic militants, the United States will destroy its nuclear bombs and missiles. But if Pakistan's nuclear bombs are not under US control, it becomes a matter of grave consequence. Pakistan's ISI is hand-in-glove with the Taliban, as the Taliban is its brainchild. There is still a significant section within the ISI that supports the Taliban, and the ISI has opened new training centers inside Pakistan to give training to Taliban recruits. The Taliban also receive money and sophisticated arms to fight in Afghanistan. The ISI funds itself independently of the Pakistani government, as mentioned, from the illegal drug trade, from which it takes in several billion dollars yearly. Although Islamic militants are not so popular in the cities, they have a following in the villages. They may be able to team up with the ISI and overthrow the civilian government, which would give them control of Pakistan's nuclear bombs and missiles. This would be a complete disaster for Western countries, Israel, and India … Armageddon. Pakistan's Gauri III, which is actually the North Korean *Taepodong-1* missile, has a range of three thousand kilometers (1,875 miles). Apart from this, Pakistan has several other nuclear-capable missiles as well.

According to the 2011 *Foreign Policy* magazine's Failed States Index, Pakistan ranks twelfth. There may be scenarios in which the United States and other Western nations want to see Pakistan, the mother of all Islamic terrorism, divided into four or five smaller countries so that its ISI can no longer promote worldwide jihad. These scenarios include:

(1) If there are several suicide bombings or car bomb explosions in crowded US malls (or even in European countries), subways, or airplanes, resulting in a number of casualties, and all these can be linked to the ISI of Pakistan;

(2) The United States faces a chemical, biological, or radiological attack, and it leads to Pakistan; or

(3) Islamic militants take over Pakistan and are in a position to obtain control of its missiles and nuclear weapons.

In these circumstances, the United States and other Western countries may provoke India into attacking and dismembering Pakistan. Pakistan has four provinces—Punjab, Sindh, Balochistan, and the North-West Frontier—as well as the Pakistan-administered portion of Kashmir called Azad Kashmir. All provinces except Punjab already have strong separatist movements. In my 1995 article, I wrote, "We might see a fragmented Pakistan … with an independent Kashmir formed by the merger of Indian Kashmir and Pakistani Kashmir."[225]

India has recently experienced several instances of terrorist activity, all sponsored by the ISI of Pakistan. In November 2008 terrorists, all trained in Pakistani terrorist camps, attacked ten different places in Mumbai, killing 178 people and wounding 308. On March 7, 2006, twenty-eight were killed and 101 were wounded in two simultaneous bombings in the Hindu holy city of Varanasi. On July 11, 2006, 209 people were killed and more than 700 were wounded in seven bomb blasts occurring over seven minutes on seven different trains in Mumbai.

On May 18, 2007, fourteen people were killed and thirty-five were wounded by bombs at a historic mosque in Hyderabad. On August 25, 2007, forty-four people were killed and more than fifty were injured in twin blasts, again in Hyderabad. In November 2007, three bombs went off simultaneously in courthouses in three cities in the state of Uttar Pradesh, killing thirteen people and injuring another sixty-one. Ten to fifteen years ago, these types of terrorist activities were limited to the troubled region of Kashmir only, but now these bombings are happening all over India, with no end in sight.

Thus, if the United States and other Western nations ask India to attack Pakistan and dismember it, India may take the risk, though if war were to occur it might become a nuclear war. But it would end a major headache for India, as Pakistan's ISI is creating terror all over India. Because of Islamic militancy, more than half of India's army has been deployed in Kashmir for two decades, and fighting the militants costs India several billion dollars annually, money that could otherwise be used for development work.

India need not physically liberate all four or five regions of Pakistan in order to dismember it, as once the bulk of the Pakistani army, which is mainly Punjabi Muslims, is defeated, the United States and other Western countries can complete the task, similar to the division of Yugoslavia. Although China will resist the division of Pakistan, it may allow the division if Islamic fundamentalists take over the reins. According to the journal *Stratfor*, Pakistan's nuclear arsenal is already under US control. After 9/11, the United States delivered a very clear ultimatum to Musharraf: unless Pakistan allowed US forces to take control of Pakistani nuclear facilities the United States would be left with no choice but to destroy those facilities, possibly with India's help.[226] If Pakistan's nuclear arsenal is under US control, then India will not have to worry at all, as the United States will destroy them (and also destroy capabilities to manufacture them) once they take the decision to divide Pakistan. According to a recent report, the United States has a "snatch and grab" plan for the Pakistani nuclear arsenals. In the process of dismembering Pakistan, however, India may have to lose its portion of the Kashmir Valley, where Muslims are in a majority, though not the Jammu and Ladakh regions, where Hindus and Buddhists are in a majority, respectively.

10

• ◆ •

EMERGENCE OF ISLAMIC EMPIRE
AND MODERNIZATION OF ISLAM

Until 2010, nobody would have thought of the drastic changes happening in Middle Eastern and North African Islamic countries, dubbed Arab Spring. After the fall of dictators such as Hosni Mubarak of Egypt, Ben Ali of Tunisia, Ali Abdullah Saleh of Yemen, and Muammar Gaddafi of Libya, every ruler in this region now looks vulnerable. As mentioned earlier, following the dissolution of the Islam-centered Ottoman Empire after World War I, Britain and France created most of the about forty nations we know there today and installed client rulers. Later on, a number of these rulers were ousted in coups, and at that time coup leaders were hailed as liberators. But these military dictators did not bring any radical changes. All the countries in these regions are now unstable and are facing Islamic militancy. Al Qaeda is not limited to Afghanistan and Pakistan only; rather, it has become a franchise. The combination of religious medievalism and sociopolitical instability indicates a transitional period is under way.

There are several Islamic hotspots around the world, including Israel-Palestine, Kashmir, Lebanon, Iraq, Chechnya, Xinjiang (in China), the Philippines, Indonesia, Kosovo, and Thailand. The most crucial among them are the Israel-Palestine issue and Iraq because Islamic militants worldwide are exploiting them to recruit new militants. Like the Treaty of Versailles, which caused the rise of Hitler and World War II but also resulted in lasting peace in Western Europe and successful independence movements in Africa and Asia, the creation of a tiny country, Israel, in the geographic heart of Islam, as well as the US-led 2003 invasion of Iraq, will ultimately give birth to the modernization of Islam worldwide.

Modernization of Islam

After the collapse of the Ottoman Empire at the end of World War I, then colonial powers Britain and France were the main power brokers in the Middle East. After World War II, the region was divided into two by the new superpowers, the United States and the USSR. The new military dictators, Nasser in Egypt, Qasim and later on Saddam Hussein in Iraq, Gadhafi in Libya, and Assad in Syria, became the front men for the USSR-led group. The remaining regimes, appointed by Britain and France, were either neutral or joined the US-led group. Of course, Israel was the main point man for the latter. After the decisive win by Israel in the 1967 Six-Day War, the Soviet group started to crumble, and finally Egypt under Sadat decided to sign the Camp-David peace treaty in 1980 when it realized that militarily it could not get its lost land, especially Sinai. The defection of Egypt, previously the strongest Soviet supporter in the region, ended the Soviet influence in the region. For the last thirty-plus years the United States has been the main power broker in the region.

Until the 2003 Iraq War, the United States (and its Western allies) was being able to impose its will, through carrots and sticks, in almost all the countries in the Middle East and North Africa, barring countries such as Iran and Syria. But the Iraq War turned out to be a disaster for the United States for its image in the region as well as for its financial capability for any future war because now it does not have money to take another large-scale military adventure anywhere. Besides Iraq, Israel, Egypt, and Jordan are the three largest recipients of direct aid from the United States. Israel, though one of the twenty richest countries in the world, receives more than $3 billion, or one-third of total direct US aid, which amounts to $500 per Israeli annually. Egypt and Jordan get $2 billion and about $450 million, respectively, each year from the United States. Bahrain is home to the administrative headquarters of the US Navy's Fifth Fleet. There are significant US military installations in Middle Eastern countries such as Saudi Arabia and Kuwait.

Syria was forced to withdraw its fourteen thousand troops from Lebanon under UN Security Council Resolution 1559, passed after the assassination of Rafik Hariri, former prime minister and billionaire, in February 2005. The United States and France played an instrumental role in the withdrawal of Syrian forces. After their withdrawal, the United States gave $280 million in military aid to the pro-Western Lebanese government in order to undermine Hezbollah.

In 2003, the Bush administration invaded Iraq, claiming that they would bring democracy in Iraq. But it was a bogus pretense because none of the regimes, except Turkey, supported by the United States, was following democracy. Their main reason was to get rid of Saddam Hussein, who was against the United States. However, reforms cannot be imposed by an outside force. They have to come from within.

The 2010 self-immolation by Mohamed Bouazizi, a Tunisian street vendor, in protest of the confiscation of his wares and the harassment and humiliation, became a catalyst for the drastic changes in the entire Middle East and North Africa. A majority of the population in almost all these countries is under thirty, as shown in Table 10.1. In the era of the Internet, these young people have come to know about the tremendous progress being made elsewhere. They view their countries as far behind when compared to others, and they blame their rulers for their backwardness. In their revolutions, they are being helped by technologies such as Facebook and Twitter, which help to sustain the organizing of these movements.

Table 10.1 Median Age and Population Under 30 in Certain Muslim Countries

Arab Country	Median Age	Population Under Age 30
Yemen	18	73%
Iraq	21	68%
Syria	22	66%
Jordan	22	65%
Oman	24	64%
Egypt	24	61%
Libya	24	61%
Saudi Arabia	25	61%
Morocco	27	56%
Algeria	27	56%
Kuwait	28	54%
Lebanon	29	51%
Tunisia	30	51%
UAE	30	49%
Bahrain	31	48%
Qatar	31	48%
All Countries	26	63%

Source: Slackman, Michael, "Arab spring's youth movement spreads, then hits wall," *The New York Times*, March 17, 2011.

Through September 2011, the Arab Spring resulted in the overthrow of dictators in Egypt, Tunisia, Yemen, and Libya. Almost all other rulers look shaky and hence they are trying to mollify their population by giving more powers to elected representatives or by providing monetary sops. The Moroccan king has unveiled his plan to make his country a constitutional monarchy with a democratic parliament. But the king will still be the head of the powerful army. Saudi Arabia is spending $130 billion raising salaries and building houses to silence its critics.

Egypt and Turkey were the two main pillars of the US policy in the region. Until the present Islamist government in Turkey, both the secular military and the government in Turkey were pro-Western. Turkey has the second-largest army in NATO, after the United States. There are signs that Egypt may unilaterally withdraw from the 1978 Camp David accords and form an alliance with Turkey.

The evolution of the Arab Spring in various countries has shown that the United States and its Western allies are no longer capable of influencing this movement. Instead, the people behind the Arab Spring in a country are using the United States and its allies to capture power. In almost all Middle East and North African countries, an Islamic fundamentalist party, being the largest opposition group, will take over. These Islamist regimes will try to impose sharia rules.

In December 2008, the Taliban captured the Swat valley, which used to be considered "the Switzerland of Pakistan" due to its great natural beauty. Instead of fighting the Taliban, the Pakistani government signed a peace accord with them in February 2009 and agreed to the imposition of sharia law in Swat and suspended military offensives against them. The Taliban set up its own parallel government in Swat valley. They have enforced strict radical Islamic rules such as a ban on female education, closing all video stores, and a ban on cutting beards. They have closed all the girl schools and burnt hundreds of them. In April 2009 the Taliban captured the Buner valley, just sixty miles from Pakistan's capital, Islamabad. Then General David Petraeus, commander of US Central Command, said that Pakistan's civilian government might fall to the Taliban. He gave only six weeks to Pakistan's civilian government to show some results. Under pressure from the United States, Pakistan's army went on the offensive against the Taliban with full force, even by dropping paratroopers from helicopters. By May 2009, the army was able to clear the Buner valley and part of the Swat valley of the Taliban. This led to a humanitarian crisis, as 150,000 to 200,000 civilians had to flee the war zone. Although the army was able to get control of some part of the valley, they were not able to kill or capture a substantial number of Islamic militants, as most of them just fled from the area.

Pakistan's civilian government and army obey US orders, as they are getting a substantial amount of money as well as military hardware from the United States. The economy of Pakistan is in very precarious condition, and it needs IMF loans to survive. Without foreign aid, its economy would collapse. Once the US economy collapses, Pakistan's economy will be nowhere, leading to the collapse of its civilian government, and its army's will have to fight the Taliban. Also, the United States will not be able to impose its will on Pakistan if it does not have economic or military clout. This will give a free hand to the Taliban in Pakistan.

It was only under US threat that Pakistan abandoned the Taliban, when after the September 11, 2001, terrorist attacks the United States decided to overthrow the Taliban government in Afghanistan. The then US deputy secretary of state, Richard Armitage, threatened General Pervez Musharraf, the then Pakistani leader, that he had to decide whether to be with America or with the terrorists, and that if he decided to go with the latter, Pakistan should be prepared to be bombed back to the Stone Age. Only then did Musharraf abandon the Taliban.[227]

Although some people in the United States, especially Republicans, claim the drastic reduction in the number of deaths of US soldiers in Iraq as the US victory, actually anti-US forces are just waiting for the United States to withdraw the bulk of its forces. By removing Saddam Hussein, the United States has virtually given control of Iraq to its archenemy Iran. Hence the United States cannot claim it as a victory.

According to Bob Woodword, the US troop "surge" of 2007, in which President Bush sent nearly thirty thousand additional US combat forces and support troops to Iraq, was not the primary factor behind the steep drop in violence there during the past sixteen months. He wrote that overall four factors were responsible for reducing the violence: the covert operations, the influx of troops, the decision by militant cleric Moqtada al-Sadr to rein in his powerful Mahdi Army, and the so-called Anbar Awakening, in which tens of thousands of Sunnis turned against al-Qaeda in Iraq and allied with US forces.[228] His assessment was based on talks with several senior American officials.

Apart from this, ethnic cleansing of Sunnis by Shiites was an important factor for the reduction of violence in Iraq. According to a study published in September 2008, satellite images taken at night showed heavily Sunni Arab neighborhoods of Baghdad began emptying before a US troop surge in 2007, graphic evidence of the ethnic cleansing that preceded a drop in violence. This study was led by geography professor John Agnew of the University of California Los Angeles. The images support the view of international refugee organizations and Iraq experts that a major population shift was a key factor in the decline in sectarian violence, particularly in the Iraqi capital, the epicenter of the bloodletting, where hundreds of thousands were killed. Minority Sunni Arabs were driven out of many neighborhoods by Shiite militants enraged by the bombing of the Samarra mosque in February 2006. Agnew's team used publicly available infrared night imagery from a weather satellite operated by the US Air Force. According to their report, the overall night light signature of Baghdad since the US invasion appeared to have increased between 2003 and 2006 and then declined dramatically from March 20, 2006, through December 16, 2007. The report said the night lights of Shiite-dominated Sadr City remained constant, as did lights in the Green Zone government and diplomatic compound in central Baghdad. Satellite studies have also been used to help document forced relocations in Myanmar and ethnic cleansing in Uganda.[229]

Using Vietnam as an example, some people claim that after the withdrawal of American troops Iraq will fall to Islamic militants but that the damage will be limited to Iraq only. In other words, other Middle Eastern nations will avoid Iraq's fate because of the failure of a domino effect to materialize after the fall of South Vietnam and the withdrawal of US troops in 1973. However, a major difference separates the two situations. In the case of Vietnam, communists lacked sufficient political power in any other country in East or Southeast Asia. In the Middle East, however, almost all countries have Muslim majorities, face active Islamic militancy, and are governed by pro-Western rulers disliked by the majority of the people. If free and fair democratic elections were to be held in any of them, Islamic militants would win. This has already occurred in the 2006 Palestinian elections (Hamas), the 1992 Algerian elections, the 2005 Egyptian elections, the 2002 and 2007 elections in Turkey, and 2011 Tunisian and Egyptian elections when Islamic militant parties won a significant number of seats. Although after the invasion the United States installed secular politicians in the

Iraq Interim Government, most lost to fundamentalists in the 2005 general elections.

Parts of South Asia are following a similar trajectory. Half of Afghanistan is already under the Taliban. The Talibanization of Pakistan is already under way as the Taliban are controlling large areas near the Pakistan-Afghanistan border, and they are trying to impose strict sharia rules in major Pakistani cities. In the 2008 Pakistani elections, the two main opposition parties, the PPP and PML(N), won the majority of seats and formed the government. But the top leaders of these two parties are well known for corruption, and it is just a matter of time before Pakistanis become disenchanted. In the past this has led to military dictatorships, yet Pakistan could fall to the mullahs.

After the withdrawal of the bulk of US troops and also the collapse of the US economy, Iraq will erupt in a free-for-all. Turkey, Iran, and Saudi Arabia will interfere by funding militias, leading to chaos.

Because of religious insurgency, Iraq, Afghanistan, and Pakistan may fall to Islamic fundamentalists. If this happens, it will set off a domino effect throughout the Islamic world, particularly in the Middle East and North Africa. Apart from this, the Arab Spring will result in Islamic fundamentalist parties coming to power after elections in these countries.

Due to economic woes, the United States will be unable to support its allies in the Middle East and North Africa either economically or militarily. The US military will suffer the same fate as that of the early-1990s USSR, when Soviet submarines and aircraft carriers rusted in their dockyards, and most ended up on the scrapheap. Following a US economic crash and the subsequent global economic depression, the intensity of Islamic militancy will surge. Economic depression will make it easier for militants to take over Islamic countries, as large-scale unemployment and acute poverty coupled with corruption in high places produce militancy.

The aforementioned domino effect will cause one after another of the pro-US and pro-Western governments in Islamic countries to fall into the hands of Islamic militants, especially in the Middle East and North Africa (in Saudi Arabia, Jordan, Algeria, Yemen, Morocco, Kuwait, Afghanistan, etc.). These radical regimes may also try to reestablish the caliphate. Here I would like to quote from my 1995 article: [230]

After the fall of oil-rich countries like Saudi Arabia to radical Islamic militants, Islamic clerics will try to establish an Islamic empire like the old Ottoman Empire.

The United States and other Western governments will impose economic embargoes against these regimes and isolate them, creating tremendous hardship for the people there. This strategy may be successful. Saddam Hussein's Iraq and Muammar al-Gaddafi's Libya are two recent examples of the success of this approach. It forced Saddam to destroy all his WMDs, and Gaddafi had to give up his two intelligence officers for the 1988 bombing of Pan Am Flight 103 as well as his WMDs. Hamas in Palestine is another example. After the January 2006 legislative elections, Hamas won a majority of seats and formed a government in March. But after the United States and EU boycott of the Hamas-led government and stoppage of funding, the government was unable to provide salaries to tens of thousands of Palestinian government employees for several months, leading to chaos.

The Islamic militants may rule for some time, say ten to twenty years (maybe even forty to fifty years), but they will never be able to turn the clock back in the present digital age (i.e., they cannot impose a seventh-century Arabian culture on the twenty-first-century population of Facebook, Twitter, etc). In the end these militants are bound to be overthrown by homegrown secular "modern-day Kemal Ataturks," i.e., when ordinary people fail to find relief from radical Islamic regimes they will force a change in leadership. These Kemals will inaugurate drastic social and religious changes, and the West will help them financially.

It is important to note that Turkey was the seat of the Ottoman Empire for six centuries, with Istanbul as its capital. Beginning in 1517, it also claimed to be the seat of the caliph, the highest Islamic authority. Kemal Ataturk dramatically altered this state of affairs in a very short span of time, however, after taking the reins of Turkey under the Treaty of Lausanne in 1923. The dynasty was abolished, and the sultan was banished. The caliphate, the spiritual and political leadership system of the Islamic world, begun after the death of Prophet Muhammad in 632, was abolished in 1924. Kemal introduced several radical political, legal, cultural, social, and economic reforms. Islamic courts were closed. In the new constitution, European laws and jurisprudence were adopted. The Turkish administration and educational systems were thoroughly secularized and modernized. The "fez," a hat worn by men introduced by Sultan Mahmud II as part of the empire's dress code in 1826, was banned, and people were encouraged to wear European dress. It became illegal for women to wear a veil or headscarf. Women were given the right to vote and own property, a right even women in several Western countries were denied at the time. Even the script was changed, and the old alphabet based on the Arabic script was replaced by one based on the Roman script used in the West.

Out of necessity, Kemal Ataturk had to take the drastic steps in modernizing Turkey after watching his country fall behind the Europeans in every aspect, whereas until the emergence of the Industrial Revolution in Europe in the eighteenth century, the Ottoman Empire was ahead of the Europeans, as described in chapter 8. In the age of swift communication technology directly available to the people, such as Facebook and Twitter, the younger generation will force the new rulers in the Islamic countries, which are right now far behind most countries in every respect, to take drastic steps like Kemal Ataturk took. The establishment of the modern Turkey was a product of World War I, the first war that left scars on the entire global population and in which millions lost their lives. Hence a drastic change in the Islamic countries, especially in the Middle East and North Africa, will not be an easy affair, and this change will take place only after a violent shake-up in these countries. Also, it will leave scars in several non-Muslim countries, especially those having sizeable Muslim population. This tremendous shake-up will be due to the struggle between the Islamic fundamentalists, especially the old guard, who will try to establish Islamic regimes based on Islamic tenets, and the new generation, who will find that the Islamic regimes are taking backward steps.

Although the present Turkish government of the Justice and Development Party, an Islamic party, is trying to get rid of the secular laws, the country will not turn back the clock in the Internet age. Turkey can never become an Islamic country like Saudi Arabia or Pakistan because the majority of its population will not accept it.

If there is no external threat or the administration is not imposed or supported by the United States or outsiders, then people will vote for political parties that will work for their development. In the 2008 Bangladesh elections, the secular Awami League-led Grand Alliance decimated its rivals by huge margins by getting 261 out of 300 seats in the National Assembly, with the Awami League taking 230 seats. The rival alliance led by BNP could get only twenty-seven seats. BNP's Islamists ally Jamaat-e Islami wiped out in the elections, with all its major leaders suffering humiliating defeats and the party getting only two seats as compared to seventeen seats in the last elections, held in 2001.

On a microscale we are witnessing this phenomenon in the North West Frontier Province (NWFP) of Pakistan also, where the top al-Qaeda leaders, including Ayman Al Zawahiri, are hiding. In the 2002 elections, Islamic parties won forty-six out of ninety-six provincial parliamentary seats and formed the government. But as they mismanaged the government and were more interested in enforcing sharia rules than providing water, health facilities, and girls' schools in this tribal area, they could win only nine seats in the 2008 elections and lost to the secular Awami National Party. But again the Taliban, who are supported by some factions within Pakistan's ISI, captured this area by attacking Pakistan's army posts and killing prominent secular Muslim leaders. Hence there is a long way to go.

The road to modernization for other Muslim nations may be less democratic. During this period of transformation, the United States, Europe, including Russia, India, and Islamic and other countries will in fact see increased Islamic terrorism, including suicide bombings. Although the transition may take several decades and be marked with violence, in the end Islam will no longer be the guiding force behind politics in the Middle East or North Africa. It is worth noting that it took almost three and a half decades (from 1914 to 1945) for Europe to make the transition from its remaining monarchies to vibrant democracies. Until the early 1900s, nobody was predicting that democracy would replace kingdoms in most of Western Europe, or that African and Asian countries would gain independence within five to six decades.

The worst is yet to come in countries like India, where there is a large Muslim population (140 million), and there is lack of modern technology of monitoring system and street-level intelligence, which countries like the United States have. India is going to witness terrorist attacks in major cities similar to the attacks on two prestigious hotels in Mumbai in 2008. The United States has a danger from homegrown terrorists (i.e., converted Muslims).

If Iran is able to produce the nuclear bomb, then it is certain that Saudi Arabia will also get it, as Saudi Arabia considers Iran a worse enemy than Israel. Saudi Arabia does not need to develop nuclear bombs. Instead it will just buy them, either from Pakistan or North Korea, who are ready to sell any technology, nuclear or missile, for hard cash. Egypt may also follow Saudi Arabia to get nuclear bombs. Hence, as soon as some or all of these countries fall to Islamic fundamentalists, it will be just a matter of time before militants will get hold of these bombs, and they will not hesitate to use them against countries such as Israel and India, or European countries, or even against China. In this case, the ensuing events will dwarf the number of people killed during World War II and can be termed as Armaggedon.

Economic collapse will also lead to a steep drop in oil demand and a crash in oil prices. This will lead to economic chaos in Middle Eastern countries such as Saudi Arabia, Iran, Iraq, Syria, and the UAE, whose economies rely on exporting oil, and further strengthen the hands of Islamic fundamentalists there. If militants take over a majority of these oil-producing nations or damage major oil-producing infrastructures, crude oil prices may also rise. These are two completely different scenarios, and we do not know which one will prevail or whether they will cancel each other out, changing the price of oil little.

Once Islam loses the patronage of people in power, it will gradually modernize and become more tolerant toward women and non-Muslims. After some time, Muslims will start to follow the spiritual aspects of Islam more than its social and militant aspects and sharia. Religions such as Christianity and Hinduism went through this transformation several centuries ago. Now it is time for Islam to do the same.

It is very difficult to predict the exact sequence of events that will lead to the modernization of Islam in these Islamic countries. In 1900, nobody would have been able to predict the exact sequence of events that would have led to the collapse of kingdoms in Europe, leading to the vibrant democracy in Western Europe, with most Asian and African countries getting independence from their colonial masters within five to six decades. Right now we are witnessing a rise of Islamic militancy globally, and with the collapse of US economy, Islamists are going to take over in a number of countries. As suggested earlier, if one discards the divinity aspects of the Muhammad's revelations (i.e., his revelations were not divines), the Quran is just the social practices of seventh-century Arabia, and it cannot be imposed on the twenty-first-century population for a long period of time. Hitler also tried to turn back the clock (i.e., he tried to create a thousand years of the Third Reich, but it lasted only a decade or so). Instead of achieving his goal, Hitler worked as a catalyst for the speedy collapse of the colonial empires as well as European kingdoms. Similarly, the present global rise in Islamic militancy is going to work as a catalyst for the modernization in Islam. Although these types of events result in the death of a large number of innocent people, they speed up the process of the changes in human civilization (i.e., the changes that would have taken several centuries to occur, take only a few decades).

11

•◆•

Multipolar World Order

The Japanese economy was constrained by the size of its population, and once labor costs increased in Japan, production units started shifting to low-wage East Asian countries. This constraint is absent in China and even in India because of their vast populations. At the end of the economic crisis, the world will become multipolar, with six superpowers—the United States, India, the European Union, Japan, China, and Russia. If China plays its cards carefully, then it may emerge as the strongest of them all. Countries such as Brazil, South Africa, and Indonesia should also emerge as regional superpowers due to their large populations and the size of their economies.

Table 11.1 shows the changing fortunes of selected countries, according to a 2007 Goldman Sachs report, over the next forty years. By 2050, China, the United States, and India will have the top three economies in the world, and the Chinese economy will be nearly twice that of the other two. Among the BRIC nations, the economies of China and India will thrive due to their large consumer base, whereas the Russian economy will thrive due to its vast natural resources. Only Brazil has the capabilities to become an economic power due to its consumer demands and natural resources.

Once projected to be the number one economy in the world, the Japanese economy is right now on decline. Due to the graying of its population and also its large public debt because of spending trillions of dollars in stimulus money in the 1990s, its economy will continue to lag behind other leading world economies. Still, it will be a global economic superpower, and it may become a regional military superpower too.

After China, the European Union will become the dominant economic player in the world. The European Union will exert its influence in the Middle East (for oil) and Latin America because of their historical connections. After the 1956 Suez fiasco, which caused the United Kingdom and France to lose their superpower status, the United Kingdom has aligned itself with the United States on international forums.

If after the collapse of the US economy, the United Kingdom leaves the US camp and aligns itself with the EU on international forums, then it will be a great loss for the United States, and, on the other hand, it will strengthen the hands of the EU globally. In 2010, France and Britain signed a military cooperation pact, including joint simulated warhead testing and research in their facilities and to form a five-thousand-member joint expeditionary force, and to make the two countries' aircraft carriers compatible for use by each other's warplanes. This shows that Britain has already started to look past its special relationship with the United States.

In any future war between two major countries, hackers will play a major role in deciding the outcome of the war. Software now plays a major role in nearly every sphere of military operations. By sending malicious codes, one can disrupt the communication as well as military satellites of its enemy. These codes can also disrupt the financial systems. Although every now and then the United States blames countries such as China for hacking its civilian and military computers, the United States itself may be doing it on a larger scale against its potential enemies both to gain information and to probe the weaknesses on their networks. Also, the countries may have already planted computer programs on each other's computers and networks that will disrupt the system once activated remotely.

Table 11.1 **GDP of Selected Countries** (*in Billions of U.S. Dollars*)

Rank 2050	Country	2050	2040	2030	2020	2010
1	China	70,710	45,022	25,610	12,630	4,667
2	US	38,514	29,823	22,817	17,978	14,535
3	India	37,668	16,510	6,683	2,848	1,256
4	Brazil	11,366	6,631	3,720	2,194	1,346
5	Mexico	9,340	5,471	3,068	1,742	1,009
6	Russia	8,580	6,320	4,265	2,554	1,371
7	Indonesia	7,010	3,286	1,479	752	419
8	Japan	6,677	6,042	5,814	5,224	4,604
9	UK	5,133	4,344	3,595	3,101	2,546
10	Germany	5,024	4,388	3,761	3,519	3,083
11	Nigeria	4,640	1,765	680	306	158
12	France	4,592	3,892	3,306	2,815	2,366
13	South Korea	4,083	3,089	2,241	1,508	1,071
14	Turkey	3,943	2,300	1,279	740	440
15	Vietnam	3,607	1,768	745	273	88
16	Canada	3,149	2,569	2,061	1,700	1,389
17	Philippines	3,010	1,353	582	289	162
18	Italy	2,950	2,559	2,391	2,224	1,914

Source: *BRICs and Beyond*, Goldman Sachs, November, 2007

Some recent hackings show the destructive nature of malicious software codes. In 2009, hackers were responsible for several power outages in Brazil. In April 2009, US government officials claimed that hackers hacked into the power grid and left computer programs that can be used later on to disrupt services. In April 2010, traffic of highly sensitive US websites, such as the Senate, NASA, and the offices of the secretary of defense and the Commerce Department, was routed through China for eighteen minutes. During those eighteen minutes, China Telecom, a Chinese government telecommunications firm, sent incorrect routing information that told US and other foreign Internet traffic to travel through Chinese servers. It was reported in October 2011 that since 2009 US drones have been found to have a virus that comes back again once removed, and its origin (i.e., who has created this virus and for what purpose) has not yet been found. The drones, unmanned serial vehicles, are used to monitor the enemies, and some of these drones, having capabilities to fire missiles, have been successful in killing senior al Qaeda members.

China

With $3 trillion FOREX, China is flexing its muscle by challenging the US domination of global financial rules. China has urged the IMF to create a "reserve currency" based on shares in the organization held by its 185 countries, known as special drawing rights (SDR). China loans money everywhere, from Asian countries such as Cambodia, Thailand, Laos, Myanmar, and the Philippines to Ethiopia and Angola in Africa. Nearly half of China's direct foreign investment, about $100 billion in 2010, goes to Latin America. China is training a number of Latin American military officers. Chinese companies have been purchasing key assets and signing long-term deals in Russia, Iran, Brazil, Australia, and Venezuela.

China is way ahead of any other country, including the United States, in green technology. The windmills for the United States are made in China. Almost half of the components of new nuclear plants in the United States are coming from China, as the United States does not manufacture them.

By 2035, according to the International Energy Agency, China will be using a fifth of all global energy, a 75 percent increase since 2008. It accounted for about 46 percent of global coal consumption in 2009, the World Coal Institute estimates, and consumes a similar share of the world's aluminum, copper, nickel, and zinc production. In 2010 China used twice as much crude steel as the EU, United States, and Japan combined. Such figures translate into major gains for the exporters of these and other commodities. China is already Australia's biggest export market, accounting for 22 percent of Australian exports in 2009. China buys 12 percent of Brazil's exports and 10 percent of South Africa's. It has also become a big purchaser of high-end manufactured goods from Japan and Germany. Once China was mainly an exporter of low-price manufactures. Today it accounts for fully a fifth of global growth. [231]

China has become Australia's number one trading partner. Due to its mineral exports to China, the average income in the state of Western Australia has increased sevenfold, from $10,000 to $70,000, in just five years. Western Australia, with Perth as its capital, is five times the size of Texas and holds the bulk of Australia's mineral wealth. Its unemployment is only 2.6 percent, whereas the national average is 5.5 percent. Despite having this close commercial relationship, the Australian government is building up its military, the largest buildup since World War II, and China is the main reason, according to a Ministry of Defense report.[232]

In the very near future, China is going to become a player in commercial airplanes also, competing with the US Boeing and European Aerospace company Airbus. By 2016, China will start production of its 156-seat passenger plane C919. GE Aviation, Eaton Corp., Parker Aerospace, Honeywell, and Rockwell Collins Inc. are participating with China in this project. China required them to set up joint ventures with Chinese firms. Half of Boeing's as well as Airbus's airplanes already have "Made in China" components. In China about six hundred thousand workers are in aerospace, which is the same figure as in the United States currently.

China's exponentially growing economy is changing the alignments, especially in East Asia, in politics as well as defense. In 1996, when the United States dispatched two carriers to the Taiwan Straits in response to China lobbing missiles over Taiwan, Australia supported the United States under the Australia, New Zealand, United States Security Treaty (ANZUS), an alliance that determines when each country will engage in war on behalf of another member. But due to the soaring business between China and Australia, Australian participation during any crisis between China and the United States is now doubtful. In 2004, Australian Foreign Minister Alexander Downer said during a press briefing in Beijing that under ANZUS, Australia was obliged to invoke the treaty only if there was a direct attack on any member's soil. When he was confronted by a US State Department aide the next year, however, he retreated from his statement.

In the early 2000s, Australia was viewing China as an emerging economic power, and Chinese growth would help propel its own economy. But now the Australian government sees China as a potential enemy. *Defending Australia in the Asia Pacific Century: Force 2030*, a 140-page white paper released by then Australian Prime Minister Kevin Rudd in May 2009, cautioned the country to raise its defense expenditure by a considerable amount to counter the growing military capabilities of China. In 2011, the United States announced that it would station twenty-five hundred troops in Australia permanently.

Due to its enormous FOREX reserves, China is able to influence countries all over the world. When twenty-two Chinese Muslims fled to Cambodia for political asylum in 2009, Cambodia sent them back to China despite protests from United States. Two days after their deportation, China signed fourteen deals with Cambodia worth $1 billion. Due to pressure from China, South Africa denied a visa in 2011 to the Dalai Lama when he had been invited by fellow Nobel Peace laureate Archbishop Desmond Tutu to attend his eightieth birthday celebrations. It was the second time in two years that South Africa denied him a visa.

China is the second-largest defense spender, after the United States. In 2010, China's defense expenditure was $114 billion, 2.2 percent of its 2009 GDP, whereas these numbers for the United States were $698 billion (which includes Iraq and Afghanistan expenses also) and 4.7 percent of GDP. Since the late 2000s, there is a phenomenal growth in Chinese military capabilities. China has state-of-the-art fighter jets from Russia, such as the Su-30s, and has Russian S-300 surface-to-air missile systems that are among the best aircraft-intercepting systems in the world. In January 2007, China successfully destroyed one of its own defunct weather satellites with a ballistic missile. In September 2006, it was reported that, using a ground-based laser, it temporarily blinded a US reconnaissance satellite tracking over China. China has a five thousand kilometer network of tunnel complexes to hide its nuclear weapons and forces, providing a massive second strike capability.

China is in the final stage of testing its carrier-killing land-based missile called Dong Feng 21D, capable of penetrating the defense of even the most advanced moving aircraft carrier at a distance of more than nine hundred miles. If China is successful in developing this missile, the United States will think twice before sending its aircraft carriers in case of a war over Taiwan. The Chinese navy is now becoming a blue-water fleet, capable of operating on the open seas. China's development of the stealth fighter is years ahead of US predictions. In 2011, China launched its first aircraft carrier, a refurbished ex-Soviet aircraft carrier that it had bought in 1998. Before the sale, Russia had stripped it of all military equipment as well as the propulsion systems.

China financed 80 percent of the $250 million in construction costs of Pakistan's second major deep-water port at Gwadar, in southwest Pakistan. After the Indian blockade of Pakistan's only major port, Karachi, during their 1971 war, Pakistan desperately wanted this second port constructed. The new port may become a major shipping center for Chinese trade with Central Asia. It may also serve as a base for Chinese submarines and surface ships to project Chinese might in the Indian Ocean, Eastern Africa, Central Asia, Western India, and the Middle East. Apart from Gwadar, China has invested in ports in Sri Lanka, Myanmar, and Bangladesh as well. China also expanded the Karakoram highway connecting China and Pakistan across the Karakoram mountain range through the Khunjerab Pass, built in the 1980s as the world's highest paved international road, at fifteen-thousand-foot-high mountain passes.

Some recent Chinese provocative actions against its neighbors have rung alarm bells all over the world. In 2010 Japan impounded a Chinese ship that strayed into the waters of disputed islands, but it had to release the ship and its captain after China barred the sale of rare earth minerals, important minerals in the electronics industry. China controls more than 90 percent of world rare earth minerals although it has only 37 percent of world proven reserves.

In a major escalation of tension with India, China has been giving visa on stapled sheet on the Indian passport to the residents of the disputed regions of Kashmir and Arunachal Pradesh. China views the growing alliance between the United States and India as a threat. In recent years, the number of US military exercises with India exceeds that of any other country.

One potential flash point for war between China and its neighbors are the 250 disputed islands in the South China Sea, having an area of 1.4 million square miles. Many of these islands are naturally under water at high tide, and some of them are permanently submerged. The dispute behind these tiny islands is because the areas around them hold huge oil and gas reserves beneath the seabed. Whoever possesses these islands will own the natural resources surrounding them. China wants to talk separately with each claimant, whereas all others favor a regional settlement. There are five main island chains (names of claimants of whole or part of the island chains are written in brackets):

(1) Spratly Islands (China, Taiwan, Vietnam, Malaysia, Brunei, and the Philippines)

(2) Paracel Islands (China, Taiwan, and Vietnam)

(3) Pratas Islands (China and Taiwan)

(4) Macclesfield Bank (China, Taiwan, and the Philippines)

(5) Scarborough Shoal (China, Taiwan, and the Philippines)

The Spratly Islands consist of more than one hundred small islands or reefs with a total land area of ten square kilometers in the South China Sea. All the islands are coral, low, and small, about five to six meters above water, spread over 160,000 to 180,000 square kilometers of sea. They are claimed in their entirety by China, Taiwan, and Vietnam, while portions are claimed by Malaysia and the Philippines. About forty-five islands are occupied by small military units from China, Malaysia, the Philippines, Taiwan, and Vietnam. The South China Sea is rich in natural resources such as oil and natural gas. Minor military confrontations among these countries have taken place over some of these islands in the past couple of decades, but the probability that they will turn into a full-scale war is small.

After being defeated by the communists, the nationalists, or *Kuomintang* forces, escaped to Taiwan in 1949. From 1949 to 1987, Taiwan was governed under martial law and one-party rule. Initially, local Taiwanese had no say in the government. First, Chiang Kai-shek (1949–75) and then his son, Chiang Ching-kuo (1975–88), ruled as president. Chiang Ching-kuo began to liberalize the political system, however. In 1984, he selected Lee Teng-hui, a native Taiwanese, to be his vice president. In 1987, he lifted martial law. After Chiang's death, Lee Teng-hui took over as president and began to democratize the government and give more power to local Taiwanese. In 1996, he was elected president in the island nation's first-ever presidential election. In the 2000 presidential election, Chen Shui-bian was elected as the first non-Kuomintang president, and he was reelected in 2004 to serve his second and last term.

China considers Taiwan a renegade province. During the 1996 Taiwan elections, China lobbed missiles over the Taiwan Strait to intimidate the Taiwanese electorate into voting against Lee. China claims that it has every right to invade Taiwan if it tries to be an independent state. China wants it to follow the Hong Kong arrangement (i.e., one country, two systems).

If Taiwan declares independence, China may attack it just to save face, but this would be a disaster for China. Although China might occupy Taiwan after only a week of battle, it will have to deal with a hostile population, resulting in a guerrilla war for the next several years, similar to what the USSR faced in Afghanistan. Its hostile neighbors, as well as the United States, will give all the needed supports to the Taiwanese who would be fighting this guerrilla war. In addition, China would face economic sanctions from the West, including the United States.

Due to its provocative actions, China may drive its neighboring countries, including India, to form a NATO type security alliance. It will be in the interest of China to lay low and let the transition process pass peacefully and emerge as the next superpower; otherwise if it tries to take advantage of a feeble United States with no military capability, say for forcible unification of Taiwan, getting Arunachal Pradesh from India, and/or grabbing some tiny islands in the South China Sea by threatening its neighbors, then the United States and the Europeans will not only destroy China economically (by economic sanctions) but may also dismember it, by creating separate countries like Tibet, Xinjiang, and Hong Kong, and by formally recognizing Taiwan as an independent nation. Although economic sanctions will hurt US and Western countries too, for them it will be worthwhile, as it will destroy China as a superpower.

China may go for war with its neighbor(s) to deflect the economic crisis at home resulting from the global economic depression. Rather than attacking Taiwan, China may take an adventure on grabbing some sparsely populated islands in the South China Sea or some sparsely populated disputed regions from India. But in the end it will be too costly, as afterwards, apart from Western economic sanctions, India may even take this war to the Chinese mainland in desperation.

According to some analysts, economic growth in China, by factors such as power consumption and volume of rail cargo in the country, is much lower than claimed by the government. According a diplomatic cable leaked by Wikileaks, Li Keqiang, then head of the Chinese province of Liaoning and tipped to be China's next prime minister, told the US ambassador in 2007 that China's GDP figure is "man-made" and "unreliable." The economic great depression worldwide is going to take a big toll on the Chinese economy, leading to social unrest, as 35 percent of its GDP depends on exports, and consumer spending constitutes only 36 percent of its GDP, whereas it is two-thirds in the United States.

It is certain that in the era of Facebook and Twitter, China will one day experience a movement like the Arab Spring. The authoritarian communist central government cannot impose its will on the lives of nearly 1.5 billion people in every sphere forever. It is said that China has at least thirty-nine million informants in the country, about 3 percent of its population. By comparison, East Germans had 2.5 percent informants for the Stasi secret police under communism.[233] A prolonged economic crisis may result in the division of China on the pattern of the collapse of the USSR when Yeltsin was able to convince the Russians that Russia was suffering due to shouldering the economic burden of the other fourteen constituent republics in the USSR. It is worth noting that in the Chinese economic miracle since the opening of the economy in 1978, only its eastern coastal regions, having about 10 percent of the entire population, is industrialized, while inland regions are much less developed.

All religions are officially banned in China at present, but it is said that nearly half of the Chinese population practice or believe in Buddhism. Until the 1949 communist takeover, Buddhism had the largest number of followers in the world, with Christianity as the second largest. Hence once China starts to move away from the communistic ideology (that considers religion as "the opiate of the masses") we will see the revival of Buddhism. As China is poised to be the world's military and economic superpower in the very near future, Buddhism may eclipse all other religions and regain the position of leading religion in the world.

It may even make an inroad into India at the expense of Hinduism. During the heyday of Buddhism in India, from the third century BC to the twelfth century AD, there were several large universities, such as Taxila (fourth century to sixth century) and Nalanda (fifth century to twelfth century), that attracted scholars and students from such faraway places as Greece, Korea, Japan, China, Tibet, Indonesia, Persia, and Turkey. Nalanda University was one of the first great universities in recorded history. It had eight separate compounds, ten temples, meditation halls, classrooms, lakes, and parks. It had a nine-story library where monks meticulously copied books and documents so that individual scholars could have their own collections. At its peak, Nalanda provided dormitories for nearly ten thousand students, perhaps a first for an educational institution, and also had accommodations for two thousand professors. It was devoted to Buddhist studies, but it also trained students in fine arts, medicine, mathematics, astronomy, politics, and the art of war. [234] In 1193, it was sacked by an invading Muslim army of Bakhtiyar Khilji, a Turk. The invading army burned thousands of Buddhist monks alive and beheaded thousands in order to uproot Buddhism. They also set fire to the nine-story library, which continued to burn for three months, and the smoke from the burning manuscripts could be seen from hundreds of miles away. Now efforts are under way to revive this grand old university. A consortium led by Singapore and Japan, with funding from India, China, and other nations, have collected $500 million for this purpose.

North Korea

It is important to study the future of North Korea, as it is going to have a long-lasting effect in the volatile region. The North Korean dictatorship is one of the last vestiges of the Cold War era. It survives due to the largesse of neighboring China, which does not want it to collapse because it would unleash a chain of events, beyond of control of China, endangering even the survival of communism in China.

The countries that will be most affected by the future of North Korea—South Korea, Japan, the United States, and China—have no say in this hermit country. The demilitarized zone (DMZ) between the two Koreas is the world's most heavily armed border, with more than two million troops. Any North Korean attack on South Korea would mean an attack on the United States because of the twenty-eight thousand American troops stationed there. The American troops would be wiped out within a few hours of an attack by North Korea's biological and chemical missiles, however. In 2003, plans were announced to move them farther south from the border. The United States may finally withdraw the entire deployment to Hawaii.

The "Great Leader," Kim Il Sung, father of the present ruler, ruled North Korea from 1948 until his death in 1994, and made North Korea the most reclusive country in the world. Until the mid-1970s, its economy outperformed both the South Korean and the Chinese economies, and its per capita income was higher than South Korea's. This changed when Deng Xiaoping dramatically altered Chinese economic policy in the late 1970s, and South Korea became a source of cheap consumer items for the United States, making it one of the four Asian Tigers. After the collapse of the USSR, which was one of North Korea's major trading partners and the main source of subsidized petroleum, food, and arms, and because of declining trade with China due to changes in Chinese economic policy, North Korea's economy collapsed in the 1990s. The collapse of the Soviet Bloc, economic mismanagement, and natural disasters resulted in large-scale famines that decade, with about two million dead. Its economy is growing now, however, partly with the help of South Korea.

North Korea's future can be described in three possible scenarios: unification with South Korea, disintegration similar to that of the USSR, or invasion of South Korea.

Unification: Neither China nor Japan wants a unified Korea with a nuclear capability and a vibrant economy like South Korea's. Japan in particular would not like to see a unified Korea under Chinese influence. Koreans have not forgotten Japanese atrocities during its colonial rule in the first part of the last century. Nor does China desire the collapse of North Korea; it is concerned that a democratic, unified Korea at its border would be troublesome.

Implosion: Due to food shortages and other economic problems, North Korea may disintegrate like the USSR. This would create a massive flood of refugees to neighboring countries South Korea, China, and Japan, as well as the possibility of merger of the two Koreas.

As both Koreas speak the same language and have the same culture, and one out of four South Korean families has relatives in the North, a majority of South Koreans want merger. The cost of unification would run into several hundred billion dollars. The cost of unification of the two Germanys is going to be more than $2 trillion. When East and West Germany reunited, the East had one-fourth the population of the West, and its economy was one-third the size. Even after two decades, the economy of eastern Germany lags far behind its western counterpart. By comparison, North Korea has nearly half as many people as South Korea, but its economy is only 7 percent of the South's.[235] Although since 1969 South Korea has had a Unification Ministry with plans for unification, including about twelve hundred public buildings earmarked for shelter for North Korean refugees, it will be costly and painful for the South.

A merger of the two Koreas will differ from the merger of the two Germanies in other ways as well. In the German case, East Germans had knowledge of the outside world, and their living standard was higher than that of North Koreans. North Koreans have no knowledge of what is happening in other parts of their country, not to speak of the outside world, for fifty years. North Korean radios and televisions are manufactured to receive only one channel, which broadcasts government programming. The government media paints a negative picture of the rest of the world in which North Korea is a heaven and other countries are worse off. Listening to foreign broadcasts is punishable by execution. International calls are prohibited. Mail is censored. All North Koreans wear the same style of shirt. People are required to get travel passes to visit another village. It will be difficult for South Korean authorities to "de-brainwash" them.

Explosion: This nobody wants, but it is likely that the "Dear Leader" will opt for it rather than suffer implosion. American analysts say that if North Korean options are either disintegration of the country due to starvation or an attack on the South, the leadership would opt for the latter. Having seen the disintegration of the USSR and the subsequent fate of its leadership, the North Korean dictator and his generals do not want to see the same happen to them. If they do invade, they will lose little: Death through battle would be preferable to death through implosion.

North Korea took Seoul within three days in 1950. If it does the same now, and takes a substantial area of South Korea, North Korea would have in its hands a bargaining chip against the United States and South Korea, possibly leading to a stalemate. Moreover, China might take the side of the North against the United States in order to retaliate against US intervention in its backyard. This would give China a chance to uproot American forces from East Asia. The Chinese leadership believes that domestic pressure would force the United States to withdraw from the conflict in the event of American deaths.

North Korea conducted its first nuclear test on October 9, 2006. According to US intelligence sources, North Korea has produced up to six or seven nuclear bombs. Unlike other rogue nations, it possesses nuclear bombs in its arsenal. In 1994, the United States and North Korea came close to war over North Korea's secret plan to build nuclear bombs. The countries finally made a deal in which North Korea promised to suspend its nuclear program in exchange for two less dangerous nuclear power plants and fuel oil worth $5 billion, mainly financed by South Korea. The 2007 US-North Korean pact is similar to the Clinton deal that the Bush administration criticized during its first term. Because of the hard-line approach taken by the Bush administration, however, North Korea has built an estimated six to seven nuclear bombs and conducted a nuclear test and missile tests, showing that this policy was a failure. In 2000, South Korea also enriched a small amount of uranium in violation of the Nuclear Proliferation Treaty.

In violation of UN sanctions against North Korea, imposed after its nuclear test, the United States allowed an arms shipment to Ethiopia from North Korea in January 2007 because Ethiopia was fighting Islamic militants in Somalia. Earlier in 2002, when Spain intercepted a ship carrying North Korean Scud missiles to Yemen, which was fighting Islamic extremists, Yemen complained to the United States, and the United States asked Spain to release the ship.

For almost a half-century, South Korea has portrayed North Korean founder Kim Il Sung as a demon, a scoundrel, and a fraud, but recently South Korean textbooks have started giving him credit for combating Japanese colonialism. In 2004, South Korean troops dismantled all loudspeakers and hundreds of signboards near the demilitarized zone that were being used to broadcast propaganda and pop music toward

North Korean troops and rice farmers. In response, North Korea also removed its loudspeakers and signboards.

South Korea is building an industrial park on the outskirts of the North Korean city of Kaesong. It is South Korea's most ambitious effort to gradually narrow the huge economic gap between the two countries. The first phase of the development is expected to include three hundred factories and employ seventy-five thousand North Koreans. According to Hong Soon Jick, an economist at Hyundai Research Institute in Seoul, it will inject $9.6 billion into the North's economy during the project's first nine years. Marcus Noland of the Peterson Institute for International Economics estimates that $1 billion to $2 billion a year is enough to keep the North on "survival rations." Small- and medium-size companies are eager to build factories in this park to get access to cheap North Korean labor to keep them competitive with rivals in China.[236]

In 2010, North Korea was accused of sinking a South Korea Navy ship, resulting in the deaths of forty-six South Korean sailors. In 2010, it fired artillery at a disputed island, killing four South Koreans.

India

Due to its large population, economy, and size, India would be able to emerge as a global player in both the economic and military fields. Among the leading economies, India trails only China in economic growth. The GDP of India is the ninth largest in the world by current prices, but the fourth largest by purchasing power parity (PPP).

In 2007, Goldman Sachs predicted that India's GDP in current prices would overtake Canada, Russia, France, and Italy by 2020, and Germany, Japan, and the United Kingdom by 2030, making it the third-largest economy of the world, behind China and the United States, and by 2050 its economy will be nearly as large as the United States' economy.

Unlike the United States, India has a high savings rate. The government's debt in India is also 80 percent of its GDP, but 90 percent of this debt is owned by its citizens. Of the other 10 percent, a significant amount is long-term debts held by agencies such as the World Bank.[237] In 2010, the external debt of India was $295.8 billion, out of which

$229.8 billion was long-term debt and the rest was short-term debt. The share of government debt in this total external debt was $72.3 billion or 24.4 percent. About 53.9 percent of the total debt was in US dollar-denominated debt, whereas the share of Indian rupee-denominated debt was 18.8 percent.[238]

After the 2008 Great Recession, $80 billion Indian stimulus in 2009–10 (less than 3 percent of GDP) resulted in growth of 6 to 7 percent, whereas China's stimulus was much larger, $585 billion (6 percent of GDP), and still resulted in only slightly higher growth. Hence India was able to weather the global recession without putting its banks at risk (for bad debts).

The bottleneck for India's economic growth is lack of infrastructure, such as transportation and power. Large-scale corruption is also affecting its economic growth. According to a Washington-based Global Financial Integrity study, India lost $213 billion in present value in illicit financial flows during 1948–2008. Based on the short-term US Treasury bill rate for the rate of return on assets, this amount translates to $462 billion, which is twice its $230 billion foreign debt in 2011.

The main engine of Indian economic growth is the growth in domestic consumption, whereas for China it is due to growing exports. India and China import 75 percent and 50 percent, respectively, of their petroleum consumptions. Both these countries are fighting all over the world for petrol and other mineral resources. Due to its $3.2 trillion FOREX, China is leaving India, having only $300 billion FOREX, far behind in this fight.

Seventy per cent of Indian technology markets such as outsourcing, back-office operations, and call centers are dependent on the United States.[239] Consequently, any severe slowdown in the US economy will adversely affect the Indian economy. Exports constitute 24 percent and 35 percent of economies of India and China, respectively. Hence a global economic depression will cost more job losses in China than India. Although India should eke out positive economic growth rates during the coming great depression because of its largely untapped consumer market, it may have a FOREX problem due to its large petroleum import bill unless it comes up with an alternative fuel like ethanol on a massive scale similar to what Brazil has done. One point worth noting is that India has the second-largest arable land after the United States.

The Indian army is the world's third largest, after the United States and China. Its defense expenditures in both total amount and percent of GDP are much lower than the United States and China. In 2010 the total defense expenditure for the United States, China, and India was $698 billion, $114 billion, and $36 billion, respectively, whereas these numbers as the percentage of their GDPs were 4.7 percent, 2.2 percent, and 1.8 percent, respectively.[240]

China has border issues with India. China accuses India of possessing ninety thousand square kilometers of Chinese territory, mostly in Arunachal Pradesh, a northeast state of India. If a senior central minister, like the prime minister, visits this state, then China lodges a protest with the Indian government. In May 2007, India had to cancel the visit of a 107-member-strong delegation of its Indian Administrative Service (IAS) officers to China when China gave visas to 106 of them and refused a visa to an IAS officer of Arunachal Pradesh state, which borders Chinese territory, claiming that as a "resident of China" no visa was needed. Some years ago, China denied a visa on the same grounds to the chief minister of Arunachal Pradesh. In 2009, China tried to block a $2.9 billion Asian Development Bank loan to India on the grounds that part of the loan was going to be used for water projects in Arunachal Pradesh.

During 2006–7, the Indian government reported more than three hundred cases of incursions by Chinese troops along the 4,000 km border. In the first quarter of 2008, there were as many as forty incursions by Chinese troops across the 206 km border along Tibet and Sikkim, a northeast state in India. China has built massive infrastructure along its India border for quick troop mobilization, whereas India has these infrastructure plans only on paper.[241] China is constructing huge blue-roofed all-weather buildings to house its hundreds of its soldiers during winter. Without any provocative episode or infrastructure built up by India in these sparsely populated areas, the massive infrastructure built by China in a very short duration points to some ulterior motive.

In 2011, Indian officials confirmed the presence of the Chinese army near the Siachen Glacier and in Pakistan-controlled Kashmir. Since April 1984, India and Pakistan have been fighting on the Siachen

Glacier in the Himalayas, the world's highest battlefield, overlooking the strategic Karakoram highway between Pakistan and China. At its highest point, the Siachen Glacier is 5,753 m (18,875 ft.) above sea level. The chance that this will explode into a full-scale war between the two countries is small, however.

China no longer views Jammu and Kashmir as part of India. According to India, they have 3,488 km common border with China, but in the last decade China has been claiming it to be only 2,000 km, as it does not consider 1,500 km in Kashmir to be part of it. In certain parts of Ladakh in the Kashmir state of India, a disputed area between India and China, the Indian government stopped construction of roads and buildings in 2010 after objections from the Chinese military. India does not want to repeat the mistake committed by its first prime minister, Jawahar Lal Nehru, in the early 1960s to provoke China. In 2011, China has deployed advanced solid-fueled CSS-5 MRBMs, replacing liquid-fueled CSS-2 IRBMs, on the Indian border.

In 2010 India suspended all military exchanges with China after it denied a visa to a top Indian general posted in Kashmir. At the end of 2010, Chinese Premier Wen Jainbao's visit to India deliberately omitted the statement supporting the one-China policy, which refers to Taiwan being a part of China, although in the past India agreed to have this statement in communiqués. China typically demands to have a statement about one-China policy in joint communiqués.

Islamabad has been asking the Karzai government in Afghanistan to ditch the United States and align with China. But China may not agree to a tripartite agreement with Pakistan and Afghanistan because if the Taliban get a foothold in Afghanistan it will worsen the Islamic militancy in its resource-rich Xinjiang. For a July 2011 deadly attack in Xinjiang, resulting in the killing of thirty people, China blamed a Pakistani-trained Islamic militant group.

China is building a "strings of pearls" around India, building ports in Pakistan, Sri Lanka, and Burma. In response, India is reopening an ex-British naval base in the Maldives to station its surveillance aircrafts, helicopters, and ships with radars all across the Maldives. In Tajikistan, India has built a small air base, which it is also using. It is India's first military base in a foreign country. Despite objections by China, India has started gas exploration in the South China Sea with Vietnam.

One potential bone of contention between India and China may be the sharing of water of the rivers originating in Tibet. China has been constructing several dams in the catchment area of the mighty eighteen-hundred-mile-long Brahamputra River, which originates from south Tibet and flows from there to the Arunachal Pradesh and Assam, two states in India, and finally into Bangladesh, where it empties into the Bay of Bengal. This river is considered to be the lifeline of the two Indian states and Bangladesh. According to some experts, China is going to divert Brahamputra to flow north toward its parched Gobi Desert, making the portion of the river in India and Bangladesh run dry.

By giving India access to international technology for its nuclear power industry in exchange for access to international inspections, the United States is trying to use India to contain China. As already mentioned, the number of US military exercises with India in recent years surpasses that with any other country. Although due to China India is aligning with the United States for mutual benefits, India will continue to have a historically close relationship with Russia. After the joint development of Sukoi Su-30MKI, a heavy, all-weather, long-range fighter, India is collaborating with Russia in the development of the fifth generation stealth jet fighter, Sukhoi PAK FA, T-50 being its initial prototype.

Keeping China in mind, India is in final stages of developing a series of ballistic missiles to strike targets at 3,500 km and more. In April 2007, India successfully tested its new, nuclear-capable Agni III missile, with a maximum range of nineteen hundred miles, putting China's major cities into range as well as the Middle East and most of Asia. In November 2011, it successfully tested the Agni-IV missile, which can hit targets up to 3,500 km. The Agni-V ballistic missile, capable of striking targets up to 5,000 km away, is in the final stage of development, and tests are expected in 2012.

As discussed earlier in this section, China may take an adventure in grabbing some of the sparsely populated disputed areas from India. India, an emerging economic and military superpower, is the only country that can match Chinese firepower in Asia. By defeating India, China will try to send a message to its neighboring countries and the

Western powers, especially to the United States, that they will have to play according to the rules dictated by China.

India is not a position to win a localized war in these areas. Hence it would be in the interest in India to widen the war by taking the fight to the Chinese mainland, as India's then prime minister, Lal Bahadur Shastri, did during the 1965 India-Pakistan war. Shastri decided to invade Pakistan all along the India-Pakistan border when he realized that India could not win a localized war in Kashmir. Although India cannot win the war by taking it to the Chinese mainland, it will leave scars in both China and India. Although this war will be a short one, it will result in the deaths of tens of thousands, maybe more, in both countries. Deaths of this many people in mainland China will cause a serious crisis, as the Chinese will blame their own government for these deaths. On the other hand, if the war ends in a stalemate, the Indians will see themselves and their government as victims and blame China for the numerous deaths in India. Apart from this, any Indian governing political party will not want to be identified as a loser in an Indo-China war, as they then will be out of power for several decades. Therefore, it is in the best interest of India to send signals to China at every international forum that in any attack in disputed areas, it will widen the war and take it to mainland China. This will make China think twice before it decides to initiate any adventure against India in disputed areas.

In late 2011 it was reported that Australia made a proposal of a trilateral security arrangement with the United States and India, which received positive response from India, although India denied the existence of any such proposal. After getting such a strong Chinese response to its impounding of a Chinese ship in 2010, it is in the best interest of Japan also to join a security pact with India, Australia and the United States. Russia also should explore a bilateral security arrangement with India because it may have to face a confrontation with China over Far East Russia in the future, as discussed in the next section. As Russia's economy depends on oil and natural gas exports, any sharp decline in their prices due to the coming global economic depression will throw the Russian economy into turmoil similar to the 1998 crisis, when its currency collapsed, and it defaulted on debt payments. This will make Russia vulnerable to Chinese aggression in

Far East Russia. A security arrangement between Russia and India will deter China from invading either of them because it cannot fight a war with these two major countries on two fronts at the same time.

Russia

Russia is flexing its muscles because of its oil and natural gas exports. With oil prices at $14 a barrel in 1998, Russia defaulted on debts worth more than $40 billion, and its currency was drastically devalued. Russian public debt was running at 96 percent of GDP in 1999, declining to 9 percent in August 2006. Due to the rise in oil prices, Russia has paid debts that were not due until 2020.[242] Its foreign currency and gold reserves are the third largest in the world.

Right now Europe gets 42 percent of its gas, a third of its oil, and a quarter of its hard coal from Russia. According to European commission estimates, by 2030 Europe will be importing 84 percent of its gas needs, up from 61 percent at present. In order to reduce dependence on Russia, the Europeans are working on six energy projects, which include two "absolute priorities" to connect the three post-Soviet Baltic states of Lithuania, Latvia, and Estonia to the European power grids and to forge ahead with the so-called "southern gas corridor," which is supposed to transport gas from the Caspian basin to Europe, bypassing Russia and Iran.[243]

In 2008, Russia thrashed its small neighbor Georgia in a limited war, resulting in the Russian recognition of the independence of two small enclaves, South Ossetia and Abkhazia. The main reason for this war was to show who controls the Caucus gas pipelines. The United States has had hundreds of its army trainers in Georgia training the Georgian army for the last several years.

Almost 80 percent of Russia's exports are natural resources such as minerals and oils. Hence a global economic depression will throw the Russian economy into turmoil. By using its FOREX reserves, Russia needs to indigenously develop the new technologies as well as get them from the Western countries, to modernize its Soviet-era industry.

Out of ten Soviet-era army units, only one survived. After decades of decline and witnessing its shortcomings in the 2008 Russo-Georgian war, Russia has announced a $650 billion massive spending program to procure one thousand new helicopters, six hundred combat planes, one hundred warships, and eight new nuclear-powered ballistic missile submarines. The Russians have already signed an agreement with France to purchase two $750 million Mistral helicopter transporting amphibious ships and two more Mistral ships to be constructed in their own shipyards. The development of their fifth generation stealth fighter F-50, also called Sukhoi PAK FA, is in its final stages. India is paying part of the cost of the development of the F-50.

A major confrontation may arise, however, in Far East Russia, where Russia has a sparse and declining population. Although area-wise it is one-third of Russia, its seven million people are only 5 percent of Russia's population, and just across the border there are three Chinese provinces with one hundred million people. Russians started leaving this area for better living conditions after the social welfare system collapsed following the Soviet Union's breakup. Farmers and factory owners, as well as administrative officials, have been inviting Chinese workers from across the border to fill empty job spots as a result. About 250,000 Chinese live there now. In a couple of decades, they will become the predominant ethnic group in the area. If the situation remains the same, China may want to possess the mineral-rich Russian Far East in the future.

12

•◆•

CONCLUDING REMARKS

The US trade deficit has been more than $600 billion per year for the last several years. Basically, the United States has been printing dollars and giving them to other nations. Apart from this, its cumulative public debt (i.e., budget deficit) is unsustainable. This cannot go on forever. Due to increasing trade deficits as well as budget deficits, the US dollar and US economy may collapse at any time, which would lead to a global economic depression. European countries are facing a similar economic crisis. Also, casino capitalism, which was creating havoc in Third World countries prior to the 2008 economic downturn, is now doing the same in the United States and Europe. Banks and investors invest in risky places where they can get maximum return, knowing that the IMF and rating agencies will get their investments back.

We can trace the roots of the present problems in the United States, both political and economic, to past administrations. The origin of Islamic militancy lies in US involvement in the funding and supply of modern arms and ammunitions to the Afghan mujahedeen in their fight against the Soviets in the 1980s during the Reagan administration. Being a holy war, this fight attracted Muslims from all over the world. After the Soviets left Afghanistan, this war became a Frankenstein for the United States and other nations.

The Reagan administration is also responsible for the chronic budget deficits. Although President Clinton tried to balance the budget, President Bush turned a projected $5+ trillion budget surplus into trillions of dollars in deficits. No administration will be able to control the ever-increasing trade deficit, however, and it will ultimately cause the US economy and global economy, as well as capitalism, to collapse.

After economic collapse in the United States, consumer prices will skyrocket as goods formerly manufactured in other countries will have to be manufactured domestically owing to the crash of the dollar and its sudden uselessness as a medium of foreign exchange. Domestic manufacturing firms will have to be restarted, and common people will be hit hard by the price shocks. It is then that people will try to find answers for their misfortune. As suggested earlier, the major media, which now avoid giving a true picture of the economy, will become a part of the ensuing upheavals and will play a major role in bringing about fundamental changes in the United States.

If the American scientific community comes up with another information technology type scientific innovation within the next few years or so, then the country can temporarily delay the collapse of its economy for another decade or two, as it did during the 1990s. During the 1990s, the advent of information technology created millions of jobs in the United States. It helped the Clinton administration to balance the budget and even having a budget surplus during its last years. But finally, due to the self-destructive nature of capitalism, the country would face the same bleak scenario as it is facing right now because Wall Street would force firms to send most of the newly created jobs overseas.

Six decades after World War II, most of Europe is moving toward unification, something unimaginable just a century ago. Similarly, although pundits try to explain the present worldwide rise in Islamic militancy in terms of Huntington's theory of a clash of civilizations, it is actually for the modernization of Islam and is a major step toward the integration of human civilization, during which moribund social structures will meet their demise. The current situation in many Islamic nations resembles that of Europe between World Wars I and II. Those two world wars changed the socioeconomic and political environment of Europe; Islamic militancy will change the Middle East and North Africa. Although fundamentalist Islamic states and powerful Islamic clerics will be the losers of a Cold or Third World War, Islam as a religion will emerge victorious and shed its seventh-century image, becoming a newer, twenty-first-century religion more tolerant to women and non-Muslims. At the end of this crisis, Islam will cease to be the guiding force in countries where it now makes policy, and a majority of Islamic nations will become secular and democratic like Turkey. Despite the approaching socioeconomic chaos, human civilization can expect a bright future.

Capitalism is not feasible

Since the 1980s, the US economy is been thriving due to foreign investment. Had the United States not imposed its financial hegemony on the post–World War II global economy via the 1944 Bretton Woods accord, which made the US dollar a global currency, the United States would have been in the same category as countries such as India, Thailand, South Korea, Indonesia, and South Africa, as the United States would not have been able to print its currency to fund its budget and trade deficits. The USSR collapsed in 1991 because of the inherent weaknesses of communism; i.e., totalitarian government and economic inefficiency. Had crude oil prices increased or had German banks decided to finance Gorbachev's reforms in the way Japan financed Reagan's deficits, the Soviet Union and communism most probably would still be with us today. The theory that this collapse occurred due to Reagan's policies is simply propaganda by conservative pundits and members of the Republican Party. Had Japan not financed American deficits in the 1980s, the US economy and capitalism might have collapsed before communism.

Two seemingly unrelated facts also suggest inherent deficiencies in capitalism and suggest that capitalism is not feasible in the long run. First, in the latest high school textbooks in Shanghai, Mao Zedong, the former communist dictator responsible for the deaths of tens of millions of Chinese, is mentioned only once—in a chapter on etiquette. The new standard world history text has eliminated wars, dynasties, and communist revolutions in favor of colorful tutorials on economics, technology, social customs, and globalization. J. P. Morgan, Bill Gates, the New York Stock Exchange, the space shuttle, and Japan's bullet train are all highlighted. The book even includes a lesson on how neckties became fashionable. The French and Bolshevik revolutions, once seen as turning points in world history, now get far less attention. Mao, the Long March, colonial oppression of China, and the Rape of Nanjing are taught only in a compressed history curriculum in junior high.[244]

Second, the percentage of workers in the American agricultural sector was reduced from 40 percent of the total workforce in 1900 to only 3 percent in 1999.[245] The percentage of manufacturing workers was reduced from 35 percent of the workforce in 1953 to 14 percent in 1999.[246] With automation and the increase in productivity that it brings, the number of workers required in the manufacturing sector as well as the service sector decreases.

The first fact tells us that China has accepted the death of communism and expects a future in capitalism. The second tells us that because over time a nation's manufacturing sector requires fewer hands, capitalism will in the long run fail in China too because of its large population. China has far too many people to employ to be able to overcome the unemployment resulting from the capital-intensive as opposed to labor-intensive techniques demanded by capitalism's profit motive and framework of competition.

Although the economies of both China and India are booming right now, they will also face large-scale unemployment as rural workers continue to migrate to urban areas due to the decline of rural economies. For the huge populations of these countries this will be a catastrophe, since right now the majority of Chinese and Indians are mostly rural, and the political and economic structures of those nations will be unable to handle the massive deluge of jobless poor clamoring for work in the only places where it is available, the cities. Therefore capitalism in the present form is not at all feasible.

Corruption in the Political System

Although individual corruption is low in the United States (as persons who commit illegal acts may expect to be caught) a corrupt political-business nexus does exist, but of a different type than the one we find rampant in India and other Third World countries. As politicians in the United States need a lot of money to run for an elected post, they have to accept donations from multinationals and the ultrawealthy. Once elected, politicians work more for these multinationals and the ultrawealthy, and less for the benefit of the average citizen. Though politicians receive only peanuts—a few thousands of dollars—in donations, their benefactors get millions, if not billions, of dollars from them in budgets and other government provisions such as tax breaks and no-bid contracts. The American political system has forced politicians to become corrupt in this way, which can better be described as systemic rather than the personal form it takes in some developing countries. Allegations of large-scale government corruption in advanced democracies such as Italy and Japan have been responsible for the fall of governments as well. This type of corruption is similar to the political corruption in Third World countries like India, except that in the US politicians legally give government funds to multinationals and the ultrawealthy via legislative procedures. Nevertheless, instead of such masked legality, this money should go the development of the country and decreasing the budget deficit or the national debt, instead of going to those who are already well-off. Although Republicans are at the forefront of this type of corruption, most Democrats also have to engage in it, as they need money to get elected. This is one of the main reasons why large corporations have been successful in sending millions of jobs overseas irrespective of whether the presidency and Congress are controlled by Republicans or Democrats. They have purchased the collusion of political officeholders even before taking office. Although common people elect the government and legislatures, the government and legislatures do not work for the common people because politicians need money to win elections, and for this very reason, they work for the ultrarich and for transnational corporations. The Wall Street investors and transnational corporations reward these politicians with millions of dollars by making them corporate consultants and lobbyists after they leave public office.

Due to rampant corruption in every walk of life, India recently witnessed a sizable movement against corruption. Due to the intervention of the Supreme Court, the investigating agencies, such as the Central Bureau of Investigation (CBI), are being forced to investigate corruption charges against senior political figures. The present government, led by the Congress Party that has been in power for fifty-three years out of sixty-four years since India's independence in 1947, is said to be the most corrupt government in the history of the country. The Supreme Court had to intervene to force out government-appointed Central Vigilance Commissioner P. J. Thomas—the top cop to investigate corruption charges in the country—due to pending corruption charges against him. Indians call the CBI "Congress Bachao (Save) Institution," as it has been filing corruption charges against the opposition party leaders, leaders of the anticorruption movement, and political leaders of small parties that are in coalition with the ruling party, but has not filed any charge against the top political leaders of the Congress Party despite pressure from the Supreme Court to do so.

Even if the present anticorruption movement (led by the aged Anna Hazare) in India becomes a success, it will only remove corruption on the personal level, which will certainly provide a big relief to ordinary Indians. But it will not be able to remove the corrupt political-business nexus, which also exists in the United States. For the removal of the corrupt political-business nexus, one needs to bring fundamental changes in the political system.

Main Street has been powerless against Wall Street, as the ultrawealthy people have money to buy the elected officials who pass the laws being used by the ultrawealthy to make money by just clicking a mouse button. Adam Smith's invisible hand has been firmly invested with the ultrarich and transnational corporations, who dictate governments and legislatures in order to create rules and regulations in their favor, thereby distorting the entire economy. They "use" the governments to enable them to make money, but when a government tries to get some of the money back in taxes, these ultrarich and transnational corporations make hue and cry.

This is not only a financial matter; money plays a big role in government policy, too, which on several occasions has hurt a country badly. For example, due to the pro-Israel lobbies the US foreign policy is always pro-Israel, even if it is against US interests.[247] Similarly in the case of the economy, the US policy is always pro-rich even if it is against US national interests, resulting in its archrival China piling up all its debts.

Corruption in politics is an ancient problem. In order to stop the meddling of businessmen in political affairs, Chānakya (350–283 BC) wrote,

> A businessman becoming excessively rich is a menace to the state. Should the king allow anyone to become too wealthy, let him reduce the bulk of his wealth and property through various kinds of direct and indirect taxes, or else, trying to acquire control of the state as a tool for their rapacious exploitation, these Vaeshyas [capitalists] may upset the whole governmental machinery.[248]

Chānakya was an adviser and the prime minister of the first Maurya emperor, Chandragupta (340–293 BC), in India, and architect of the latter's rise to power. Also known as Kautilya, he wrote a political treatise called *Arthahāstra*, and is considered "the world's pioneer economist" and "the Indian Machiavelli."

There should be full state funding of the entire election process so that all candidates have an equal opportunity to present their positions. No individual or private funding of elections should be allowed so that wealthy people will be unable to buy influence or be elected on their own money.

It is an irony that for-sale politicians get only peanuts for their betrayal of the democratic trust compared to the millions and billions of dollars wealthy tycoons and multinationals get in return. For the latter, investing in the political process might be better than investing on Wall Street. They are parasites lodged firmly in the body politic, however, looting government funds, the nation's resources, and the pockets of ordinary Americans with the help of their political cronies. Similar situations resulted in violent revolutions like the 1776 American Revolution, the 1789 French Revolution, the 1917 Bolshevik Revolution in Russia, and the 1949 Communist Revolution in China. At those times, monarchies instead of democracies were the object of revolt. The days of violent revolution are gone, however. We live in the digital age, and the time has come for an intellectual revolution that will unburden us of the drawbacks of democracy. Its present form is a disfigured caricature of what it could be, be it in the United States, the world's wealthiest nation, in India, the world's most populous democracy, or anywhere in between.

Democracy Needs a Tune-up

Like communism, universal political democracy is a relatively new phenomenon. In several Western nations, women were denied voting rights until early in the last century—United States (in 1920), the United Kingdom (in 1928), France (in 1944), and Italy (in 1945). In Switzerland, women obtained suffrage in 1971. In one part of the country it happened as late as in 1990 by central governmental decree.

Although democracy is the best of all "-cracies," it has deficiencies, because of which incompetent persons like Reagan and Bush Jr. can get elected. Democracy in the present form is not truly successful either in the United States, the world's most developed democracy, or in India, the world's largest democracy. More than half of the elected officials in India at both the state and central levels, for example, are noted criminals. Almost 99 percent of Indian cabinet ministers would go to prison if corruption and criminal charges were impartially and vigorously investigated. Democracy needs major reforms.

According to P. R. Sarkar, democracy has two organs—political democracy and economic democracy. Liberal democracy, as defined by Western standards, incorporates political democracy only and fails to recognize its second organ, economic democracy. According to Sarkar's definition of economic democracy, everyone living in a region should have equal rights over its natural resources. Right now both the organs of democracy are controlled by the ultrarich people and transnational corporations (TNCs). Although common people elect the politicians, the elected officials work for the ultrarich and TNCs. Apart from this, the money power brainwashes voters with false propaganda through the commercial media and otherwise. Therefore, due to the nonexistence of economic democracy, Western liberal democracy is a failure everywhere.

As discussed earlier, at the time of independence of the colonies (in Asia, Africa, and elsewhere) after World War II, there was only transfer of political power from the colonial country to a handful of local politicians. Everything else, including the exploitative economic system, remained the same. The new postcolonial rulers were first hailed as liberators and heroes by the common people, but later it was found that these new rulers were in fact worse than the erstwhile colonial rulers because the new exploiters were their own people, who were using the divide and rule policy to remain in power. How could the ordinary people now unify the country to fight exploitation as they did against the colonial power? According to Sarkar, freedom fighters should have fought for both political and economic democracy while fighting against the colonial rulers.

Russia also experimented with the Western form of liberal democracy and saw its fortune sinking during 1990s, when its GDP dropped by more than 45 percent (Figure 12.1). Soviet industrial production fell by 24 percent in World War II, whereas from 1990 to 1998 in Russia it fell by 42 percent, and GDP by 45 percent. Only 2 percent of Russians were living in poverty in 1989. By 1998 that number had leapt to 24 percent. From 1992 to 1994 life expectancy of Russian males dropped from 63.8 to 57.7 years. Female life expectancy dropped from 74.4 years to 71.2 years.[249] In 2004, the life expectancies for Russian males and females were 58.6 and 73 years, respectively.[250] After the collapse, people and industries resorted to bartering, since they were strapped for cash. One glass firm, Bor Glassworks, traded glass for autos with a big Russian automaker. Bor in turn used the autos to settle up with its sand suppliers. Another customer, a factory near Moscow once owned by the Singer sewing machine company, paid for Bor's glass with sewing machines, which were then given to employees in lieu of wages.[251]

In the United States, incompetent persons like Ronald Reagan and George W. Bush win elections and become president of the world's superpower because of massive media propaganda using hundreds of millions of dollars donated by big corporations and the ultrarich. People like Reagan and Bush Jr. are not capable to make decisions that are in the "best interests" of the country. Any realistic president would try to control the soaring national budget deficit for the long-term interests of the country. For this reason, despite having said, "Read my lips: no new taxes" during the 1988 Republican National Convention, President George H. W. Bush (Sr.) raised taxes in the 1990 budget in order to reduce the deficit. Further, not only did President Clinton balance the budget, his administration had budget surpluses during its final two years. Incompetent persons like Reagan and Bush Jr., on the other hand, ran the nation into massive financial black holes by gifting tax cuts to the rich. When the economy booms and there is a budget surplus, their administrations gave tax cuts to corporations and wealthy people, claiming that the extra money belonged to all Americans. But when the economy was in recession, they gave tax cuts to corporations and wealthy people, claiming that they were needed to jump-start the economy. It can be seen in any economic situation, therefore, who their administrations really worked for. The loser was always the average American.

Figure 12.1 **Russia GDP Growth**

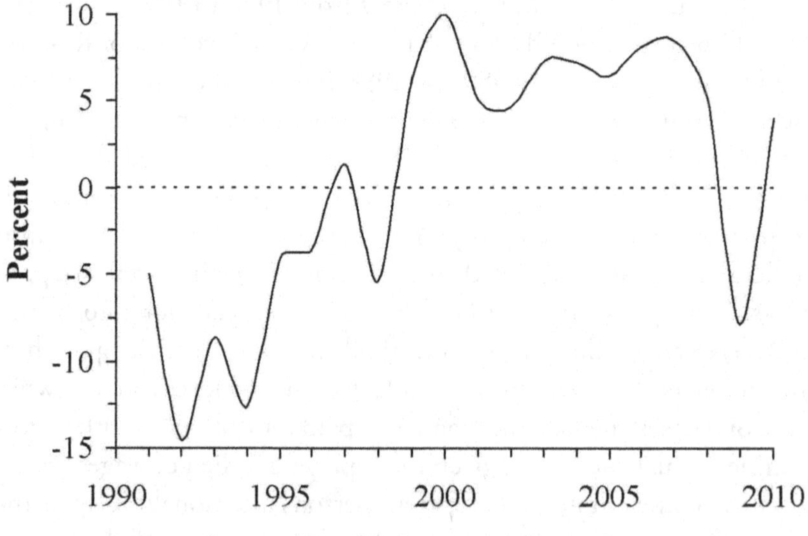

Source: *World Economic Outlook* , IMF

According to Peter W. Galbraith, until two months before President Bush ordered troops to invade Iraq in March 2003, he was unaware that there were two major sects (Sunni and Shiite) of Islam.[252] Galbraith is former US ambassador to Croatia and is a son of the late economist J. K. Galbraith. It seems astonishing that a president would lack this knowledge before taking such an important step. After the 1991 Gulf War, the United States had created the northern and southern no-fly zones in Iraq precisely on this basis: the southern zone had been created to protect Shiites from the Hussein regime, which was Sunni.

On the other hand, on September 12, 2005, the *Wall Street Journal* ran an article entitled "President Bush Is 'Average,' but Far From Ordinary." In it James Taranto, editor of OpinionJournal.com (the online editorial page of the WSJ) ranked Bush nineteenth among forty presidents and in the average category, ahead of both his father, George H. W. Bush, and Bill Clinton. In an article published in 2004, Taranto even wrote, "George W. Bush could eventually end up joining the ranks of the greats."[253]

Though some pundits would like to place Ronald Reagan in the "near great" category, the truth is that had there been no Japan, which financed the US debt during his tenure of office, Reaganomics would have collapsed. Nor did the collapse of Soviet communism occur because of his policies. Communism has inherent weaknesses, as discussed in earlier chapters, and collapsed for economic and financial reasons. Let us see what Henry Kissinger says about Reagan:

Reagan knew next to no history. He treated biblical references to Armageddon as operational predictions. Many of the historical anecdotes he was so fond of recounting had no basis in fact, as facts are generally understood. In a private conversation, he once equated Gorbachev with Bismarck, arguing that both had overcome identical domestic obstacles by moving away from a centrally planned economy toward the free market. I advised a mutual friend that Reagan should be warned never to repeat this preposterous proposition to a German interlocutor.

The details of foreign policy bored Reagan. He had absorbed a few basic ideas about the dangers of appeasement, the evils of communism, and the greatness of his own country, but analysis of substantive issues was not his forte. All of this caused me to remark, during what I thought was an off-the-record talk before a conference of historians at the Library of Congress: "When you talk to Reagan, you sometimes wonder why it occurred to anyone that he should be president, or even governor. But what you historians have to explain is how so unintellectual a man could have dominated California for eight years, and Washington already for nearly seven."[254]

Reagan did, however, want to avoid nuclear war:

No one could "win" a nuclear war. Yet as long as nuclear weapons were in existence they would always be used ....

My dream, then, became a world free of nuclear weapons ....[255]

According to his biographer, Lou Cannon:

Speaking as if he were describing a movie scene, he related a terrifying episode in the Armageddon story where an invading army from the Orient, 200-million strong, is destroyed by a plague. Reagan believes that the "plague" was a prophecy of nuclear war, where "the eyes are burned from the head and the hair falls from the body and so forth." He believes this passage specifically foretold Hiroshima.[256]

Reagan came close to realizing his dream of a world free of nuclear weapons in 1986. During the Reykjavik Summit with Soviet General Secretary Gorbachev, Reagan committed the United States to destroying all its ballistic missiles and abolishing all nuclear weapons. It was a nightmarish situation for senior US administration officials. The Reykjavik deal failed, however, because Gorbachev linked the deal to a ban on the Strategic Defense Initiative (SDI, also called "Star Wars"), which Reagan resisted. When Gorbachev started insisting on a ban on SDI testing for ten years, Reagan left the room, and the talks collapsed. Years later, when Kissinger asked a senior Gorbachev adviser who had been present at Reykjavik why the Soviets had not settled for what the United States had already accepted (the destruction of all ballistic missiles within ten years and the abolition of all nuclear weapons), he replied: "We had thought of everything except that Reagan might leave the room."[257]

The SDI was proposed in 1983 and entailed using ground- and spaced-based systems to protect the United States from nuclear ballistic missiles. It is still nonfunctional twenty-eight years later. Emphasis later shifted from national missile defense to theater missile defense and from global to regional coverage. Had Gorbachev known at the time that Star Wars was just a fictional idea and incapable of being implemented, he would have accepted Reagan's deal, and the United States might have had to undergo a disaster worse than the 2003 invasion of Iraq. Without its ballistic missiles and nuclear bombs, the United States would have lost its superpower status, and its allies and interests would have become more vulnerable to military aggression. Not only was Reagan's judgment poor, he used to fall asleep during cabinet meetings. Yet, a person of his caliber was allowed to become president.

The issues of military misadventure and economic mismanagement should lead to a discussion of how our leaders are elected and what qualifications they should have in order to serve in office. Wealthy donors have hidden agendas and hire incompetent people to do their dirty work. Once in office, their hirelings—Reagan, Bush Jr., etc.—engage in policies that will make the United States and other countries, such as Iraq, suffer for decades.

PROUT

Wall Street currently dictates the location of manufacturing units (in China, Japan, South Korea, Taiwan, etc.), the location of service centers (in India, the Philippines, Ireland, etc.), and now the location of certain medical facilities (in India), across approximately eight time zones, approximately thirteen if Latin America is included. In a process more similar than not, the USSR had a planning commission, appointed by the Politburo, which decided where in the Soviet Union to produce what across eleven time zones. The Soviet economy was similar to the present global economy (i.e., none of the Soviet regions was self-sufficient economically). For this reason, capitalism and communism are two faces of the same coin, and capitalism is also bound to fail, as Soviet communism did.

Under their five-year plans, communist countries gave importance to large industries. In the USSR, the center dictated the establishment of factories all over the country. Third World countries such as India have also used five-year plans. According to Jawahar Lal Nehru, India's first prime minister, the large industries these plans created were like modern-day temples. People migrated in droves from rural to urban areas for work, resulting in places like Dharavi, the world's largest slum, near Mumbai (Bombay), and home to more than a million poor people. It is true that modern industry is necessary for economic development, but because it is not labor-intensive it resulted in large-scale unemployment in India and is now disrupting China after the withdrawal of the state-funded welfare system.

Not only has the United States lost millions of jobs due to Wall Street dictates, several of the Third World countries are now losing their manufacturing jobs to East Asia, mainly China, as well. These countries will consequently follow America's path and over the years face growing trade deficits, which will cause them to seek financial aids from the IMF frequently.

The global economic crisis has proved that the current capitalistic system, based on TNCs exploiting the natural resources (both minerals and humans) and exporting them to far different places, is not feasible at all. It has only resulted in the concentration of money in a few hands, creating a small number of billionaires and millionaires here and there, and has left the rest of the world in misery.

If the US economy collapses, economic conditions in China and other East Asian nations will become similar to those of the former Soviet Union. Service sector jobs in India and other nations will have a similar fate. Demand for commodities such as crude oil and minerals will also plummet, causing the economies of countries such as Australia, Russia, Canada, Brazil, and Venezuela, which rely significantly on these commodities, to collapse.

A primary lesson in all of this will be that we need an economic model that avoids dependency on external factors. An economy cannot survive by export alone. It has to be a self-sufficient consumption-oriented country. Jobs should be created by using local resources, and instead of giving importance to increasing GNP it should be devoted to increasing people's purchasing power. Every region in a country has some natural resources that can be harnessed to give full employment to local people. Based on this, importance should be given to making regions self-sufficient using local resources that can generate local employment.

In advanced countries such as the United States and Japan, people talk about getting the latest gadgets, such as flat-panel televisions, iPods, iPhones, and iPads. It is true that the quality of living of developed countries has increased tremendously in the last couple of decades, but poor people around the globe still struggle just to survive. The World Bank uses an income of one dollar per person per day, measured at purchasing power parity, to determine the numbers of extreme poverty, and income between one and two dollars per day to indicate moderate poverty. According to a 2004 World Bank study done by economists Shaohua Chen and Martin Ravallion, roughly 1.1 billion people were living in extreme poverty in 2001, down from 1.5 billion in 1981. The overwhelming share of the world's extreme poor, 93 percent in 2001, live in three regions: East Asia, South Asia, and Sub-Saharan Africa. Since 1981, the numbers of extreme poor have risen in Sub-Saharan Africa but have fallen in East Asia and South Asia. Almost half of Africa's population is deemed to live in extreme poverty, and that proportion had risen slightly over the period. The proportion of extreme poor in East Asia has plummeted, from 58 percent in 1981 to 15 percent in 2001; in South Asia progress has also been marked, although slightly less dramatic, from 52 percent to 31 percent. Latin America's extreme poverty rate is around 10 percent, and is relatively stuck there. Eastern Europe's rose from a negligible level in 1981 to around 4 percent in 2001, the result of upheavals from the communist collapse and economic transition to a market economy. East Asia, South Asia, and Sub-Saharan Africa have about 87 percent of the world's 1.6 billion "moderately" poor.[258]

According to the propounder of the Progressive Utilization Theory (PROUT), P. R. Sarkar, nature has been kind enough to provide abundant natural resources to all regions of the world, but she has not given any guidelines on how to distribute these resources among the members of society. This duty has been left to the discretion and intelligence of human beings. In light of how many people suffered under communism and still suffer under capitalism, it would appear that these two systems represent less than the best in discretion and intelligence, and so Sarkar developed the theory of PROUT with numerous practical directions and suggestions.

In its political teachings, PROUT outlines major reforms that can be incorporated into democracy. The theory also proposes several major economic changes, changes that will become more and more necessary as the United States heads down the path of economic self-destruction. PROUT is based on increasing the purchasing power of the individual instead of the gross national product. It is also based on economic decentralization and on the optimum utilization of local resources to generate full employment for local people.

According to PROUT, most industries should be run as cooperatives owned by workers as shareholders, and management experts will be there to provide the needed help to guide them in their goals similar to the pattern in several German firms. The industries will work for the stakeholders and not shareholders. Despite bearing the pains of German unification, costing more than $2 trillion over the last twenty-plus years, Germany came out of the 2008 Great Recession first in Europe, and its unemployment rate is the lowest since the unification.

In the United States are a number of large cooperatives that are very successful—notable among them are the Green Bay Packers and the Seattle-based Group Health Cooperative. The Green Bay Packers is one of the most successful football franchises among professional sports teams. Generally professional sports teams are located in big cities, as they need a large fan base to be commercially viable. But the Packers is the only NFL team based in a small city, Green Bay, with a population of only 104,057 people as of the 2010 census. The Packers has won thirteen league championships, more than any other team in the NFL, as well as four Super Bowl victories and nine NFL championships in the pre-Super Bowl era. Founded in 1919, it is the third-oldest team in the NFL. It is also the only nonprofit, community-owned major league professional sports team in the United States. While the team is operated as a nonprofit organization, technically it is a for-profit corporation because under Wisconsin law nonprofit corporations cannot issue stock. As of 2011, its 4,750,937 shares are owned by 112,158 stockholders—none of whom receives any dividend on the initial investment. To protect against someone taking control of the team, the articles of its incorporation prohibit any person from owning more than two hundred thousand shares.

Seattle-based Group Health Cooperative in Washington State holds 20 percent of the market, the third-largest stake in the state, and has served six hundred thousand people for more than six decades. The increase in rates is always lower than for-profit health insurers. Complaint rates against Group Health are less than a third of that for the two largest insurers in the area.

The main driving point for private banks is profit and not the development of a region or welfare of people. They provide loans only to an extent that they can get the maximum interest rate from the paycheck of a person. Generally these banks offer a teaser rate, as low as 0 percent, for a short duration of time and then will increase the interest rate to even 30 percent if they think that the person is deep in debt.

The Bank of North Dakota (BND), the only state-owned bank in the United States, is a unique success story. Apart from agriculture being the largest industry, North Dakota has major petroleum and food processing industries. Since 2008, North Dakota has the lowest unemployment rate in the nation, and in August 2011 it was just 3.5 percent, nearly one-third of the national unemployment rate. Alaska has nearly the same population as North Dakota and produces 1.6 times more oil than North Dakota, but its unemployment rate in August 2011 was 7.7 percent.[259] In the last two decades, North Dakota's unemployment rate has never been above 5 percent.

BND was established by legislative action in 1919 as a venture to promote agriculture, commerce, and industry in North Dakota. The state and state agencies are required to place their funds in the bank; local governments are not required to do so.[260] It works like a central bank in the state. The state deposits its tax revenues in this bank, which invests a major portion of it in the state economy, whereas other states deposit their tax revenues in private banks that invest this money in places (including in other states as well as in other countries) where they get maximum return. BND have four established business areas: student loans, lending services, treasury services, and banking services. It guarantees student loans, business development loans, and state and municipal bonds. Deposits in the bank are guaranteed by the general fund of the State of North Dakota itself and the taxpayers of the state, and not by the Federal Deposit Insurance Corporation. It always has been profitable, even during the 2008–9 years, when nearly every other bank went into the red. BND's profit is revenue for the state. In the last decade (i.e., 2001–10), its net income was $448 million, with record-breaking incomes year after year since 2003, and it bucked the national trend of record losses since the 2008 economic downturn by having record net incomes in the last three years—$57 million (2008), $58.1 million (2009), and $61.9 million (2010). At the end of 2010, BND had the highest capital level in its history at just over $325 million, and it returned 19 percent return on equity (ROE), which represents the state's return on its investment.[261]

A number of other mineral-rich states were initially not affected by the economic downturn, but they lost revenues with the later decline in oil prices. North Dakota is the only state to be in continuous budget surplus since the banking crisis of 2008. Its balance sheet is so strong that it recently reduced individual income taxes and property taxes by a combined $400 million, and is debating further cuts. It also has the lowest foreclosure rate and lowest credit card default rate in the country, and it has had no bank failures in at least the last decade.[262]

According to PROUT, a central bank should be run as a public utility and form the monetary policy for the country or region, providing services to small cooperative banks and providing services to local people. Like BND, the main driving force behind this bank will be the development of the region and the welfare of its people and not the profit.

The miracle of North Dakota's economy and its state-run bank can be emulated in underdeveloped and developing countries worldwide. During the 1980s, P. R. Sarkar provided examples of how local resources could be utilized by socioeconomic zones in South Asia in order to show how the people there could obtain their minimum requirements without the investment of significant amounts of money.

PROUT promotes economic democracy and economic decentralization, and in this way contrasts with the economic authoritarianism and centralization of capitalism and communism. According to PROUT, the optimum utilization of local resources can generate full employment for local people. In so far as we are headed for a new world order, it need not be defined by either capitalism or communism, and in order to achieve complete global integration, PROUT deems it necessary to establish self-reliant economic zones, defined by common cultural and economic factors, in order to develop the indigenous strengths of various societies and their peoples so that they can participate on a more equal basis in the world to come.

Countries or communities should not import a product if it can be produced locally. No jobs should be outsourced. According to PROUT, there should be a rational distribution of wealth, with a constantly adjusted income policy.

PROUT deems that a country should be divided into socioeconomics zones, each of which will have enough natural resources for its population to become economically self-sufficient. In order to realize the goal of self-sufficiency, local people will hold economic power, enabling local raw materials to be used to promote their economic prosperity. The raw materials of one socioeconomic unit will not be exported to another unit, as they often are in the free market system, but rather, industrial centers will be built up wherever raw materials are available. Following this policy will create industries based on locally available resources and provide full employment for local inhabitants. Goods essential to local life, such as basic food items and clothing, will not be targeted for export, either to other zones or to other countries, but instead will satisfy local demand first and foremost. Trade, rather than being the centerpiece of economic policy as it is under neoliberal globalization ideology, will focus more on demi-essential items (nonbasic food items, antiseptic soaps, etc., that are not luxury items) and nonessential, refined wares (luxury items). Guaranteed employment and productivity improvements will increase the purchasing capacity of all residents, ensuring rising standards of living, the goal of any economic philosophy that plans systematically, not haphazardly, for the welfare of all people, not just a few.

PROUT promotes economic democracy. Economic democracy will give local people the power to make all important economic decisions, such as producing commodities on the basis of collective necessity and how to distribute agricultural and industrial commodities. Currently, the only economic decisions most people make are to some extent what to purchase and where to work.

PROUT also promotes economic decentralization. Each sector of the economy must strive for maximum development, and all sectors must strive for maximum decentralization. This policy leads to diversity of production in goods and economic sectors and diversity of production location. Economic decentralization is impossible under capitalism, because capitalist production always aims at maximizing profit. Capitalists prefer centralized production, which leads to regional economic disparity and imbalances in the distribution of the population. In the decentralized economy of PROUT, emphasis is on production for general consumption, and the minimum requirements of life will be guaranteed to all. All regions will get ample scope to develop their economic potentiality, so the problems of floating and migrant populations and overcrowding in urban centers will melt away.

Rather than emphasizing state ownership of industry, which characterized communism, or stimulating private ownership of industry, the raison d'être of capitalism, PROUT's economic structure has three tiers:

- Government controlled key industries
- Cooperatives
- Small, privately owned enterprises

The majority of industries will be cooperatives and will be worker-owned. Very large industries, too large to be managed by cooperatives, will be managed by the local government. Small industries will be privately owned. These days the United States is losing jobs overseas because CEOs have to demonstrate quarterly profits to Wall Street. Suppose a high-tech firm of five hundred employees in the Silicon Valley is owned entirely by its employees running it as a cooperative. Its decisions will not be dictated by Wall Street since it is not vulnerable to the stock market. Nor will it be controlled from Moscow or Beijing like a communist enterprise. Large retail and department stores such as Wal-Mart will be replaced by consumer cooperatives owned entirely by local consumers. They may form regional or national groups, but they will be owned by their members only. Consumer cooperatives will buy consumer goods from producer cooperatives that will be owned entirely by producers. Although stores such as Wal-Mart claim they provide cheap goods to American consumers by getting them manufactured overseas, they have also sent millions of manufacturing jobs overseas, making the country vulnerable economically, as the United States is going into debt by more than $600 billion a year due to its trade deficit.

According to Sarkar, per capita income is an insufficiently reliable, scientific index for determining the economic status and progress of a particular socioeconomic unit. Rather, it is misleading and deceptive because it refers to a simple mathematical calculation of total national income divided by total population. It is unable to convey an accurate picture of the standard of living in a particular socioeconomic unit because it conceals the degree of wealth disparity. When using per capita income as the measurement of economic status and progress, great income disparity can result in the same average standard of living as a more equitable disparity.

This measure also lacks any inherent relation to the ability to buy, or not buy, desired goods and services. That is, even though people may have high incomes, they may be unable to purchase the necessities of life. If per capita income is low, however, but people have great purchasing capacity and can buy a lot with that money, they are much better off. So purchasing capacity, the measure of the ability to purchase something with a given amount of money, and not per capita income, which is nothing more than average income, is the true measure of economic prosperity.

Purchasing capacity is the more accurate index, since it shows to what extent people's needs are being met by their income. All of PROUT's programs in the socioeconomic sphere aim at increasing this particular capacity. In addition, policies will ensure that the sum total of costs for each person's minimum requirements falls within his or her purchasing capacity, or "pecuniary periphery," as it were.

PROUT is a ground-up approach, similar to what Franklin D. Roosevelt indicated in his April 1932 "Forgotten Man" radio address, where he gave importance to "purchasing power" of the people. He said, "A real economic cure must go to the killing of the bacteria in the system rather than to the treatment of external symptoms ... one of the essential parts of a national program of restoration must be to restore purchasing power to the farming half of the country." FDR's famous speech was considered to be the turning point of his 1932 Democratic Party's presidential campaign, which finally led to his election as US president.

At present, economic power in democratic countries is concentrated in the hands of a few individuals and groups. In socialist countries, economic power is concentrated in a small group of party leaders. In both cases, handfuls of people manipulate the economic welfare of all of society. When economic power is vested in the hands of the people, the supremacy of these small groups will be terminated.

Fundamental Rights

The roots of our fundamental rights can be traced to the Magna Carta. Under the threat of civil war, King John signed an English charter of civil liberties, called the Magna Carta, in 1215. It required the king to renounce certain rights, respect certain legal procedures, and accept that his will could be bound by law. Clause 39, for example, defined the right of *habeas corpus*, and states that "no freeman shall be ... imprisoned or disseised [dispossessed] ... except by the lawful judgment of his peers or by the law of the land." In the United States, both the national and state constitutions contain ideas and even phrases directly traceable to this document.[263]

The constitutions of a majority of countries generally consider fundamental rights to include the right to equality, freedom of expression, freedom of religion, cultural and educational rights, etc. According to Sarkar, it is now time to raise the bar. Rights pertaining more to the material level of life should also receive constitutional guarantee: "Every individual must have equal rights to the dot in respect of things such as food, clothes, housing, medical aid and education that are absolutely necessary for existence."[264]

PROUT, unlike European social democracy or American liberalism, is not a social welfare system. It promotes a policy of 100 percent employment for local people utilizing local resources as the basis of service and industry. A basic right of all people in the PROUT view, as mentioned, is to be guaranteed provision of the minimum essentials for their existence. Further, what counts as the minimum will vary and increase with the development of the economy. A cave man could live without telecommunications and education, but for modern people that is unthinkable. This basic right should be arranged through fully guaranteed employment, however, not through dole-outs. Unemployment is a critical economic problem in most places in the world today. Hundred percent employment is the only way to solve it.

Welfare, utilized to support poor and unemployed people in many nations, is poor policy. Even though, in the PROUT view, society has the responsibility to ensure everyone his or her minimum necessities, if this is done gratis or unilaterally through gifts of things such as food and shelter, individual initiative becomes stunted. People gradually become lethargic and may even start to demand an income simply because they exist, as has happened in northern Europe. To avert this form of deterioration, as well as to cultivate a reciprocal spirit of willingness to contribute to others' well-being and prosperity through work, society has to make such arrangements that people may earn the money they require to purchase the minimum necessities through labor they can perform according to their capacity. PROUT promotes welfare through work, not welfare for free, except in cases where someone is severely disabled for one reason or another.

Guaranteeing the availability of the basic necessities of life has another advantage and purpose. If sufficient purchasing capacity is ensured in a way that avoids the monopolization of people's time and energy, they will be able to use their surplus time and energy, which in some countries is nil owing to the resources required just to procure life's necessities, in subtler pursuits. People will be progressively freed from the struggle to conquer need and scarcity, and both individuals and society will benefit as they use their surplus resources in art, the accumulation of knowledge, leisure (possibly alleviating stress and health problems), sports, spiritual development, etc.

The minimum requirements of every person are generally the same (food, living quarters, clothing, etc.). Still, diversity is also the nature of creation. Special amenities should therefore be provided in the form of incentives so that diversity in skill and intelligence is fully stimulated and utilized, and talent is encouraged to contribute its best for human development. What counts as an amenity or incentive will vary according to the society and the times. But at the same time there should be a constant effort to reduce the gap between the amount of special incentives a society offers and the minimum requirements a society ascertains to be the bare necessities at any given time. The guaranteed supply of minimum requirements must be liberalized, in other words, by gradually increasing the amenities given to the many so that they approach the level of amenities given only to the few. If economic adjustment is pursued along these lines, it will assist in the physical, mental, and spiritual evolution of humanity, and allow humanity to develop a cosmic sentiment for world fraternity in place of narrower sentiments such as the marked modern tendency to emphasize personal acquisition.

The cosmic sentiment finds its clearest description in P. R. Sarkar's philosophy of Neohumanism. Neohumanism represents an evolution of ordinary humanism. While the latter is centered on human beings in their generic sense, Sarkar based Neohumanism on the most expansive sentiment of living beings, one that sympathetically embraces everything in the universe. It is an application of his spiritual philosophy, a form of monism in which matter occupies a derivative position. According to Sarkar:

> All molecules, atoms, electrons, protons, positrons and neutrons are the veritable expressions of pure consciousness. Those who remember this reality, who keep this realization ever alive in their hearts, are said to have attained perfection in life .... When the underlying spirit of humanism is extended to everything, animate and inanimate, in this universe—I have designated this as Neohumanism. This Neohumanism will elevate humanism to universalism, the cult of love for all created beings of this universe.[265]

It is a sentiment or philosophy like Neohumanism that will help people progress beyond selfishness into a socioeconomic system that incorporates social or shared benefit as one of its defining factors.

Surplus goods and services, after distributing the minimum requirements, are to be given according to the social value of the individual's production. Note that the measure of value is social rather than economic. Here, the "social value" of a person means how valuable he or she is to society, whereas "economic value" indicates how valuable a person is to the economy. Those with social value benefit society noneconomically, and those with economic value benefit society in terms of their direct economic contributions. For example, Mother Teresa, and other Nobel Peace and Literature Prize winners, teachers, spiritually elevated people, and the like may have more social value than the CEO of a firm, whereas a CEO has more economic value. This principle provides a rational social basis for material incentives and expands their scope so that they are less focused on market services and commodities. It is, of course, better for society if moral incentives and the desire for social service motivate people in their productive work. However, the practical reality is that productivity is, to a large extent, proportional to material rewards. The Marxist slogan "Serve according to capacity and earn according to necessity" may sound good but will reap no harvest in the hard soil of the world. The need, rather, is for a framework that controls incentives and contains them within bounds that best serve the collective interest, which transcends pure market considerations. Incentives should also be provided in the form of goods and services that can be applied to social purposes, rather in the form of wealth that is likely to be hoarded.

To be more concrete, today common people in poorer countries need bicycles, for example, while meritorious people need motorcars, but there should be efforts to provide common people with motorcars also. While all are being provided with motorcars, it may be necessary to provide meritorious people with airplanes so that their incentive to work is maintained. After providing each meritorious person with an airplane, efforts should be made to provide ordinary people with airplanes also, etc. This principle is applicable in poor as well as in developed nations.

If the maximum amenities of meritorious people become excessively high, however, then the minimum requirements should immediately be increased. For example, if a person with special qualities has a motorbike and an ordinary person has a bicycle, there is a balanced adjustment. But if the person with special qualities has a car, then we should immediately try to make motorbikes part of the minimum requirements. There is a proverb that refers to plain living and high thinking, but what is plain living? Plain living eighty years ago was not the same as it is today, so plain living changes from age to age. The standard of value also varies from age to age. Thus, both the minimum requirements and the maximum amenities will vary from age to age, and both will be ever-increasing. If this were not so, economic progress would falter.

The PROUT approach, in sum, is to provide the minimum requirements of the age to all, the maximum amenities of the age to those with special qualities according to the degree of their merit, or social value, and the maximum amenities possible to ordinary people as well. As per their monetary value, the minimum and maximum requirements of the age are to be fixed, refixed, fixed again, and so on. The PROUT amenity system is thus a process both for providing incentives for extra effort and skill and for raising the level of minimum necessities. Because it is a permanent part, or fundamental principle, of PROUT, any society organized in this way will steadily raise its level of material prosperity in perpetuity, and humanity will thereby develop as well.

India has seen some progress on this front. Since 1972, villagers in the state of Maharashtra, on India's west coast where Mumbai is located, can demand work from the state government if they are unable to earn their livelihood under the state government's Employment Guaranteed Scheme. The central government implemented this program under the National Rural Employment Guarantee Act (NREGA) in 2005. Under NREGA, every household in India's rural areas shall have a right to at least one hundred days of guaranteed employment every year for at least one adult member to do public work-related unskilled manual work at the statutory minimum wage. In early 2012, the central government in India is considering free medicine for all through public facilities and health facilities across the country to reduce the indebtedness, especially for the rural people, as medicine costs are nearly 50 percent to 80 percent of health-care costs. By purchasing medicines directly from manufacturers, the cost of medicines can be reduced drastically. A similar plan is already being implemented by the state government in Tamil Nadu, and three other states are in process of implementing it.

Even though the advancement of science and technology has made enough resources available so that everyone can get the minimum requirements necessary for life, material wealth is still in limited supply, or finite, at any given point in time. PROUT, therefore, advocates a maximum limit to wealth too, not only minimum levels. According to Sarkar, "No individual should be allowed to accumulate physical wealth without the clear permission or approval of the collective body." The term "the collective body" here means society. Setting maximum limits will allow more rational and effective application of policies that increase both minimum requirements and amenities, both of which would tend to stagnate if wealth was concentrated in a few hands.

This would include capping salaries and other forms of compensation at a reasonable maximum level. According to renowned economist J. K. Galbraith, "The most forthright and effective way of enhancing equality within the firm would be to specify the maximum range between average and maximum compensation."[266] Currently, however, the gap between the wages of average workers and the salary and compensation package of a typical CEO in America is increasing yearly. Japanese and Taiwanese CEOs make about eleven and fourteen times more than their average employee, respectively, whereas German, French, and Polish CEOs make about twenty, twenty-three, and twenty-five times more, respectively.[267] But, as mentioned earlier, the average American CEO earns 262 times more than the average worker—more in a day (there are 260 workdays in a year) than an average worker earns in a year. In 1965, American CEOs in major companies earned twenty-four times what the average worker earned. This ratio grew to thirty-five in 1978 and to seventy-one in 1989. The ratio surged in the 1990s, and hit three hundred at the end of the recovery in 2000. A fall in the stock market then temporarily reduced CEO stock-related pay, causing it to moderate to 143 times that of the average worker in 2002. Since then, however, it has exploded, and by 2005, the average CEO was earning $10,982,000 a year, 262 times the average employee, who received $41, 861.[268]

Ceaseless efforts should be made to increase both the minimum and maximum amenities provided as well as to reduce the gap between the two, but the size of this gap will never shrink to zero. If the minimum vehicle provided is a six- to ten-year-old used car, for example, the vehicle provided as a maximum amenity may be a luxury car worth, say, $100,000. With the advancement of science and technology, if the minimum vehicle provided is a brand new car, the maximum amenity might be a private airplane.

Differences Among PROUT, Capitalism, and Communism

Capitalists want to produce commodities at the lowest cost and sell them at the highest price. To produce commodities cheaply requires efficient transportation, cheap raw materials, cheap labor, cheap energy, adequate water supply, etc. No matter what form capitalism takes—individual capitalism, group capitalism, or state capitalism—capitalists will always prefer centralized production. All these forms of capitalism are essentially the same in this regard.

Communism is state or governmental capitalism, which is why it shares some of the defects of individual capitalism. State capitalism, like individual and group capitalism, controls industries in a centralized manner. It centralizes production and other economic functions through state-controlled industries, rather than through private ownership. Thus, while communism appears to differ from capitalism on the question of personal liberties, the two are the same internally. They both put all or most control of the economy in a few hands. Fruits of the same variety may have different color skins, but their seeds are the same. Capitalism and communism are fruits of the same variety.

PROUT, capitalism, and communism differ in numerous ways, of which the following are among the most important:

(1) The PROUT economic system is three-tiered: The cooperative sector occupies the middle industrial tier; local governments run key industries, industries that are huge, complex, or focused on the extraction of raw materials; and small, private enterprises conduct business too small in scope for the other sectors to run and where entrepreneurship is to be encouraged. The latter, as well as cooperatives in their true sense of being directly worker-owned and run, were outlawed under communism. Capitalism is committed only to the interests of the private sector.

(2) PROUT's approach to cooperative enterprise is based on voluntary, not forced, cooperation. Soviet farmers were forced to join agricultural collectives, which was extremely unpsychological, and were not paid according to their individual output, which was nonproductive. Capitalists, to

compare, want to minimize the costs of production in order to maximize their profit. In the United States, for example, they now use millions of illegal immigrants, who are paid only a fraction of the wages of legal workers, in agriculture and other labor-intensive industries. They are trying to legalize these immigrants as well. Once immigrants are legalized and their families move up the economic ladder in one or two decades, capitalists will find more millions, also illegal, to work at low wages. If allowed to continue, it will be a never-ending saga.

(3) Communism's industrial approach was centralized, with huge factories producing one item to be widely distributed, whereas capitalism's approach is to locate production units where they can maximize their profit. PROUT's approach is based on complete and wholesome decentralization and local self-reliance.

(4) Communism dictated all decisions from above, such as five-year plans for industry; it was a party dictatorship. All economic planning was highly centralized and controlled by the state. Capitalism centralizes the major part of economic planning in huge corporations that now span continents. In PROUT, economic governance is bottom-up: local people have all the say regarding the development and utilization of local resources, etc. PROUT decentralizes the planning authority to the level at which people are most aware of economic problems and potentialities, and therefore best able to plan for their common welfare.

(5) Workers in both communist and capitalist economies are alienated due to lack of ownership and control of their workplaces. PROUT's enterprise system is based on worker participation in decision-making and cooperative ownership of assets, conditions that increase motivation and enhance possibilities for personal fulfillment.

(6) Communism's command economy was responsive to production quotas. Capitalism's free market economy is

profit-motivated. PROUT's economy is consumption-oriented. It aims at increasing consumer purchasing power and the availability of consumer goods as the primary means of meeting people's basic and amenity needs and maintaining economic vitality.

According to Sarkar, it is incorrect to say that advanced scientific technology, such as mechanization, is a main cause of unemployment. This is rather misinformation, or propaganda, carried out by leaders having little knowledge of socioeconomics. The question of unemployment arises only in the capitalistic framework, where industry is for profit. In an economic structure based on cooperation, where industry stands for consumption and not for profit, the question of unemployment will not arise. Automation and other advances in technology will not reduce the number of laborers; rather, working hours will be reduced, and the remaining hours will be used in nonwork pursuits. A reduction in working hours depends not only on productivity, but on the demand for commodities and the availability of labor. In 1930 John Maynard Keynes proposed the same when he said that the goal of future societies should be the reduction in working hours. He said that by the start of the twenty-first century, the working hours would be only fifteen hours a week, and the goal of the society would be focused on how to use freedom from economic concerns.

Those who want to promote public welfare without antagonizing the owners of capital will have to oppose mechanization. This is because when the productive capacity of machinery is doubled, the human labor required is decreased by half, such that capitalists retrench large numbers of workers from their factories. A few optimists may say, "Under circumstantial pressure other ways will be found to employ these surplus laborers in different jobs, and the very effort to find these alternatives will accelerate scientific advancement, so the ultimate result of mechanization under capitalism is, in fact, good." This view, though not useless, has little practical value, because it is impossible to arrange new jobs for retrenched workers as quickly as they become surplus laborers in consequence of rapid mechanization.

In a collective economic system, no scope for such an unhealthy situation will arise; rather, mechanization will lead to less labor and more prosperity. With a twofold increase in the productivity of machines, for example, working hours will be reduced by half. A reduction in working hours will, of course, have to be determined keeping in view the demand for commodities and the availability of labor. Science will thus be used benevolently, for the purpose of human welfare. It is possible that as a result of mechanization no one will be required to work more than five minutes a week. Not always being preoccupied with the problems of acquiring food, clothing, etc., people's psychic and spiritual potentialities will no longer be wasted. They will be able to devote ample time to activities like sports, literary pursuits, and spiritual practices.

Democracy and PROUT

As explained earlier, political democracy has become a great hoax for many people around the world. It promises peace, prosperity, and equality, but in reality creates criminals, encourages exploitation, throws common people into an abyss of sorrow and suffering, and, in some nations, such as the United States, is a participant in ever-new wars. According to Sarkar,

> There are several forms of government structure and among them the democratic structure is highly appreciated. Democracy is defined as government of the people, for the people and by the people. But in fact it is the rule of the majority. Hence democracy means mobocracy because the government under a democratic structure is guided by mob psychology. The majority of society are ignorant or fools. The wise are always in a minority. Thus finally democracy is nothing but "foolocracy".[269]

Government of the people, by the people, and for the people will only mean government of fools, by fools, and for fools.

We are witnessing this phenomenon in the United States. As noted earlier, although after a sixteen-month, $900-million-plus investigation, American weapons hunters known as the Iraq Survey Group declared in 2004 that Iraq had dismantled its chemical, biological, and nuclear arms programs in 1991 under UN oversight, a Harris Poll released on July 21, 2006, found that a full 50 percent of American respondents said they believed Iraq did possess forbidden weaponry when US troops invaded in March 2003. A poll conducted in March 2006 by Steven Kull of WorldPublicOpinion.org found that seven in ten Americans perceive the administration as still saying Iraq had a WMD program. On July 21, 2006, when Hezbollah guerrillas were fighting the Israeli army in Lebanon, Fox News—without any evidence—suggested another enemy of the Bush administration also had WMDs by displaying the following headline on the television screens of millions of Americans: "Are Saddam Hussein's WMDs Now in Hezbollah's Hands?"[270] Democracy is a mockery of good government in a country where many people are uneducated or gullible.

If one tells a lie one hundred times, it becomes a truth for uneducated and gullible people. The taxes are historic low in 2010, but according to a 2010 Gallop poll, 48 percent of people thought that taxes are "too high" and 45 percent thought that taxes were "about right." In 2009, federal, state, and other taxes—including income, property, sales and other taxes—consumed 9.2 percent of all personal income in 2009, the lowest since 1950. It is far below the average of 12 percent for the last half century.[271] In the 2010–11 budget year, federal tax revenue will be 14.8 percent of GDP, the lowest since the late 1940s, and in Bush's last year in office, tax receipts were 17.5 percent, just below their forty-year average.[272]

This is generally the case with most Third World nations. In much of the Third World, cunning and fraudulent persons very easily secure or purchase the votes of illiterate people. Moreover, the general public is easily misled by the propagation of casteism or religious communalism. Democracy, however, requires educated, sensible voters; the spread of education is thus of the highest priority. To facilitate its spread and strengthen democracy, the educational system must be free of cost.

Democracy has been likened to a puppet show where a handful of power-hungry politicians pull strings from behind the scenes. In liberal democracies such as America, capitalists manipulate people through the mass media, while in socialist democracies like India, corrupt politicians and bureaucrats lead the country into lawlessness and economic collapse. In both forms of democracy, little scope exists for honest, competent leaders to emerge, and there is virtually no possibility for the economic liberation of the people.

Because of relatively insignificant factors like the "3 Gs" ("Guns, Gays, and God"), incompetent persons such as George W. Bush win elections and ruin the country for decades by committing massive blunders like invading Iraq and turning a projected ten-year, $5.6 trillion budget surplus into a deficit. Elections, like beauty contests, have become popularity contests. Political parties try to find candidates such as Bush who can get votes by fooling the people.

For the welfare of people in general, it is not fitting to leave the onus of the administration in public hands, even through representative democracy. Suppose a certain couple has five children. All of them are happy and comfortable. But if the children, on the plea of being in the majority, suddenly claim full authority and the right of management of the family, does that make it feasible? Let us say they call a meeting and pass a resolution to smash the glasses and dishes. Is this a wise resolution? To take another example, the number of students is always greater than the number of teachers. If students, on the plea of being in the majority, demand a right to draw up their own examinations, would this make sense? Such is the logic that results, however, when majority rule is made the central criterion for the functioning of a society. Democratic reforms are thus urgently needed.

Democracy was introduced over twenty-five hundred years ago in the ancient state of Vaishali, in East India. Called the Licchavii democracy, it drew up the first written constitution. Prior to that, the word of the king was law, and kings ruled according to the advice of their ministers. Under the Licchavii system, only the elites, not the people in general, could exercise and enjoy adult franchise. The representatives of the people were known as Licchaviis, and they formed an executive body known as Mahalicchaviis through elections. The Mahalicchaviis controlled the power in Vaishali that had previously been controlled by the monarchy.

If people want to drive automobiles, they need to know traffic rules and have to pass driving tests in order to get a driving license. If the government decides that everyone above the age of eighteen will automatically, without proof of skill, get a driving license, then that government is playing with the lives of its citizens. Similarly, by giving everyone the right to vote on the basis of age irrespective of political consciousness, problems are bound to arise. In order to be eligible to vote, a person needs to have some political awareness.

PROUT proposes the formation of an electoral college as the voter list. It should consist of several tiers—local, state, and central, or federal. For local elections (mayoral posts, etc.), the franchise should be universal adult if the population is small. But to vote in state- and central-level elections (and in cities with populations in the millions), people should have some basic political consciousness. They should have basic knowledge of the political system and of the manifestos of various political parties, and they should know what persons elected in the previous election have done for the city, state, or country. Determining whether people possess this knowledge can be done through voter-eligibility examinations. Exam questions should depend on the election level, and should include the option of being taken orally or in written form. Preparation for the exam will be provided by governmental bodies free of charge. And just like driving tests, a "democracy test" should be able to be taken as many times as a person needs until s/he passes it. Children should be taught the country's constitution in schools so that as they grow up and become able to vote, they will be politically conscious.

In order to expand the scope of the electoral college beyond knowledge of politics and the political system, PROUT also suggests that institutions be established to provide moral, social, and basic economic education, qualifying them as voters. Such institutions should be free from political influence. They should be administered by an independent body, such as an election commission, and their curricula should be carefully designed by experts—educationalists, sociologists, philanthropists, and spiritualists, among others. To enter into the electoral college, a voter needs to take this examination before every major election or at periodic intervals.

If people have the right to vote, it should be their duty to vote, too. In some countries, such as Belgium and Australia, if voters avoid voting they must either pay a fine or explain their nonparticipation. This principle could be introduced in other countries.

Electoral candidates should be required to pass an examination as well, but for them passing marks should be higher than those for voters. Candidates in Western countries usually face each other in televised debates for the general public to gauge their knowledge. But in Third World countries such as India, this concept is nonexistent, and voters have little knowledge about candidate qualifications. Most state-level candidates lack any idea about the Indian constitution, fiscal policy, etc., but after getting elected to state assemblies they are supposed to be the constitution's guardians.

Usually society's top layer (in terms of intelligence) avoids fighting elections and joining the political system for several reasons: lack of economic security, the need for money and muscle power to get elected, and the lack of a secure career outlook. Instead, they join the bureaucracy or the private sector. In Third World countries, people from the bottom layer of society, who are incapable of getting jobs, usually join the political system and lead the country's affairs. The chief minister of Bihar, the second most populous state in India, once said publicly that most of his cabinet ministers were incapable of getting even an orderly's job. Politicians like these have legislative powers, however, and wide authority over bureaucrats, who take tough examinations and belong to the intellectual elite.

In the Proutist system, the role of the electoral college will remain unfinished even after it has elected members of various political bodies. It will continue to remain in touch with the people and apprise them of the points and counterpoints of various socioeconomic issues. Constant vigil will be required to make sure that all arms of government function efficiently and honestly, and this vigil will have to be exercised by the ever-watchful electoral college.[273]

In many contemporary democratic systems, governmental actions and policies are carefully examined by opposition parties and the press. This is a healthy practice that serves to keep official arbitrariness under control. But it also has its faults. Quite often the opposition engages in destructive criticism or plays upon narrow tendencies in the public mind. The party in power counters with the same game, and, as a result, the country does get two viewpoints on an issue, but not necessarily the best viewpoint. The electoral college that PROUT calls for will have a different role to play. Since it will not belong to any faction or party, it will be able to offer constructive criticism of government policies.[274]

PROUT also proposes full state funding of the entire election process so that all candidates have equal opportunity to present their positions. It allows no individual or private funding of elections, so wealthy people will be unable to buy influence.

Candidates will need to produce their programs in black and white. They will furthermore be required to stick to their programs; if they do not, they will be legally liable and may be tried in court on breach of promise or similar charge. If an elected official is found guilty of deceiving the public, his or her election will be cancelled. During an election in Bihar, the state's leader, Laloo Yadav, promised villagers that he would construct rural roads so that they were as smooth as the cheek of a beautiful leading actress in Bollywood. After he formed his government, people asked him to fulfill this promise, and he replied that poor villagers did not need smooth roads because they did not have any cars.

Prout advocates nonparty-based elections like in Nebraska, where state assembly members are elected with no party affiliation next to their names on the ballot.

Compartmentalized Democracy

A properly constituted democracy should have four compartments of government—a legislature, executive, judiciary, and public exchequer, or treasury—and each of them should be independent from one another. To strengthen their legitimacy, certain reforms need to be undertaken.

The democratic system allows elected officials from one party to comprise more than 50 percent of the officeholders even though the number of votes secured by their party may be less than 50 percent. In such a condition, their party is sometimes said to form a majority, but in reality it is government by a minority. Moreover, since governments are formed by particular parties, the opinion of other parties may not be respected in the legislature. Though all parties participate in passing legislation, bills may be passed according to the wishes of the party that is in the majority. When this occurs, that party often derives benefit from the enacted law while the people at large may derive little benefit at all.

In democracy as it is now practiced, securing the highest number of votes is proof of a person's qualification to hold office in most countries.

However, this qualification is not adequately examined in all cases. The popularity of a candidate securing the highest number of votes needs to be tested again if he or she polls less than half the total number of votes cast. In this test, arrangements will have to be made so that people can vote either for or against the candidate in a second vote. If the candidate polls more favorable than unfavorable votes, only then should he or she be declared elected.

Nor should a candidate be elected without a contest. In some Third World countries, wealthy and influential people can sometimes compel other candidates, by financial inducements or intimidation, to withdraw their nomination papers. So in cases where only one candidate is running, that candidate's popularity will have to be tested. If he or she fails the test, the candidate and all those who withdrew their nomination papers will forfeit the right to contest the subsequent by-election for that constituency and will have to wait until the next election to run again.

The manner in which the civil service is selected is also important, so that government can run well. In the United States, the majority of public service jobs on the federal, state, and local levels are awarded on the basis of the spoils system; after winning an election, the party in power dispenses public service positions to donors and campaign workers, awarding posts as if they were rewards for political battle. This contrasts with the merit system, under which jobs are awarded on the basis of ability, irrespective of a candidate's party affiliation. Federal appointments had been made according to merit before 1829, but this changed when President Jackson started the spoils system to reward his supporters. The process in India, to compare, is quite different, and might prove instructive. Even though poverty and political corruption are widespread, the country does maintain a few jewels in polished condition, and the civil service is one of them. The country's civil service candidates undergo a yearlong examination at more than forty-five different locations to select about five hundred top-level bureaucrats. This is done on an annual basis, and more than three hundred thousand candidates between twenty-one and thirty years of age contend for the few positions available. Once they are selected, they represent the executive branch of the Indian government and hold all top government jobs. This attracts the best brains of India to the executive branch. If they were not subject to corrupt politicians, the government might run well. Victorious parties in American elections, once again, are, however, allowed to nominate anyone they choose. This results in major donors and party members being nominated to posts for which they often lack any experience at all, because of which the nation sometimes has to pay dearly. As previously discussed, when Hurricane Katrina devastated New Orleans in 2005, FEMA was unable to do anything, largely because five of its eight top officials had no experience in handling disasters. Although for major executive posts Senate confirmation is required, the president can bypass this process by nominating a person for one year during Senate recesses. PROUT prefers the merit system for the executive branch.

According to PROUT, to provide a fearless and independent character to the administration, the executive branch, or secretariat, should be kept free from pressures from the cabinet. The executive branch should be run by experts in their respective fields; for example, the department of health should be run by a group of eminent health experts, not staff choices dictated by someone nominated by the legislature. The cabinet should confine itself to legislation, passage of the budget, the implementation of its plans and policies, defense, etc. The power of ministers should remain confined to the parliament, and they should refrain from poking their noses into the workings of the executive branch. The chief secretary or the head of the entire executive branch should not be subordinate to the president or prime minister and should act independently as the executive head. All the secretaries should work under the chief secretary. A secretary is head of an executive department. Free from cabinet pressures, every department will serve the people well.

Judiciary is one of the three pillars of democracy. PROUT supports the independence of the judiciary. In the present system, judges are either elected along party lines or selected by elected officials, such as by the governor or president in the United States. The US judiciary is not working as an independent organ because an elected judge has to cater to the voters so that he or she can get elected in the next elections. In the Bush victory in the 2000 presidential elections, ultimately decided by the narrow 5–4 Supreme Court decision in the Florida ballot case, the majority decision was written by conservative judges. Late night talk show hosts joked that the court had selected the president, and now the president would select it. Judges should abstain from fighting elections along party lines, however, because the judiciary should be above party politics (i.e., impartial). And for the nomination of judges to higher courts, a committee of experts, consisting of distinguished lawyers and members of the Supreme Court, needs to be consulted, and will have veto power over judicial nominees. In India, the judges are not elected. Instead, the government nominates the judges for high courts in states and for the Supreme Court, the highest court in nation, on the advice of the Supreme Court judges. The Supreme Court judges in India, who are exposing corruptions in the government, are held in high esteem by Indians. If people fail to keep this issue under close scrutiny, justice will give way to injustice.

Finally, for the proper utilization of the treasury, or public exchequer, the independence of the audit department too is a must. Only an independent audit department can keep proper accounts of every department. The auditor general should be independent of the president or prime minister. An example of this is the comptroller and auditor general (CAG) of India, established by the Constitution of India, who audits all receipts and expenditure of the government of India and the state governments, including those of bodies and authorities substantially financed by the government. Since the latter half of the 2000s, the CAG of India has brought to light large-scale corruption in several projects of central as well as state governments. This has resulted in filing of corruption charges against several political figures.

ENDNOTES

•◆•

Chapter 1

(1) Joseph Stiglitz, "The Insider: What I Learned at the World Economic Crisis," *New Republic*, April 17, 2000.

(2) Joseph E. Stiglitz, *Globalization and Its Discontents* (New York: W.W. Norton, 2003), 208.

(3) George Monbiot, "Clearing Up This Mess," *The Guardian*, November 18, 2008.

(4) Benjamin M. Rowland and W. H. Brittain, eds., *Balance of Power or Hegemony: The Interwar Monetary System* (1976), 220.

(5) Paul Blustein, "U.S. Trade Deficit Hangs in a Delicate Imbalance," *Washington Post*, November 19, 2005.

(6) Ibid.

(7) Lori Montgomery, "U.S. Debt Expected To Soar This Year," *Washington Post*, January 3, 2009.

(8) "Weakening rupee burdening Indian oil cos' finances: Reddy," *Indian Express* (India), October 10, 2011.

(9) "Oil cos lose Rs 14.57 a litre on diesel sale," *The Hindu (PTI),* January 17, 2012.

(10) Floyd Norris, "The Euro's Uneven Benefit in Europe," *The New York Times*, December 17, 2010.

(11) Niall Ferguson, "In China's Orbit," www.niallferguson.com, December 2, 2010.

(12) "Trade deficit spans to $117 b in April-Nov period," *Deccan Herald*, January 2, 2012.

(13) Prabhjot Singh, "India biggest beneficiary of remittances," *The Tribune* (India), January 7, 2012.

(14) Vikas Bajaj, "With Econmomy Slowing, the Indian Rupee Tumbles," *The New York Times*, November 25, 2011.

(15) "Rupee fall may make India Inc foreign loans costlier by $5-bn," *Economics Times* (India), November 20, 2011.

(16) Justin Webb, "Don't be distracted by Greece: Americans must also face financial facts," *Telegraph* (UK), June 25, 2011.

(17) Paul Krugman, "The Third Depression," *The New York Times*, June 27, 2010.

(18) Dennis Cauchon, "Why home values may take decades to recover," *USA Today*, December 12, 2008.

(19) Ibid.

(20) Daniel Gross, "Boston's Incredible Shrinking Skyscraper," *Newsweek*, September 4, 2009.

(21) Pallavi Gogoi, "Failing loans for commercial real estate threaten small banks," *USA Today*, September 10, 2009.

(22) Paul Krugman, "Block those metaphors," *The New York Times*, December 12, 2010.

(23) Blake Ellis, "Home values tumble $1.7 trillion in 2010," *CNNMoney.com*, December 9, 2010.

(24) Michael Snyder, "The Middle Class in America is radically shrinking. Here are the stats to prove it," *Business Insider*, July 15, 2010.

(25) Mark Trumbull, "Eight ways the Great Recession has changed Americans," *The Christian Science Monitor*, June 30, 2010.

(26) John W. Schoen, "Slow economy is a worse problem than any downgrade," *msnbc.com*, August 8, 2011.

(27) Eric J. Weiner, "China's giant economic sway," *Los Angeles Times*, October 6, 2010.

(28) Ibid.

(29) Craig Whitlock, "Financial Crisis Leaves Romania Reeling," *Washington Post*, November 5, 2008.

(30) "Did Speculation Fuel Oil Price Swings?" *CBS 60 Minutes*, January 11, 2009.

(31) Rudy Ruitenberg, "World food prices rise to record, may gain further, UN says," *Bloomberg*, March 3, 2011.

(32) Omer Farooq, "Gadkari demands stop to commodities trading," *The Pioneer* (India), June 7, 2010.

(33) "BJP demands probe into price rise," www.rediff.com, April 6, 2010.

(34) Roger Lowenstein, *When Genius Failed: The Rise and Fall of Long-Term Capital Management* (Random House, 2000), 211.

(35) Ron Suskind, *The Price of Loyalty* (New York: Simon & Schuster, 2004), 291.

(36) Josh Voorhees, "More than half of GOP voters still doubt Obama born in U.S." *The Slate.com*, May 10, 2001.

(37) Tom Bawden and Kevin Shalvey, "The era of owned by China," *The Guardian*, January 12, 2011.

(38) Ferguson, "In China's Orbit."

(39) Lee Chyen Yee, "China tops U.S, Japan to become top patent filer," *Reuters*, December 21, 2011.

(40) Peter Whoeiskey, "U.S. losing high-tech manufacturing jobs to Asia," *Washington Post*, January 17, 2012.

(41) Robin Wright, "Top focus before 9/11 wasn't on terrorism," *Washington Post*, April 1, 2004.

(42) Susmit Kumar, "Christian vs. Islamic Civilization—Another Cold War?" *Global Times*, (Copenhagen, Denmark), December 15, 1995.

(43) Dan Murphy, "Hillary Clinton compares parts of Israel to Jim Crow south," *Christian Science Monitor*, December 5, 2011.

(44) The theory of the clash of civilizations predicts alignments and wars among various civilizations—Western, Islamic, Chinese, Japanese, Orthodox/Russian, Hindu, African, and Latin. The term "clash of civilizations" was first used by Bernard Lewis in an article in the September 1990 issue of *Atlantic Monthly* titled "The Roots of Muslim Rage."

(45) Peter Baker and Susan B. Glasser, "The Rollback of Democracy in Vladimir Putin's Russia," *Washington Post*, June 7, 2005.

(46) Michael Wines, "China fortifies state businesses to fuel growth," *New York Times*, August 29, 2010.

(47) Paul O'neill interview on PBS, November 24, 2008.

(48) Rebecca Leung, "Bush Sought 'Way' To Invade Iraq?" *CBS. com*, February 11, 2009.

(49) Ron Suskind, *The Price of Loyalty* (New York: Simon & Schuster, 2004), 126, 148–49, 169.

(50) Henry Kissinger, *Diplomacy* (New York: Touchstone Book, 1994) 794–95.

(51) Donald T. Regan, *For the Record: From Wall Street to Washington* (St. Martin's Press, 1989).

(52) Yves Smith and Rob Parenteau, "Are profits hurting capitalism," *New York Times*, July 2, 2010.

(53) Spencer Soper, "Workers complain of harsh conditions in Amazon warehouse," *Tribune Newspapers*, September 23, 2011.

(54) Stu Woo, "Retired 'Workampers' Flock to Remote Towns for Temporary Gigs; RV Parks Are Full," *Wall Street Journal*, December 21, 2011.

(55) Steven Mufson and Jia Lynn Yang, "Companies use fuzzy math in job claims; candidates still buy in," *Washington Post*, October 10, 2011.

(56) Sheeran J. Thomas, "Ohio shale drilling spurs job hopes in Rust Belt," AP, November 27, 2011.

(57) Charles Duhigg and Keith Bradsher, "How U.S. Lost Out on iPhone Work," *New York Times*, January 21, 2012.

(58) Paul Blustein, "Mideast Investment up in U.S.," *Washington Post*, March 7, 2006.

(59) David R. Fracis, "The U.S. is for Sale — and Foreign Investors are Buying," *Christian Science Monitor*, June 9, 2008.

Chapter 2

(60) "India to reclaim Mughal-age economic aura," *PTI* (India), August 26, 2008.

(61) Nicholas D. Kristof, "China, the World's Capital," *New York Times*, May 22, 2005.

(62) Jeffrey D. Sachs, *The End Of Poverty* (New York: Penguin Press, 2005), 26–27.

(63) Ibid., 28–30.

(64) Ibid., 176.

Chapter 3

(65) Batuk Vora, "Overseas Chinese Outperform NRIs," *Times of India*, May 10, 1997.

(66) James Fallows, *Looking at the Sun* (New York: Vintage Books, 1995), 10.

(67) Robert Brenner, *The Boom and the Bubble* (London: Verso, 2002), 84–85.

(68) David Barboza, "Some Assembly Needed: China as Asia Factory," *New York Times*, February 9, 2006.

(69) Geoff Hill, "Cheap imports batter Africa's businesses," *Washington Times*, May 6, 2007.

(70) Emily Wax, "An Ancient Indian Craft Left in Tatters," *Washington Post*, June 6, 2007.

(71) "CEO Churn Hits Record High in 2005," *Reuters*, May 18, 2006.

(72) Paul Kennedy, *The Rise and Fall of the Great Powers* (New York: Vintage Books, 1989), 429 and references therein.

(73) Jeffrey D. Sachs, *The End Of Poverty* (New York: Penguin Press, 2005), 132.

(74) Jeannine Aversa, "Even as economy mends, a jobless decade may loom," AP, December 26, 2009.

(75) Peter S. Goodman, "Millions of unemployed face years without jobs," *New York Times*, February 21, 2010.

Chapter 4

(76) US Department of Commerce (Bureau of Economic Analysis).

(77) Ron Scherer, "What recovery? Budget deficits get worse for states," *Christian Science Monitor*, December 18, 2009.

(78) Stanley White, "Are Japan's public finances at tipping point?" *Reuters*, January 28, 2011.

(79) Chris Isidore, "The rich are much richer than you and me," CNNMoney.com, December 23, 2010.

(80) David J. Lynch, "Global financial crisis may hit hardest outside U.S.," *USA Today*, October 30, 2008.

(81) Neil Irwin, "The signs don't point to a typical recovery," *Washington Post*, August 17, 2009.

(82) Patrice Hill, "American reliance on government at all-time high," *Washington Times*, March 1, 2010.

(83) *World Economic Outlook*, IMF, April 2008, 258, 266.

(84) Louis Uchitelle, "China and the U.S. Embark on a Perilous Trip," *New York Times*, July 23, 2005.

(85) Blaine Harden and Ariana Eunjung Cha, "Japan, China Locked In by Investments," *Washington Post*, September 20, 2008.

(86) "CEOs and the rest of us," *Boston Globe*, March 11, 2007.

(87) Lawrence Mishel, "CEO-to-worker pay imbalance grows," *Economic Policy Institute*, June 21, 2006.

(88) Bob Herbert, "The Worst of the Pain," *New York Times*, February 9, 2010.

(89) David Leonhardt and Geraldine Fabrikant, "Rise of the Super-Rich Hits a Sobering Wall," *New York Times*, August 21, 2009.

(90) Maurice Leven, Harold G. Moulton, and Clark Warburton, *America's Capacity to Consume* (Washington, DC: Brookings Institute, 1934).

(91) Robert S. McElvaine, *The Great Depression, America 1929–1941* (New York: Three Rivers Press, 1993), 38.

(92) Ibid., 38–39.

(93) Ibid., 50.

(94) Ibid., 27–28.

(95) Les Christie, "30% of mortgages are underwater," CNNMoney.com, February 9, 2011.

(96) Blake Ellis, "Home values tumble $1.7 trillion in 2010," CNNMoney.com, December 9, 2010.

(97) Dina ElBoghdady and Sarah Cohen, "The Growing Foreclosure Crisis," *Washington Post*, January 17, 2009.

(98) Lori Montgomery, "U.S. Debt Expected To Soar This Year," *Washington Post*, January 3, 2009.

Chapter 5

(99) Jenny Anderson, "Wall Street Pursues Profit in Bundles of Life Insurance," *New York Times*, September 6, 2009.

(100) Tomoko Yamazaki and Komaki Ito, "Hedge funds eye $740 billion Japan pensions pool post-quake," *Bloomberg*, June 27, 2011.

(101) Peter Whoriskey, "Economists: State, local pension funds understate shortfall by $1.5 trillion or more," *Washington Post*, March 3, 2011.

(102) Stephen Labaton, "Agency's '04 Rule Let Banks Pile Up New Debt," *New York Times*, October 2, 2008.

(103) Peter S. Goodman, "Taking Hard Look at a Greenspan Legacy," *New York Times*, October 8, 2008.

(104) David Jolly, "Global Financial Troubles Reaching Into Gulf States," *New York Times*, October 26, 2008.

(105) Manav Tanneeru, "How a 'perfect storm' led to the economic crisis," CNN.com, January 1, 2009.

(106) Cauchon, "Home values."

(107) Peter S. Goodman and Gretchen Morgenson, "Saying Yes, WaMu Built Empire on Shaky Loans," *New York Times*, December 28, 2008.

(108) Elliot Blair Smith, "Bringing Down Wall Street as Ratings Let Loose Subprime Scourge," Bloomberg.com, September 24, 2008.

(109) Tomoeh Murakami Tse and Renae Merle, "The Bonuses Keep Coming," *Washington Post*, January 29, 2008.

(110) Louise Story, "On Wall Street, Bonuses, Not Profits, Were Real," *New York Times*, December 18, 2008.

(111) Peter S. Goodman and Gretchen Morgenson, "Saying Yes."

(112) David Cho, "1 Man, 1 Year: $3.7 Billion Payout," *Washington Post*, April 17, 2008.

(113) Robert Lenzner, "The Top 0.1% of the Nation Earn Half Of All Capital Gains," Forbes.com, November 20, 2011.

(114) William Selway and Martin Z. Braun, "JPMorgan Swap Deals Spur Probe as Defualt Stalks Alabama County," Bloomberg.com, May 22, 2008; Kyle Whitmire and Mary Williams Walsh, "High Finance Backfires on Alabama County," New York Times, March 12, 2008.

(115) Ibid.

(116) Mark Landler, "U.S. Credit Crisis Adds to Gloom in Arctic Norway," New York Times, December 2, 2007.

(117) Edward Cody, "Norwegian Hamlets Seek Wall Street Amends," Washington Post, August 25, 2009.

(118) "Did Speculation Fuel Oil Price Swings?," CBS 60 Minutes, January 11, 2009.

(119) Howard Schneider and Annys Shin, "Gloom Goes Up Around Globe as Signs Point Down," Washington Post, November 14, 2008.

(120) "Did Speculation Fuel Oil Price Swings?"

(121) Testimony of Michael W. Masters, Managing Member/ Portfolio Manager, Masters Capital Management, LLC before the Committee on Homeland Security and Governmental Affairs, US Senate, May 20, 2008.

(122) "Did Speculation Fuel Oil Price Swings?"

(123) Ibid.

(124) R. S. Eckaus, "The Oil Price Really Is A Speculative Bubble," Center for Energy and Environmental Policy Research, Massachusetts Institute of Technology, June 2008.

(125) Graham Bowley, "U.S. commodity regulator sues oil traders," New York Times, May 24, 2011.

(126) Robert Brenner, *The Boom and the Bubble* (London: Verso, 2002), 156.

(127) Joseph E. Stiglitz, *Globalization and Its Discontents* (New York: W.W. Norton, 2003), 208.

(128) Ibid., 129–30.

(129) Ibid., 109.

Chapter 7

(130) Susmit Kumar, "Forgotten Victims of U.S. Crusades to Save the World from Communism," *Global Times* (Copenhagen, Denmark), October 1996.

(131) Russell Gordon, "A People Beyond Suffering: Afghanistan After the Holy War," *Washington Report on Middle East Affairs*, November/December 1994, 59.

(132) Ibid.

(133) John Burns, "Kabul's misery wears a single face," *Guardian* (UK), February 6, 1996, originally published in *New York Times*.

(134) Ibid.

(135) Susmit Kumar, "Christian vs. Islamic Civilization— Another Cold War?" *Global Times* (Copenhagen, Denmark), December 15, 1995.

(136) Joe Stephens and David B. Ottaway, "From U.S., the ABC's of Jihad; Violent Soviet-Era Textbooks Complicate Afghan Education Efforts," *Washington Post*, March 23, 2002.

(137) Craig Davis, "'A' is for Allah, 'J' is for Jihad," *World Policy Journal*, March 22, 2002.

(138) Stephens and Ottaway, "The ABC's of Jihad."

(139) Babak Dehghanpisheh, "Where 'J' Is for Jihad," *Newsweek Web Exclusive*, April 19, 2003.

(140) Ibid.

(141) Davis, "'A' is for Allah."

Chapter 8

(142) Reza Aslan, *No God But God* (New York: Random House, 2006), 17.

(143) Fatima Mernissi, *The Veil and the Male Elite* (Cambridge, MA: Perseus Books, 1991), 44.

(144) H. A. R. Gibb, *Muhammadenism* (London: Oxford University Press, 1949–50), 79, referenced in Mostafa Vaziri, *The Emergence of Islam* (New York: Paragon House, 1992), 50.

(145) Shahrastani, Muhammad b. Abdulkarim b. Ahmed, *Al Milal wal-Nihal*, vol II, 2nd ed. (Tehran: Offset Co., 1979), 373–416, referenced in Vaziri, *Emergence of Islam*, 14–15.

(146) Montgomery W. Watt, *Muhammad at Medina* (Oxford, 1956), 268, referenced in Karen Armstrong, *Muhammad: A Biography of the Prophet* (San Francisco, New York: Harper, 1992), 230.

(147) Daniel Howden, "Shame of the House of Saud: Shadows over Mecca," *Independent* (UK), April 19, 2006.

(148) Bernard Lewis, *The Crisis of Islam* (New York: Modern Library, 2003), 31–32.

(149) Ann Elizabeth Mayer, *Islam and Human Rights* (Boulder, CO: Westview Press, 1999), 97–98; Fazlur Rahman, "The Status of Women in the Qur'an," in *Women and Revolution in Iran*, ed. Guity Nashat (Boulder, CO: Westview Press, 1983), 38.

(150) Bernard Lewis, *What Went Wrong?* (New York: Oxford University Press, 2002), 72 and references therein.

(151) Al-Bukhari, *Al-Sahih*, vol. 4 (Collection of Authentic Hadith) (Beirut: Dar al-Ma'rifa, 1978), 137, referenced in Mernissi, *Veil and the Male*, 76.

(152) Lewis, *What Went Wrong?*, 72.

(153) Al-Tabari, *Tafsir*, Dar al-Fikr edn., vol. 8, 107, referenced in Mernissi, *Veil and the Male*, 120–21.

(154) Armstrong, *Muhammad*, 190–91.

(155) Albert Hourani, *A History of the Arab Peoples* (New York: MJF Books, 1991), 121–22.

(156) Ibn Warraq, "Islam Supports Gender Inequality," in *Islam Opposing Viewpoints*, ed. Jennifer A. Hurley (Greenhaven Press, 2001), 89. Originally published in *Free Inquiry*, vol. 17, no. 4, fall 1997.

(157) Ibid.

(158) Armstrong, *Muhammad*, 190.

(159) Hourani, *History of the Arab Peoples*, 121.

(160) Caesar E. Farah, *Islam*, 6th ed. (Hauppauge, NY: Barron's Educational Series, 2000), 67.

(161) Ibid., and references therein.

(162) Hourani, *History of the Arab Peoples*, 121.

(163) Vaziri, *Emergence of Islam*, 15.

(164) Asqalani, *Fath al-bari*, vol. 13 (Cairo: Al-Matba'a al-Bahiya al-Misriya, n.d.), 46, referenced in Mernissi, Fatima, op. cit., 56–57.

(165) Mernissi, *Veil and the Male*, 3 and references therein.

(166) Armstrong, *Muhammad*, 12–13.

(167) Marcel Simon, *Versus Israel: A Study of the Relations between Christians and Jews in the Roman Empire (AD 135–425)*, trans. from French by H. McKeating (Oxford, 1986), 226; referenced in Bat Ye'or, *Islam and Dhimmitude: Where Civilizations Collide*, translated from French by Miriam Kochan and David Littman (Associated University Press, 2002), 34.

(168) Jean Juster, "La Condition Legale des Juifs sous les sous Rois Visigoths," in *Etudes d'Histoire Juridique Offertes a Paul F. Girarad*, Paris, 1912–13, 289–95, referenced in Ye'or, *Islam and Dhimmitude*, 34.

(169) Ye'or, *Islam and Dhimmitude*, 34.

(170) Armstrong, *Muhammad*, 28.

(171) Hourani, *History of the Arab Peoples*, 217.

(172) Lewis, *The Crisis of Islam*, 55–56.

(173) Hourani, *History of the Arab Peoples*, 267.

(174) Ibid., 267–68.

(175) Ibid., 281–83.

Chapter 9

(176) "Mapping the global Muslim population: A report on the size and distribution of the world's Muslim population," PewResearch Center, October 2009.

(177) "Saudi jailed for discussing the Bible," *Washington Times*, November 14, 2005.

(178) Neil MacFarquhar, "Anti-western and extremist views pervade Saudi school," *The New York Times*, October 19, 2001.

(179) Valerie Strauss and Emily Wax, "Where two worlds collide," *Washington Post*, February 25, 2002.

(180) David Crawford, "West's relations with Saudis face growing strains," *Wall Street Journal*, December 7, 2004.

(181) Ibid.

(182) Yaroslav Trofimov, "In a switch, Saudis let some dissidents speak their minds," *Wall Street Journal*, May 9, 2002.

(183) Simon Romero, "Algeria shows willingness to abandon its violent past," *New York Times*, February 16, 2004.

(184) "IAEA says Iran probably 3–8 years off nuclear bomb," *Reuters*, May 24, 2007.

(185) Neil MacFarquhar, "Heavy hand of the secret police impeding reform in Arab world," *New York Times*, November 14, 2005.

(186) Alan Sipress, "Tiny Qatar discovers the pitfalls of its alliance with U.S.," *Washington Post*, March 19, 2003.

(187) Benny Morris, *Righteous Victims: A History of the Zionist-Arab Conflict 1881–2001* (New York: Vintage Books, New York, 2001), 10.

(188) Charles D. Smith, *Palestine and the Arab-Israeli Conflict*, 4th ed. (Boston: Bedford/St. Martin's, 2001), 490.

(189) Glenn Kessler, "Old Legal Opinion Raises New Questions," *Washington Post*, June 17, 2009.

(190) Gershom Gorenberg, "Israel's tragedy foretold," *New York Times*, March 10, 2006.

(191) Chris McGreal, "Israel's colonization of Palestine blocking peace, says Jimmy Carter," *Guardian* (UK), March 18, 2006.

(192) "Israel could become pariah state, warns report," Agencies, *Guardian*, October 14, 2004.

(193) William Dalrymple, "Syria's shades of gray," *New York Times*, June 7, 2003.

(194) Douglas Frantz, "Turkey, well along road to secularism, fears detour to Islamism," *New York Times*, January 8, 2002.

(195) Christopher Cooper, "Terror friendly isn't a label Yemen cares to wear these days," *Wall Street Journal*, October 9, 2001.

(196) Susan Sachs, "Yemen fears being singed by a home-grown firebrand," *New York Times*, February 15, 2002.

(197) James Risen and Judith Miller, "Pakistani intelligence had links to Al Qaeda, U.S. officials say," *New York Times*, October 29, 2001.

(198) Craig S. Smith, "China, in harsh crackdown executes Muslim separatists," *New York Times*, December 16, 2001.

(199) Elaine Ganley, "Shoe Bomber Sent E-Mails Before Flight," washingtonpost.com/ap, January 22, 2002.

(200) Souad Mekhennet and Michael Moss, "Europeans get terror training in Pakistan," *New York Times*, September 10, 2007.

(201) David Rohde and Carlotta Gall, "In a corner of Pakistan a debate rages: Are terrorist camps still functioning?" *New York Times*, August 28, 2005.

(202) Sebastian Rotella, "Who guided London's attackers?" *Los Angeles Times*, March 6, 2006.

(203) Mekhennet and Moss, "Europeans get terror training."

(204) Sebastian Rotella and Janet Stobart, "Terrorism Defendant Cites Fear of Pakistan," *Los Angeles Times*, September 20, 2006.

(205) Craig Whitlock, "In Morocco's 'Chemist,' A Glimpse of Al-Qaeda," *Washington Post*, July 7, 2007.

(206) Dirk Laabs and Sebastian Rotella, "Terrorists in training head to Pakistan," *Los Angeles Times*, October 14, 2007.

(207) "US think tank: Pakistan helped Taliban insurgents," AP, June 9, 2008.

(208) John Lancaster, "Pakistan struggles to put army on moderate course," *Washington Post*, April 4, 2004.

(209) Seymour M. Hersh, "Defending the arsenal," *New Yorker*, November 16, 2009.

(210) James Risen and Judith Miller, "Pakistani Intelligence had links to al-Qaeda, U.S. Officials Say," *New York Times*, October 29, 2001.

(211) Ibid.; Bill Clinton, *My Life* (New York: Alfred A. Knopf, 2004), 902.

(212) Jane Perlez and Salman Masood, "Terror Ties Run Deep in Pakistan, Mumbai Case Shows," *New York Times*, July 27, 2009.

(213) "ISI creating trouble in India," *Press Trust of India*, April 23, 2007.

(214) Ralph Joseph, "Pakistan fights to end 'Kalashnikov culture'; Afghan arms find way into terrorists' hands," *Washington Times*, August 20, 2002.

(215) Richard Pendlebury, "Get out fast, Britons told; 'We can get any weapon except an atomic bomb' Tibal chief Haji Ahmad Khan Kukikhel," *Daily Mail*, September 17, 2001.

(216) Peter W. Singer and John M. Olin, "Pakistan's Madrassahs Ensuring a System of Education not Jihad," *America's Response to Terrorism Analysis Paper #14*, The Brookings Institution, November 2001.

(217) Anwar Iqbal, "Mastering the madrassas," *Washington Times*, August 17, 2003.

(218) Peter Fritsch, "Religious schools in Pakistan fill void and spawn warriors," *Wall Street Journal*, October 2, 2001; Owais Tohid, "Pakistan, U.S. take on the madrassahs," *Christian Science Monitor*, August 24, 2004.

(219) Tohid, "Pakistan, US."

(220) Iqbal, "Mastering the madrassas."

(221) Zahid Hussain and Jay Solomon, "al-Qaeda gaining new support," *Wall Street Journal*, August 19, 2004.

(222) Rakesh K. Singh, "Fidayeen implode on Pakistan," *Pioneer* (India), March 2, 2008.

(223) Shahan Mufti, "Suicide attacks a growing threat in Pakistan," *Christian Science Monitor*, October 10, 2008.

(224) "2010 bloodiest year for Pakistan since 2001: Report," *Times of India/PTI*, December 24, 2010.

(225) Kumar, "Another Cold War?"

(226) "Geopolitical Dairy: The Pakistani Army's Scattered Signs of Dissent," www.Stratfor.com, November 20, 2007.

Chapter 10

(227) Pervez Musharraf, *In the Line of Fire* (New York: Free Press, 2006), 201.

(228) Bob Woodward, *The War Within: A Secret White House History, 2006–2008* (Simon & Schuster, 2008).

(229) Maggie Fox, "Satellite images show ethnic cleanout in Iraq," *Reuters*, September 19, 2008.

(230) Kumar, "Another Cold War?," 27.

Chapter 11

(231) Niall Ferguson, "In China's Orbit," www.niallferguson. com, December 2, 2010.

(232) John Pomfret, "Australia welcomes China's investment, if not its influence," *Washington Post*, February 14, 2010.

(233) Malcolm Moore, "Chinese police admit enormous number of spies," *Telegraph* (UK), February 9, 2010.

(234) Jeffrey E. Garten, "Really Old School," *New York Times*, December 9, 2006.

(235) Anthony Faiola, "South Koreans weigh burden of massive assistance for North," *Washington Post*, July 25, 2005.

(236) Gordon Fairclough, "South Korean aid to North increases tensions with U.S.," *Wall Street Journal*, March 21, 2005.

(237) Vikas Bajaj and Keith Bradsher, "Asia sails smoothly through debt waters," *New York Times*, February 8, 2010.

(238) "External debt grows 12.8% to $296 bn in H1," PNS, *Pioneer (India)*, January 1, 2011.

(239) Anthony Faiola and Jill Drew, "Slowing Economy Gives Way to Global Role Reversals," *Washington Post*, July 17, 2008.

(240) Military Expenditure Database for 2010, Stockholm International Peace Research Institute (SIPRI).

(241) "Chinese incursions do happen, admits Pranab," timesofindia.indiatimes.com, January 18, 2008; "China using Sikkim to push Arunachal claim?," timesofindia.indiatimes. com, April 6, 2008.

(242) Peter Finn, "Oil Profits Help Russia Pay Off Soviet-Era Debt," *Washington Post*, August 22, 2006.

(243) Ian Traynor, "EU unveils energy plan to reduce dependence on Russia," guardian.co.uk, November 13, 2008.

Chapter 12

(244) Joseph Kahn, "Where's Mao? Chinese Revise History Books," *New York Times*, September 1, 2006.

(245) Michael W. Cox and Richard Alm, *Myths of Rich and Poor: Why We're Better Off Than We Think* (New York: Basic Books), 128.

(246) Ibid., 129.

(247) John J. Mearsheimer and Stephen M. Walt, *The Israel Lobby and U.S. Foreign Policy* (New York: Farrar, Straus and Giroux, 2007).

(248) P. R. Sarkar, *Prout In A Nutshell, Parts 1–3* (Calcutta, India, AMPS, 1987), 54–55.

(249) Natalia S. Gavrilova, Galina N. Evdokushkina, Victoria G. Semyonova, and Leonid A. Gavrilov, "Economic Crises, Street and Mortality in Russia," paper presented at The Population Association of America 2001 annual meeting, Session 106, Violence, Street, and Health, March 28–31, 2001, Washington, DC.

(250) Mark McDonald, "Health crisis ravages Russia's men," *Seattle Times*, February 13, 2005.

(251) Guy Chazan, "Fueled by Oil Money, Russian Economy Soars," *Wall Street Journal*, March 13, 2007.

(252) Peter W. Gallbraith, *The End of Iraq: How American Incompetence Created a War Without End* (New York: Simon & Schuster, 2006).

(253) James Taranto, "What Makes a President Great?" *Wall Street Journal*, June 10, 2004.

(254) Henry Kissinger, *Diplomacy* (New York: Touchstone Book, 1994), 794–95.

(255) Ronald Reagan, *An American Life* (New York: Simon & Schuster, 1990), 550.

(256) Lou Canon, *President Reagan: The Role of a Lifetime* (New York: Simon & Schuster, 1990), 289.

(257) Kissinger, *Diplomacy*, 783.

(258) Sachs, *End of Poverty*, 20–21.

(259) Bureau of Labor Statistics, United State Department of Labor; Aaron Clark, "North Dakota Crude Output Poised to Pass Alaska: Chart of Day," Bloomberg.com, January 12, 2011.

(260) http://www.banknd.nd.gov/.

(261) http://www.banknd.nd.gov/financials_and_compliance/annual_report_2010/financials2010.pdf.

(262) Ellen Brown, "Solution to the Economic Crisis? North Dakota's Economic 'Miracle'—It's Not Oil," *Yes Magazine*, September 2, 2011.

(263) *The New Encyclopaedia Britannica*, vol. 7, 15th ed. (Chicago: 1991), 673.

(264) P. R. Sarkar, *Prout*, 48.

(265) P. R. Sarkar, *The Liberation of Intellect—Neo-Humanism*, 4th ed. (Calcutta, India, AMPS, 1999), 6–7.

(266) John K. Galbraith, *Economics and the Public's Purpose* (New York: New American Library, 1973), referenced in Dada Maheshvarananda, *After Capitalism* (Copenhagen, Denmark: Proutist Universal, 2003), 75.

(267) "CEOs and the rest of us," *The Boston Globe*, March 11, 2007.

(268) Lawrence Mishel, "CEO-to-worker pay imbalance grows," *Economic Policy Institute*, June 21, 2006.

(269) P. R. Sarkar, *Prout In A Nutshell, Part 4* (Calcutta, India: AMPS, 1987), 14.

(270) Chales J. Hanley, "Half of U.S. Still Believes Iraq Had WMD," Associated Press, August 6, 2006.

(271) Dennis Cauchon, "Tax bills in 2009 at lowest level since 1950," *USA Today*, May 11, 2010.

(272) Stephen Ohlemacher, "By one measure, federal taxes lowest since 1950s," AP, February 7, 2011.

(273) Ravi Batra, *The Political System of Prout* (Calcutta, India: Proutist Universal).

(274) Ibid.

INDEX

Britain 85
budget 107
budget deficit 54, 84, 93, 237
Bush Jr. administration 33, 91
capitalism 54
China 70, 81, 85
collapse 108
consumer spending 83
cooperatives 252
corporations 50
current account deficit 70
debt 6, 81
deregulation 116
dollar a Ponzi scheme 6
dollar devaluation 95
economic disaster during Bush Jr.
    administration 79
exports 87
federal debt 12
financial sector 97
foreign investment 81
France 85
Free Trade 53
gdp 35, 95
gdp after WWII 5
Germany 85
global goods and services market 91
government debt 107
Great Depression II 39
household debts 21
housing bubble 22, 116
imports 87
income growth 101
information technology 72
interest rate 2, 70, 94, 107
its collapse 133, 250
its history 67
Japan 85, 108
job losses 22
major holders of Treasury Bonds 95
mortgage crisis 120
Obama administration 91
per capita income 35, 58
productivity 72, 98
Quantitative Easing (QE) 31, 91

Russia 81, 85
shares of income groups 101
stimulus 82
trade deficit 1, 3, 54, 69, 81, 86, 93,
    237
Treasury Bonds 7
unemployment 51, 84
unemployment in various income
    groups 101
World War I 66
World War II 66
Uzbekistan 151, 189

V

Vaishali 269
Vaishya 39
Venezuela 126, 129, 218, 250
Vietnam 9, 38, 69, 87, 138, 144, 207,
    222, 232
    balance on current account 13
    China trade 14
    currency devaluation 3, 14

W

wages 84
Wahhabism 144, 153, 154, 170, 194
Wall Street 13, 26, 72, 97, 98, 111,
    120
401(k) 53
2008 crisis 116
Amazon (firm) 51
bailout 115
bettings 112
commercial real estate 20
commodity price 30
federal tax 28
Free Trade 53
gold price 29
life insurance 112
location of jobs 249
outsourcing 256
pension funds 113
regulation 28
vs Main Street 242